Llewellyn's 2001 Astrology Datebook

DAILY PLANETARY GUIDE

Copyright © 2000 Llewellyn Publications. All rights reserved.
Printed in the United States of America.
Typography property of Llewellyn Worldwide, Ltd.
ISBN: 1-56718-971-7

Edited by Michael Fallon. Cover design by Lisa Novak. Line art by Kathleen Edwards. Special thanks to Leslie Nielsen for astrological proofreading.

Set in Eastern and Pacific Standard Times. (Note: Although starting and ending dates for Daylight Saving Time are marked, all times listed in this datebook are standard time.) Ephemeris and aspect data generated by Astro Communications Services, San Diego, CA 92123. Re-use is prohibited.

LLEWELLYN PUBLICATIONS
P.O. Box 64383, Dept. 971-7
St. Paul, MN 55164-0383, U.S.A.

2000

JANUARY
S	M	T	W	T	F	S
						1
2	3	4	5	6	7	8
9	10	11	12	13	14	15
16	17	18	19	20	21	22
23	24	25	26	27	28	29
30	31					

FEBRUARY
S	M	T	W	T	F	S
		1	2	3	4	5
6	7	8	9	10	11	12
13	14	15	16	17	18	19
20	21	22	23	24	25	26
27	28	29				

MARCH
S	M	T	W	T	F	S
			1	2	3	4
5	6	7	8	9	10	11
12	13	14	15	16	17	18
19	20	21	22	23	24	25
26	27	28	29	30	31	

APRIL
S	M	T	W	T	F	S
						1
2	3	4	5	6	7	8
9	10	11	12	13	14	15
16	17	18	19	20	21	22
23	24	25	26	27	28	29
30						

MAY
S	M	T	W	T	F	S
	1	2	3	4	5	6
7	8	9	10	11	12	13
14	15	16	17	18	19	20
21	22	23	24	25	26	27
28	29	30	31			

JUNE
S	M	T	W	T	F	S
				1	2	3
4	5	6	7	8	9	10
11	12	13	14	15	16	17
18	19	20	21	22	23	24
25	26	27	28	29	30	

JULY
S	M	T	W	T	F	S
						1
2	3	4	5	6	7	8
9	10	11	12	13	14	15
16	17	18	19	20	21	22
23	24	25	26	27	28	29
30	31					

AUGUST
S	M	T	W	T	F	S
		1	2	3	4	5
6	7	8	9	10	11	12
13	14	15	16	17	18	19
20	21	22	23	24	25	26
27	28	29	30	31		

SEPTEMBER
S	M	T	W	T	F	S
					1	2
3	4	5	6	7	8	9
10	11	12	13	14	15	16
17	18	19	20	21	22	23
24	25	26	27	28	29	30

OCTOBER
S	M	T	W	T	F	S
1	2	3	4	5	6	7
8	9	10	11	12	13	14
15	16	17	18	19	20	21
22	23	24	25	26	27	28
29	30	31				

NOVEMBER
S	M	T	W	T	F	S
			1	2	3	4
5	6	7	8	9	10	11
12	13	14	15	16	17	18
19	20	21	22	23	24	25
26	27	28	29	30		

DECEMBER
S	M	T	W	T	F	S
					1	2
3	4	5	6	7	8	9
10	11	12	13	14	15	16
17	18	19	20	21	22	23
24	25	26	27	28	29	30
31						

2001

JANUARY
S	M	T	W	T	F	S
	1	2	3	4	5	6
7	8	9	10	11	12	13
14	15	16	17	18	19	20
21	22	23	24	25	26	27
28	29	30	31			

FEBRUARY
S	M	T	W	T	F	S
				1	2	3
4	5	6	7	8	9	10
11	12	13	14	15	16	17
18	19	20	21	22	23	24
25	26	27	28			

MARCH
S	M	T	W	T	F	S
				1	2	3
4	5	6	7	8	9	10
11	12	13	14	15	16	17
18	19	20	21	22	23	24
25	26	27	28	29	30	31

APRIL
S	M	T	W	T	F	S
1	2	3	4	5	6	7
8	9	10	11	12	13	14
15	16	17	18	19	20	21
22	23	24	25	26	27	28
29	30					

MAY
S	M	T	W	T	F	S
		1	2	3	4	5
6	7	8	9	10	11	12
13	14	15	16	17	18	19
20	21	22	23	24	25	26
27	28	29	30	31		

JUNE
S	M	T	W	T	F	S
					1	2
3	4	5	6	7	8	9
10	11	12	13	14	15	16
17	18	19	20	21	22	23
24	25	26	27	28	29	30

JULY
S	M	T	W	T	F	S
1	2	3	4	5	6	7
8	9	10	11	12	13	14
15	16	17	18	19	20	21
22	23	24	25	26	27	28
29	30	31				

AUGUST
S	M	T	W	T	F	S
			1	2	3	4
5	6	7	8	9	10	11
12	13	14	15	16	17	18
19	20	21	22	23	24	25
26	27	28	29	30	31	

SEPTEMBER
S	M	T	W	T	F	S
						1
2	3	4	5	6	7	8
9	10	11	12	13	14	15
16	17	18	19	20	21	22
23	24	25	26	27	28	29
30						

OCTOBER
S	M	T	W	T	F	S
	1	2	3	4	5	6
7	8	9	10	11	12	13
14	15	16	17	18	19	20
21	22	23	24	25	26	27
28	29	30	31			

NOVEMBER
S	M	T	W	T	F	S
				1	2	3
4	5	6	7	8	9	10
11	12	13	14	15	16	17
18	19	20	21	22	23	24
25	26	27	28	29	30	

DECEMBER
S	M	T	W	T	F	S
						1
2	3	4	5	6	7	8
9	10	11	12	13	14	15
16	17	18	19	20	21	22
23	24	25	26	27	28	29
30	31					

2002

JANUARY
S	M	T	W	T	F	S
		1	2	3	4	5
6	7	8	9	10	11	12
13	14	15	16	17	18	19
20	21	22	23	24	25	26
27	28	29	30	31		

FEBRUARY
S	M	T	W	T	F	S
					1	2
3	4	5	6	7	8	9
10	11	12	13	14	15	16
17	18	19	20	21	22	23
24	25	26	27	28		

MARCH
S	M	T	W	T	F	S
					1	2
3	4	5	6	7	8	9
10	11	12	13	14	15	16
17	18	19	20	21	22	23
24	25	26	27	28	29	30
31						

APRIL
S	M	T	W	T	F	S
	1	2	3	4	5	6
7	8	9	10	11	12	13
14	15	16	17	18	19	20
21	22	23	24	25	26	27
28	29	30				

MAY
S	M	T	W	T	F	S
			1	2	3	4
5	6	7	8	9	10	11
12	13	14	15	16	17	18
19	20	21	22	23	24	25
26	27	28	29	30	31	

JUNE
S	M	T	W	T	F	S
						1
2	3	4	5	6	7	8
9	10	11	12	13	14	15
16	17	18	19	20	21	22
23	24	25	26	27	28	29
30						

JULY
S	M	T	W	T	F	S
	1	2	3	4	5	6
7	8	9	10	11	12	13
14	15	16	17	18	19	20
21	22	23	24	25	26	27
28	29	30	31			

AUGUST
S	M	T	W	T	F	S
				1	2	3
4	5	6	7	8	9	10
11	12	13	14	15	16	17
18	19	20	21	22	23	24
25	26	27	28	29	30	31

SEPTEMBER
S	M	T	W	T	F	S
1	2	3	4	5	6	7
8	9	10	11	12	13	14
15	16	17	18	19	20	21
22	23	24	25	26	27	28
29	30					

OCTOBER
S	M	T	W	T	F	S
		1	2	3	4	5
6	7	8	9	10	11	12
13	14	15	16	17	18	19
20	21	22	23	24	25	26
27	28	29	30	31		

NOVEMBER
S	M	T	W	T	F	S
					1	2
3	4	5	6	7	8	9
10	11	12	13	14	15	16
17	18	19	20	21	22	23
24	25	26	27	28	29	30

DECEMBER
S	M	T	W	T	F	S
1	2	3	4	5	6	7
8	9	10	11	12	13	14
15	16	17	18	19	20	21
22	23	24	25	26	27	28
29	30	31				

Table of Contents

Astrology *by Kim Rogers-Gallagher*.................................4
   The Four Astrological Building Blocks.........................5
      The First Building Block: Planets and Asteroids 5
      The Second Building Block: Signs 15
         Genders: Masculine and Feminine...................15
         Qualities: Cardinal, Fixed, or Mutable...............16
         Elements: Fire, Water, Air, and Earth................16
      The Third Building Block: Astrological Houses 22
      The Fourth Building Block: Aspects and Transits.........25
   Retrogrades of Mercury and Other Planets...................29
      Mercury Retrograde: A Communication Breakdown 29
      Retrogrades of the Other Planets 30
   The Influence of the Moon 30
         The Quarters................................31
         The Moon through the Signs.........................32
         The Void-of-Course Moon.........................35
2001 Eclipses 37
Astronomical Phenomena 2001...............................38
Time Zone Conversions.......................................40
World Time Zones..41
Planetary Stations for 2001 42
2001 Weekly Forecasts *by Kim Rogers-Gallagher* 43
Planetary Business Guide......................................68
How to Use Your Daily Planetary Guide 69
2001 Calendar and Aspect Pages................................70
Monthly Ephemeris..176
The Planetary Hours...188
Quick Table of Rising Signs...................................193
Blank Horoscope Chart 194
Telephone Directory Blanks...................................195
Directory of Products and Services.............................199

Astrology

by Kim Rogers-Gallagher

Some folks say that Earth is a school—a place to learn, take tests, and earn our degrees. They say that each of us is born at a selected moment, when all conditions are right for an evolutionary lesson to begin. In other words, we're planning our trip even before we arrive. We don't jump onto the Evolution Express until All The Right Stuff is in all the right places.

What stuff? Well, Cosmic Stuff. Our universe is chock-full of all kinds of amazing energies. Astrology allows us to interpret these energies. It's not a religion—so we aren't required to start or stop believing in anything, and we don't need to believe in it for it to work. (That's Tinkerbell, not Saturn…) Astrology blends science and intuition, magic and mathematics, cycles and symbols. There's no hocus-pocus involved. Astrology focuses on planets and their seasons, and planets are real. In fact, they're so real that their movements are consistent and recordable. Astrology allows us to draw parallels between the orbits of heavenly bodies and events down here on Earth. It allows us to surf the cosmic waves by glancing at our own "tidal tables," or planetary ephemerides, and by figuring out how to get the best ride from the tide that's en route. It validates our hunches and supports what we already know. Astrology is a language, a symbol set, and a guide to understanding the world, life, and the cosmos.

What's in a Horoscope?

Your astrology chart or your horoscope is your personal map, calculated using the date and time you were born from the perspective of your birth location. From that information, a circular, clock-shaped diagram emerges that shows where every planet, star, asteroid, and comet was located at the moment you made your debut. Your chart is a cosmic snapshot that freeze-frames the universe exactly as it was from your perspective. You carry that same perspective around with you throughout life. The horoscope chart is your blueprint—your cosmic backpack, an owner's manual that shows what you packed into your "tool-kit" for this lifetime and how best to use it. It's the circular lens that colors the way you see what's Out There. Everybody's got one, and no two are ever the same, which is pretty amazing. But there's more—since the chart is a map, everybody's got one of everything. Everybody's got a Venus, a Moon, and a Pluto. Everybody's got a bit of Virgo in there, and some Sagittarius, too.

The Four Astrological Building Blocks

Each chart is composed of the same elements, rearranged. I like to think of them as the four astrological building blocks: planets, signs, houses, and aspects. Each block represents a different level of human existence.

The planets (the eight other planets in our solar system, along with the Sun and Moon) are actual physical bodies. They represent urges or needs we all have by virtue of our decision to take up residence inside our physical body. Chiron and the asteroids also fall into this category.

The twelve signs of the zodiac (which correlate loosely with the twelve constellations) are sections of sky—30 degrees each—that act as filters or flavors for planets' energies. They describe the style of behavior a planet or house will use to express itself. They've also been compared to an actor's costumes.

The twelve houses in a chart—the twelve "pie-wedges" which divide the circle—describe the area of life or set of life circumstances in which our planets, dressed in their sign costumes, will come to life. Houses represent the twelve sides of our personalities, each of which comes out during the life situation that calls for it.

Aspects are angles. When we freeze-frame the planets in their orbits to create a chart, some of those planets will be positioned an exact number of degrees apart, forming angles to one another. The angles we use in astrology are most often those that divide a circle into equal parts. For example, 180 degrees, an opposition, is a circle divided by two. A square is 90 degrees, and divides a circle by four. A trine is 120 degrees and divides a circle by three, and so on. Aspects show which planets are "hot-wired" or engaged in constant dialogue with one another. The particular aspect that joins them describes the nature of their "conversation." Not all planets will aspect all other planets, but those that do have a very specific relationship.

The First Building Block: Planets and Asteroids

First, we'll look at the planets. Each of these heavenly bodies represents an urge you must express or something you need to do. Each planet acts as the director of a department in a very busy corporation. The corporation, of course, is you. You have a Communications Department, run by Mercury; a Love and Appreciation Department, run by Venus; and an Abundance, Generosity, and Growth Department, run by Jupiter. So when you have an urge or need to express yourself, you call on your Mercury; when you want to show love, you reach for your Venus; and when it's time to risk, extend, or grow, you use your Jupiter. Let's meet each of the planets individually and take a closer look at which job duties fall under each planet's jurisdiction. We'll go right to the top and start with the big boss: the Sun.

The Sun

Every corporation needs someone at the helm—a head honcho who makes all the final decisions. In other words, an executive director. The executive director of your corporation is the Sun. Just as the Sun itself is the core of the solar system, the source of heat and light around which all the other planets revolve, the Sun in your chart is your core, your reason for being, your true self. Although each of the planets in your chart is important in its own right, they all take their orders, figuratively speaking, from the Sun.

Everyone's Sun has the same inner goal: to shine. The Sun's spot in your chart shows where you really want to do good, where you want to be appreciated, loved, and patted on the back. The Sun is where you keep your supply of pride and confidence, where you store your identity and hold your ego. The Sun is you at your creative best, enjoying life to the fullest. If you never, ever again had to do anything that you didn't want to do, if you could spend the rest of your life pursuing only those activities that give you joy, you'd be acting out your Sun freely. To get in touch with how the Sun "feels," think of how you feel on your birthday, when the Sun returns to the same degree as when you were born and gives you a double dose of Sun energy. It's your day, a day when, whether or not you admit it, you really feel as if the world should treat you special. Well, that's the way the Sun inside us feels all the time. The Sun corresponds with gold, the rich, royal metal that adorns kings and queens. In the physical body, the Sun rules the heart, the back, and the circulatory system. On a daily basis, the Sun acts like a flashlight of sorts, illuminating each degree of sky it passes through. The Sun shows the focus of the moment, where the world's attention will be directed on that particular day. In fact, in horary and electional astrology—the two branches that pertain most to timing and prediction—the Sun represents the day, the Moon the hour, and the Midheaven the moment.

The Moon

Let's meet the Moon. First off, to "feel" the Moon, go stand by a body of water on a clear night when she's Full. Let your gaze shift back and forth between the Moon herself and the reflection she casts on the water. Whether you're looking up at her, or at that silvery patch she creates as it shivers and dances on the water, take a deep breath and allow yourself to be still. Take it all in, and you'll feel the Moon. In truth, when the Moon is Full, it's hard not to look at her—she invites us to look. She hypnotizes us silently, makes us sigh, and brings back memories. She's the soft inner side of each of us, the side that cries, fears, and dreams.

She's the head of the Department of Feelings and the bringer of "moods"—a great Moon word. She's a lovely lady in silver who circles our planet protectively in her monthly orbit. We see her subtle power in the tides as she calls the ocean to her and sends it away. We feel her influence ebb and flow through the ever-changing moods we experience, both en masse and individually, as she appears and disappears. She's the place in our chart where we keep our instincts, emotions, memories, and abilities to express our feelings. She is the ultimate feminine energy, the part of us that points to how we were nurtured and how we nurture. She's got a lot to do with our mothers, since our first emotional impressions of the world came through their bodies during the nine months they carried us. The Moon's the side of us that decides what's safe and what's not, the side that shows how we'll cope when we're hurt, the piece of us that responds to the outside world. The Moon corresponds with the silver color she creates. In the body, the Moon has jurisdiction over the breasts, ovaries, and the womb, all necessary for creating and nurturing life. She also rules our body fluids, the internal ocean that keeps us alive.

Mercury

Remember Mercury back in the ancient days, when gods and goddesses were thought to be in charge of the affairs of humanity? Back then, his job title was Messenger of the gods, and his duties included carrying messages back and forth between immortals and mortals. Although his official title has changed, his job description hasn't. He's now the head of your Department of Communications, and he still carries information back and forth. The only difference is that now he's known for being the "tool" you reach for when it's time to get information from out there to here. He's the computer that's at work inside you twenty-four hours a day, constantly feeding you data about the world. Whatever you're aware of, you're aware of it because of Mercury. He's the side of you that shows how you'll think and reason and how you'll express yourself to others. You'll recognize him in your speech patterns, your handwriting, and in the way you walk. He operates through your five senses and your brain, and makes you conscious of opposites—light and dark, hot and cold, up and down. He's what you use when you have a conversation, exchange a glance or gesture, and interpret a symbol. Mercury's specialty is the Here and Now. He's the side of you living totally in the present, your automatic pilot mechanism, the part of you that has the world memorized and can perform routine tasks without stopping to think how—tasks such as blinking, swallowing, answering the phone, or writing your name.

In the body, Mercury also acts as messenger—he transmits messages for you physically through the central nervous system. He is the "internal switchboard" that lets your eye and your hand collaborate. He corresponds to the metal named for him, and if you've ever tried to collect mercury after it's escaped from a broken thermometer, you've had an irreplaceable lesson on Mercury. Just as your Mercury never stops collecting data, those tiny beads you tried so hard to collect didn't come back without some information of their own—they brought back a bit of everything they contacted: dog hair, crumbs, and grains of dirt.

Venus

♀ You know the warmth that spreads across your chest when you're looking across the room at your significant other, asleep in the Sun? The same feeling you get when you look at your new car? You know how warm and happy you feel when someone leaves an "I love you" message on the answering machine? All this is due to the Lady Venus, the part of you that describes who, what, and how you love. Whenever you're pleased, satisfied, or content, it's your Venus who made you feel that way. Anything or anyone that you come into contact with on the outside that makes you feel just great on the inside—well, that makes Venus happy. She's a very sensual kind of planet. She's the head of the Department of Nice. Supplying your favorite people, places, and things is her job. If you want chocolate, music, flannel sheets, or the coworker you've got a mad crush on, it's your Venus that tells you how to get it. Venus shows how you act when you're out to attract what you love, especially people. When you're being charming, whether by using your manners or by adorning yourself because you want something, that's Venus, too. She loves doing things with someone and being with a partner. She's in charge of all behavior that is pleasing to others—light chit-chat, polite small talk, smiles, hugs, and kisses. The Lady is an expert at drawing others to you. Since money is one of the ways that we draw the objects we love to us, she's also in charge of finances. Copper is the metal that correlates with Venus, the metal that mixes most easily with other metals, and the one that wears pastels—in other words changes to pink, and green, and purple when it's heated. Copper is a perfect "alloy"—which sounds an awful lot like "ally," doesn't it? In the body, Venus relates to the sensory organs, the body's receptors—which makes sense, because these are the spots that tell us what feels good and what doesn't.

Mars

♂ Mars is one tough planet. He's the head of the Department of Self-Defense, Aggression, and Action. He's your sword, the warrior who fights back when you're attacked—your own personal SWAT team. This is the side of you that's brave, courageous, daring, and downright fearless. He describes how you act on your own behalf. He's not concerned with anyone or anything but you, and he doesn't consider the size, strength, or abilities of whomever or whatever you're up against. He's totally spontaneous, the side of you that initiates all activity. He's in charge of how you assert yourself, and how you express anger. In fact, one of the best ways to get in touch with Mars is by thinking of all the ways we describe anger. Examples are "hot under the collar," "seeing red," and "all fired up." The color red, fire, adrenaline, muscles, blood, and action are Mars' words. Remember, he's the ancient god of war, so he's not for the faint of heart. At best, he's what you use to be passionate, adventurous, and bold. At worst, he's violent, accident-prone, and cruel. Wherever he is in your chart, you need constant action to keep him "fed." Just as Venus attracts, Mars pursues. He charges through situations. He shows how you take action, how you do anything. He's where you're competitive and combative, where you're not afraid to take a stand on your own behalf. The metals that correspond to Mars are iron and steel, both used to make weapons, tools, machinery, and automobiles—things we use to enforce our will over that of another or over our environment. In the body, this headstrong planet corresponds to the head, the blood, and the muscles.

Jupiter

♃ Jupiter is the largest planet in the solar system, so large in fact that all of the other planets could fit inside him. He's been called "The Greater Benefic" and "King of the Gods" since time began. Jupiter is also the head of the Department of Expansion, Growth, and Incorporation. He's the side of you that's ultrapositive, optimistic, and generous to a fault—the astrological equivalent of Santa Claus. He's where you keep your supply of laughter, enthusiasm, and high spirits. Whenever you try something new, take a risk, or hear yourself say, "Oh, what the heck"—that's Jupiter. This is the side of you that's always ready to boldly go where you have never gone before. He prompts you to travel, take classes, get involved, and meet new people because he wants you to grow through new experiences. He's a big fan of networking, so wherever he is in your chart is a place where you'll have an extensive network of friends and associates. On the other hand, your Jupiter is also what you're using when you find yourself being excessive and wasteful, and when you're being extravagant or blowing something out of proportion. As a result, Jupiter is also the side of you that will probably have terminal "grass-is-greener" syndrome and will never be satisfied with what you've got. Words like "too," "very," and "most" are the property of Jupiter, as are "more" and "better." In general, this planet loves to make things bigger. Jupiter corresponds to tin—a most malleable, expandable metal. In the body, Jupiter works with the liver, the organ that filters what we take in and rids us of excess. Jupiter also handles the growth of the physical body.

Saturn

♄ As much as Jupiter represents the urge or need to expand, risk, and grow, Saturn is the side of you that withholds, contracts, refuses to take chances, and resists change. Saturn is head of the Department of Walls, Boundaries, and Rules, the honorary principal wherever he goes. Saturn is where you build walls to keep change out, where you may segregate yourself at times, where you'll be most likely to Just Say No to just about anything. Your Saturn is the critical parent inside you, the spot where you may delay, inhibit, or stall yourself throughout life. Because your fear of failure is so strong here, you'd often rather not act at all than act inappropriately or incorrectly.

This is the planet that prefers just the facts, ma'am, that likes reality delivered with a capital "R." This is where you are keenly aware of what's socially acceptable and what's not. This planet teaches you to respect your elders, follow the rules, and do it right the first time. Wherever Saturn is in your chart is where you'll feel respectful, serious, and conservative, and where you'll never embellish the facts or act until you're absolutely ready. In Saturn, you'll never expect something for nothing, and you'll be keenly aware that you earn what you get. Saturn is also where you're at your most disciplined, where you'll teach yourself the virtues of patience, endurance, and responsibility with another capital "R." In fact, your Saturn is well aware of concepts like doing the right thing, listening to your conscience, and being decent and respectable. Because this planet is so fond of boundaries, it's also the planet in charge of structures and guidelines. In the physical body, Saturn correlates with the bones and the skin—the structures that keep your body together. The metal that correlates with Saturn is lead, which is dull on the outside but quite shiny when it's polished and worked.

Uranus

♅ There's a spot in everyone's chart where independence is the order of the day, and where rules are made to be broken regardless of the consequences. This is where you're at your rebellious best, and where you'll surprise yourself at the things you'll say and do. Meet Uranus, the head of the Department of One Never Knows—the place in your chart where surprises and sudden reversals are regular fare. As much as Saturn is the technology you use when it's time to conform and act appropriately, Uranus is the side that you take out when it's time to do the unpredictable and erratic. Remember, this is the planet that just can't stand "shouldn'ts," and considers "no" and "don't" invitations to act. Of course, life provides plenty of situations where we can't act as we really want, but your Uranus is the piece of you that can only hold back for so long and that breaks you out of your rut and sets you free.

This is the side of you that delights in breaking tradition and shocking the masses. The more sudden and surprising your behavior is when you use your Uranus, the more restricted, captive, and repressed you've been feeling. Uranus loves suddenness—everything from lightning and tornadoes to winning the lottery. He's also a computer wizard, the planet who's most involved in mass communications. Here is where you'll have genius potential, where you'll be bold enough to ignore the old way to solve a problem and instead find a whole new way—maybe even invent something in the process. Major scientific and technological breakthroughs like the space program, the World Wide Web, and the Information Superhighway were all inspired by Uranian-type genius. In the body, Uranus rules the circulation and the involuntary nervous systems, as well as all the automatic functions our bodies are constantly performing, such as breathing, blinking, and digesting.

Neptune

Next time you hear yourself sigh or feel yourself slip into a daydream, think of Neptune. This is the planet in charge of romance, nostalgia, and magic. She's the side of you that delights in glamour and illusions, the side of you that's wistful and that wishes and believes dreams will come true. Neptune's place in your chart is a fuzzy, vague spot where you keep your pink smoke machine, where you're equally capable of fooling all of the people all of the time or of being fooled yourself. You're a psychic sponge where Neptune is in your chart, and here you will have an amazing ability to infiltrate your environment and be infiltrated as well. This is where you're capable of amazing compassion and sensitivity for creatures less fortunate than yourself, and where you'll be drawn into charity or volunteer work because you realize that we're all part of a bigger plan. Since sensitivity and harsh reality don't always mix too well, this may also be a place where you'll try to escape—seeking anything that takes you away from the real world. Sleep, meditation, and prayer are the highest uses of Neptune's energies, but alcohol and drugs are also under her jurisdiction. Any time you "leave" the planet, whether by losing yourself in a movie or just refusing to see the truth, you're using your Neptune. Neptune in your chart is where you'll always be tempted to believe that whatever you want is already just exactly the way you want it to be. The problem is that when reality does arrive with its sharp edges, Neptune's where you're vulnerable to disappointment.

Although her official title is Head of the Department of Altered States, Reality Avoidance, and Fantasy, Neptune's also one of the most creative energies you own. This planet is a well of receptive energy that helps you cast magic onto other folks. In the body, Neptune and the Moon corule the fluids. Neptune is connected with the body's immune system and with poisons and viruses that invisibly infiltrate our bodies.

Pluto

Of all the planets in your corporation, Pluto is the one with the most unenviable job description. He holds the dubious distinction of being head of the Department of Death, Destruction, Decay, and other unavoidables. He's the side of you that handles these topics and others not usually heard around the dinner table—sex and reincarnation, for example. He's also in charge of recycling, regeneration, and rejuvenation, but nobody sticks around much to hear those parts of his job duties after they hear about death and destruction. Yes, Pluto has a tough job, but a necessary one. He's not a planet that handles "maybes." Pluto is in charge of anything that absolutely has to happen. He disposes of situations that have gone past the point of no return and where the only solution is to let go. As we humans are notoriously bad at handling total, complete, and unavoidable change, so Pluto's spot in your chart is where you'll necessarily learn to firewalk, where intense and inevitable circumstances will teach you about agony and ecstasy. He's a planet of extremes, where you'll always be in a state of turmoil or evolution and where there will be a constant shedding of skin. When it's time to end a situation, whether it's because you've lost a relationship or a job, or because someone dear to you has died, your Pluto is the tool you reach for. This is the side of you that realizes life goes on after tremendous loss, and that will reflect on your losses down the road and try to make sense of them. It's also here that you'll crave intense experiences—from horror movies to deep, soul-baring conversation and physical intimacy. Most importantly, since Pluto rules life, death, and rebirth, here's where you'll understand the importance of process. You'll be amazingly strong where your Pluto is—he's a well of concentrated, transformative energy. In the body, Pluto is associated with the reproductive organs, since here is where the invisible process of life and death begins. He is also in charge of sexual maturity and puberty.

Chiron

Chiron is a huge comet that makes a 50.7-year orbit between Saturn and Uranus, occasionally nipping into Jupiter's orbit. Discovered on November 1, 1977, by Charles Kowall of the Hale Observatory in Pasadena, California, Chiron was originally thought to be our newest planet. He was named for the great centaur who foster-parented such heroes as Hercules, Achilles, and Aesclepius, and so, immediately after his discovery, astrologers began to work with Chiron. In 1981, Chiron was classified as an asteroid, and was discussed as a "maverick" of sorts, since he'd chosen an orbit apart from most of the other asteroids that circled the Sun in the lane between Mars and Jupiter. However, once it was classified as a comet in 1988, Chiron's problems began. Many astrologers were skeptical whether comets counted. First of all, there are millions of them—how could we study them while our sky already had eight planets, the Sun and Moon, millions of fixed stars, and more than 5,000 asteroids? However, Chiron's shape-shifting attracted attention. The fact that he changed form several times fit beautifully with his myth and, later, his astrological meaning.

According to the story, Chiron was born from a union between the sea-nymph Philyra and Chronos-Saturn. It seems Saturn, though married, saw Philyra one day and became rather smitten with her. She did not feel the same, however, and changed into a horse to escape Saturn's advances. Not to be put off, Saturn changed himself into a stallion, chased Philyra down, and raped her—Philyra becoming pregnant as a result of the encounter. Naturally, Philyra was horrified when she saw her child and thought she was being punished for her "sins." She begged the gods to allow her to escape from this monster child, so they let her change into a linden tree. Chiron, a tiny half-colt, half-human, became an orphan, deserted by his father Saturn and abandoned by a mother repulsed by his physical form.

Rather than concentrate on his problems, however, Chiron studied all kinds of things—music, poetry, hunting, war, healing, even astrology. In time, his talents became famous, and the gods and goddesses began to send him their children to foster. He spent his life teaching until he was wounded by a poisoned arrow as he handed it to Hercules—it was a poison of his own creation. Since his father was a god, Chiron didn't die from the poison, living instead in agony from a wound that would not heal. After trying to cure himself, Chiron gave up and asked Zeus to allow him to die. Zeus agreed, and Chiron exchanged places with Prometheus. He was elevated to the constellation Centaurus, in honor of all he'd done.

Many themes in Chiron's myth will play out in our lives according to where Chiron is located in a chart. The main theme in his story is the incurable or unsolvable wound, a physical defect that may make us feel as if we are "different" from others. We handle this wound in one of three ways: by becoming The Healer, The Wounded One, or The One Who Wounds. Our choice depends on whether we choose to recognize our wound consciously, project it onto others, or refuse to admit we're hurt and turn on others when they get too close. Chiron is our "sore spot," a place where we often feel prejudiced or stigmatized by others.

Chiron in our charts also points to a place where we feel as if we are handicapped, disabled, or "broken" in some way, or where we may find ourselves dealing with people or animals who have been injured or abandoned. Chiron's correlation with the concept of being handicapped also shows quite well through the similarity of his symbol (⚷) and the Handicapped Symbol of Access (♿)—a symbol which was adopted in 1968 when Chiron was just crossing over 0 degrees Aries, the first degree of the zodiac that corresponds with birth. This symbol tells a handicapped person (particularly someone using a wheelchair) that they can be free to conduct their business independently, without fear of being blocked by architectural barriers. This definition in itself is amazing, since Chiron is the bridge between Saturn and Uranus, linking the limitations of the past to the freedom of the future. As with the other planets, there are a variety of "symptoms" you'll find in Chiron's spot in your chart: healing others but not yourself, dealing with addictions, avoiding problems by running away (as Chiron's mother did), feeling as if you have a "tragic flaw," and coming to terms with a physical imperfection. While Chiron's placement is a very tender spot, remember that here is where we're quite gifted—we are capable of deep compassion where we are hurt. We cannot heal what we have not experienced.

Asteroids

Between the orbits of Mars and Jupiter, there's a spot where, according to what's known as Bode's Law, there ought to be a planet, mathematically speaking. Although there isn't a planet in this lane, it's far from empty. In fact, there are more than 5,000 asteroids of varying size that orbit the Sun. Since they're named by whomever finds them, the asteroid belt is inhabited by all manner of creatures—places, people, even objects (from "California" to "DuDu" to "Pizza"). Regardless of their size, these celestial bodies turn up in the most amazing places: attached to your Sun, wearing your husband's name, or right on your Moon with your mom's name. Of the 5,000, astrologers have used four since the 1970s when Eleanor Bach inspired the first asteroid ephemeris. Those four are Juno, Vesta, Pallas, and Ceres—all named for the great goddesses who were worshipped with as much respect and honor as their male counterparts after whom our planets were named. Each of them seems to point to a different face of femininity, but they also represent subtle qualities of both men and women.

Juno: The Wife

Juno (Hera in Greek mythology) was the wife and sister of Jupiter (Zeus). He was notoriously unfaithful, yet she remained constant and refused to break her vows. Here is where we find the happiness of absolute commitment in a relationship, and the rage and jealousy that accompany betrayal. A strong Juno personality lives for the spouse, regardless of how abusive the relationship, because of the strength of commitment.

Ceres: The Mother

In mythology, Ceres (Demeter) was the grain goddess who went on strike and caused the Earth to become barren after Pluto kidnapped her daughter Persephone. The girl was allowed to rejoin her mother, but only for half of the year. During these six months, Ceres allows the Earth to be fruitful, but during the other six months she mourns, and the Earth is without food. Ceres carries a Moon/Pluto tone and relates to possessiveness and loss. She also deals with eating disorders, nurturing, and rewards.

Pallas Athena: The Daughter

Pallas Athena was Zeus' child, and Zeus alone parented her. She was born from his head, arriving full-grown and in full armor. She was his favorite child, and has come to represent the father-daughter bond as well as mentor relationships. Her placement is where we are logical, witty, and diplomatic; where we champion our heroes; possess wisdom, intelligence, and common sense; and where we operate impartially because we're not emotionally attached to anyone or anything.

Vesta: The Virgin

Vesta (Hestia) was a "virgin" or "single" goddess—the last child born to Saturn (Chronos) and Rhea. Her brother Zeus gave her rulership of the sacred gift of fire. She protected homes with her warmth, offered hospitality to strangers, and united communities. Vesta's priestesses, the Vestal Virgins, tended temple fires and remained chaste until called upon to give themselves in sacred rituals. The penalty for intimacy at any other time was to be buried alive in an underground chamber. Vesta's spot is where we guard our passions and are aware that every action carries a sacred tone. We withhold our energy for long periods in the area of the chart Vesta inhabits, use it up in one intense moment, then draw back to regroup.

The Second Building Block: Signs

Every sign is "built" of three things: genders, qualities, and elements. Understanding each of these primary building blocks offers a head start toward understanding the signs themselves, so let's take a look at them.

Genders: Masculine and Feminine

"Masculine" and "feminine" are often misunderstood. Although the contemporary meanings of these words are "manly" and "womanly," in reality, masculine means that an energy is assertive, aggressive, and linear. Feminine means that an energy is receptive, magnetic, and circular.

Qualities: Cardinal, Fixed, or Mutable

Qualities show the way a sign's energy flows. They describe how the sign will act—quickly, steadily, or erratically. The cardinal signs are energies that initiate change, since the Sun passes through cardinal signs during the first month of each season. Cardinal signs operate in sudden bursts of energy, while fixed signs are unstoppable. They're the energies that endure and that correspond with the Sun's passage during the second month of every season. They take projects to completion and tend to block change at all costs. They keep at things. Finally, the mutable signs are versatile, flexible, and changeable, though they can also be scattered, fickle, and inconstant. They correspond with the third month of the Sun's journey through a season, when one stage of growth is about to recede and give way to another.

Elements: Fire, Water, Air, and Earth

As with all astrology, the best part of learning the elements is you can use what you already know to remember new concepts. Fire, for example, acts just as you'd expect it to: It's uncontainable, spontaneous, impulsive, and immediate—think of how quickly a match leaps to life when you strike it. The fire signs correspond with the spirit and the spiritual aspect of life. They inspire action, attract attention, and love spontaneity. Earth, too, is just as you know it to be: It's solid, practical, supportive, and as reliable as the ground under our feet. The earth signs are our physical envoys and are concerned with our tangible needs, such as food, shelter, work, and other responsibilities. Air signs are all about the intellectual or mental sides of life, and like air itself they are light, elusive, and uncontainable. They love conversation, communication, and mingling; the air signs are the social directors of the zodiac. The water signs correspond to the emotional side of our natures, and are just as changeable, subtle, and able to infiltrate as water itself. Water signs gauge moods, feel the ripples in a room when they enter and operate on what they sense from their environment.

Aries

♈ March 20–April 19 Planet: Mars
Element: Fire Quality: Cardinal

Aries is ruled by Mars, and it's cardinal fire. This sign turns any planet it touches into a bullet—red-hot, impulsive, and ready to go. Aries planets are not known for their patience—in fact, they hate waiting more than anything. There are no obstacles in the mind of an Aries planet. There's only where they are and where they want to be, and the shortest distance between those two points is a straight line. These planets prefer cutting to the chase over any other tactic. Planets done up in Aries boldly charge in where few would dare to go. They are brave, courageous, impetuous, and direct. Your Aries planet will always be exactly what it seems to be. This is the first sign, so Aries planets are often very good at initiating projects or starting things up. They aren't as eager to finish—that's more of a fixed quality—so they often leave projects undone. Aries planets need physical outlet for their considerable Mars-powered energy—otherwise their need for action can turn to stress. Exercise, hard work, and competition are food for their little Martian souls.

Taurus

April 19–May 20 Planet: Venus
Element: Earth Quality: Fixed

As fast and impulsive as Aries is, here's Taurus, the fixed earth sign next door. Taurus is a sign that loves to wait. It has endless patience and turns your planet into a solid, thorough force to be reckoned with. Taurus planets never quit—even when they probably should. They're responsible, reliable, honest as they come, practical as the day is long, and not afraid of hard work. They are fixed, so their reputation for stubbornness isn't accidental. However, the opposite side of the coin of stubborn is "solid"—and that they are. Planets in Taurus are regular rocks, endowed with a "stick-to-itiveness" other planets envy. Since Taurus is ruled by Venus, it's not surprising to find that these planets are sensual and luxury-loving, too. They love to be spoiled—whether with good food, fine wine, or a Renoir. Taurus planets need peace and quiet like no others. They don't like their schedules to be disrupted, and they often need to be reminded that comfortable habits can become ruts.

Gemini

May 20–June 21 Planet: Mercury
Element: Air Quality: Mutable

Gemini is ruled by Mercury, so it's a communication specialist. If something involves talking, writing, gesturing, or working hand-to-eye, your Gemini planet will love it. Mercury also rules short trips, of course, so any planet in Gemini is an expert at how to make their way around the neighborhood in record time. This, in fact, is the sign that's famous for its incredible lightness of being, the sign that loves variety and new experiences. Gemini is mutable air, which translates into changing your mind, so expect your Gemini planet to be chatty, entertaining, and versatile. This sign knows a little bit about everything. Scattered? Maybe somewhat—but no sign enjoys "just a taste" more. Gemini planets are experts at duality, too—they display at least two distinct sides of their personalities at all times. They're changeable, even fickle at times, and wonderfully curious.

Cancer

June 21–July 22   Planet: Moon
Element: Water   Quality: Cardinal

This Moon-ruled sign rules the home, family, motherhood, and children. It's also in charge of emotions, so expect your Cancer planet to operate "from its gut." Cancer specializes in instinct. It's cardinal water—good at emotional beginnings and keeping private. But the world is a scary place to Cancer planets—they're emotionally vulnerable, sensitive, and easily hurt. Cancer planets often long for their safe nests. Because they love with the energy of the Moon, Cancer planets say "I love you" by tending to your needs for food, warmth, or a place to sleep. They offer the very best hugs in the zodiac. The problem with Cancer planets is that they often become needy or unable to function unless they feel someone or something is dependent on them. They are moody, but it's their job to be—they're Moon-ruled.

Leo

July 22–August 22   Planet: Sun
Element: Fire   Quality: Fixed

Leo rules the pride and the ego, while it's ruled by the Sun. Leo planets want to shine, and you can use them to perform if you own them. In fact, you should find a stage, take the center spot, and get used to it, because, like it or not, your Leo planets will attract attention even when they don't necessarily want it. After all, this is fixed fire. Fortunately, Leo planets are only too happy to reciprocate any attention they receive. They'll repay the adoration of their fans a thousand times over with lavish compliments, lovely gifts, and wonderful, creative outings designed especially to amaze and delight. Leo's specialties are entertaining, having fun, and making big entrances and exits. Planets in this sign are into drama, and since the Sun is the center of the solar system, occasionally your Leo planet may forget others are out there or that not every action is planned with them in mind. In other words, they can be a bit too touchy and "high-maintenance" at times. Above all else, Leo planets cannot help but live to be loved and appreciated and gather up any attention that comes their way.

Virgo

August 22–September 22   Planet: Mercury/Vulcan
Element: Earth   Quality: Mutable

This sign has had a bad rap for far too long. Virgo has been called picky and "critical" ever since the first astrologer—but here's where it ends. Although it's true that Virgo is an automatic fault-finder, Virgo is Mercury-ruled like Gemini and is the sign with the keenest eye for details. When you're that good at particulars, it's natural to see tiny flaws in things. Your Virgo planet is a trouble-shooter extraordinaire. It exercises discrimination because that's its job—to analyze and suggest remedies to problems. This sign is also wonderful at lists and schedules. More than anything, your Virgo planet will delight in helping, and since it's a mutable earth sign, it's willing to adapt to any task. Keep your Virgo planet happy by keeping it busy.

Libra

September 22–October 23   Planet: Venus
Element: Air   Quality: Cardinal

Libra is associated with balance and harmony, but your Libra planets won't necessarily arrive that way. It's Libra's job to restore balance, create harmony, and cooperate with all—not easy jobs. Both balance and harmony require an entity to give and take equally. Again, no easy task. Fortunately, your Libra planets are up for the job. No sign is more charming, social, and able to coax the same out of another. Libra is cardinal air, so it wants to start conversations. Libra planets are experts at behavior that's pleasing to others. They're Venus-ruled, so they specialize in manners, courtesy, and small talk. Libra planets fit into any social situation and get along with just about everyone. They don't want to be alone, and, because they're gifted with the ability to pacify, they may sell out their own needs or the truth to buy momentary peace and a companion. Their real work is to see both sides of a situation, weigh the options, and keep their inner balance by remaining honest.

Scorpio

October 23–November 21   Planet: Pluto
Element: Water   Quality: Fixed

Water signs are gifted by being able to sense. Cancer uses its instinct, and Pisces uses its intuition. However, Scorpio operates on its perceptive abilities. Planets in this sign are detectives, experts at the delicate art of strategy. Your

Scorpio planets sift through every situation for subtle clues, which they analyze carefully to determine what's really going on. Because they're good at spotting clues, they're also gifted at sending equally subtle signals back into the environment, and at imperceptibly altering a situation by manipulating it with the right word or movement. Scorpio planets are constantly searching for intimacy. They want the real stuff from all encounters. No lighthearted Libra chit-chat—they want to bare their souls. They seek out intensity and crises. They can be relentless, obsessive, and jealous—remember, this is fixed water, so Scorpio feels things deeply and forever. Give your Scorpio planets what they crave: the opportunity to walk fire and to experience life-and-death situations. They're wells of limitless energy.

Sagittarius

November 21–December 21   Planet: Jupiter
Element: Fire   Quality: Mutable

This third fire sign is ruled by Jupiter, the largest planet. It's mutable fire, so its enthusiasm can spread at times like a brushfire. Scattered? Well, maybe—this sign is out to experience everything life has to offer. Sagittarius planets tend to have terminal grass-is-greener syndrome. They are adventurous, bored by routine, and generous and optimistic to a fault. They can also be excessive, tending to overdo and overindulge. These planets adore foreign places, foreign people, maps, and outdoor activities. They're not known for neatness or for accepting just a sliver of anything. They're only too happy to preach, advertise, philosophize, and learn by having the big picture explained. Sag planets are also quite prophetic at times, since Jupiter is the planet that rules higher learning. They absolutely believe in the power of laughter and aren't above embarrassing themselves to make someone laugh.

Capricorn

December 21–January 20   Planet: Saturn
Element: Earth   Quality: Cardinal

Your Capricorn planet has a tendency to build things. It's ruled by Saturn, so it erects structures or buildings and creates a career or starts up an organization. These planets know how to run things. They're authority figures—constantly marching, shaking their fingers and saying things like "better not," "shouldn't," and "let's not rush into this." Capricorn has a need to exercise caution and discipline, to set down rules and live by them, to set boundaries, and to put plans in motion from within those limits. Contrary to popular opinion, they're not humorless: Capricorn is the sign with the driest wit out there. Here's where your sense of propriety and tradition will be strong, where doing things the old-fashioned way and paying respect to the elders will be the only way to go. Your Capricorn planets are also starved in some way. They want a return for the time they invest.

Aquarius

January 19–February 18 Planet: Uranus
Element: Air Quality: Fixed

This sign is ruled by Uranus, the bringer of the unpredictable and head of the Department of One Never Knows. So as wild and crazy a planet as Uranus is, this sign, his envoy, is just about always ready to shock and amaze the masses and to rebel against whatever everyone else is doing. Planets in this sign are into their personal freedom. They insist on creating their own rules, fighting city hall whenever possible, and deliberately breaking tradition. They adore change, especially of the sudden kind. Abrupt reversals are their specialty, so others often perceive them as erratic, unstable, or unreliable energies. But as changeable as it seems to be, Aquarius is a fixed air sign. When it commits to a cause or to an intellectual ideal, it's really committed. Aquarian planets are often much better at friendship than love—they value like-minded folk and need to be with kindred spirits to recharge.

Pisces

February 18–March 20 Planet: Neptune
Element: Water Quality: Mutable

Pour a glass of water onto a table, and you'll see how mutable water flows into every corner. With no walls to contain it, Pisces, like this water, bonds itself emotionally to whatever it's exposed. This is the source of Pisces' well-deserved reputation for compassion, and it is also the source of a tendency to escape reality. Planets in this sign are ultrasensitive—they feel anything and everything. They're psychic sponges that often need time alone to unload and reassemble themselves. Exposure to others, especially crowds, is exhausting to your Pisces planet. It's in this sign that you may find a tendency to take in stray people and animals, but also where you'll need to watch for the possibility of being victimized or taken advantage of in some way. Pisces planets are not known for their realistic view of the world—they see the best in any person or situation—but when reality steps in they sometimes can be disappointed. These planets are the romantics of the zodiac. Let them dream in healthy ways.

The Third Building Block: Astrological Houses

Houses are twelve pie-shaped wedges in a horoscope chart. They reflect the actual life circumstances we create and encounter as we pass through life. Think of the twelve houses as twelve rooms in a house where twelve different sides of our personalities live. There's a room where you keep the side of you reserved for work, another room where you keep the shopper in you, and yet another where you keep the romantic lover. The sign on the cusp of each house in your chart—that is, the sign that appears alongside the line that precedes a house—is like the door to that room. This sign influences your behavior when the appropriate life circumstances turn up. Since the signs on each of the houses are determined by the time of day you were born, it's important to have an accurate birth time when having a chart erected. Let's look at the side of you that resides in each of your twelve houses.

The First House and Your Rising Sign

The first house is the area of the chart that shows which sign was ascending over the horizon at the moment you were born. It's known as the Rising Sign, or Ascendant, and if you think of your chart as a big house and of the astrological houses as "rooms," then your first house is the front door of your big house. It is the first impression you make. The sign on this house cusp and the planets in this house describe your physical appearance—the way you dress and decorate yourself and the overall condition of your body and health. This house is purely superficial in many ways, since it's easy to change your appearance, but it's also a very important spot. As with all front doors, its condition can make or break the impression others have of the house in general. If it's uninviting or unfriendly in some way, no one will visit. In other words, it's important to keep the first house in good condition so that others will want to step inside and get to know you.

The Second House

This is the side of you that handles possessions and what you hold dear. This means money, material objects, and qualities you respect and admire in yourself and in others. This house also holds the side of you that takes care of what you've got. What you buy for yourself, the amount of money you earn, and what you're willing to do for it are a matter of self-worth—so this house is also a description of your self-esteem.

The Third House

This house corresponds with our neighborhoods. If we pictured familiar places, we'd see the physical side of our third house that operates on automatic pilot and performs unconscious tasks. It also refers to childhood and school when we learned many of our automatic skills, and it shows our relationships with siblings, our communication styles, and our attitudes toward short trips.

The Fourth House

This spot at the very base of the chart shows your symbolic foundation—your childhood home, family, and parents. Here's where you find the side that decorates and maintains your nest and decides how much privacy you'll need. This house deals with matters of real estate and also has been seen as describing the conditions at the end of life. Most importantly, this house holds the emotional warehouse of subconsious memories.

The Fifth House

Here's the side of you that comes out when there's fun to be had, when work's done and it's time to party and be entertained. This is the charming, creative, delightful side of you, where your hobbies, interests, and playmates are found. If something gives you joy, it's contained here. Your fifth-house side is shining anytime you create something that allows you to see a bit of yourself in it—anything from your child's smile to a piece of art. This house also traditionally refers to speculation and gambling.

The Sixth House

This house describes the rhythm of our days and how we function. It's where we keep the sides of us that decide how we like things to go along over the course of a day. Since it describes duties we perform on a daily basis, it also refers to the nature of our work, our work environment, and how we take care of our health. Pets are also traditionally a sixth-house issue, since we tend to them daily and incorporate them into our routine.

The Seventh House

Although it's traditionally known as the house of marriage, partnerships, and open enemies, this house really holds the side of you that only comes out when you're in the company of one other person. This is the side of you that handles relating on a one-to-one basis. Whenever you use the word "my" to describe your relationship with another, it's this side of you talking.

The Eighth House

Here's the crisis expert side of us that emerges when there's an emergency, or when it's time to handle extreme circumstances. This is the side of us that deals with agony and ecstasy, with sex, death, and all manner of mergings, financial and otherwise. The house also holds information on surgeries, psychotherapy, and the way we regenerate and rejuvenate after loss.

The Ninth House

This house holds the side that handles brand-new experiences requiring you to be completely aware and on your toes. Foreign places, long-distance travel, and legal matters are among the situations that call on this side of you. You use this side of yourself whenever you leave behind the automatic routine of the third-house world. Higher education, publishing, advertising, and opinion-forming are handled here, as are big-picture issues such as politics, religion, and philosophy.

The Tenth House

This highest spot in your chart, the symbolic "roof" of your house, describes public knowledge about you—your career, reputation, and social status. This is the side of you that takes time to learn and become accomplished. It describes the behavior you exhibit when you're in charge and the way you act with an authority figure. Most importantly, this house describes your vocation and your life's work—whatever you consider your "calling."

The Eleventh House

Your friends and allies make a strong statement about how you see yourself. This house shows the type of organizations you're drawn to, the kind of folks you consider kindred spirits, and how you'll act in group situations. Here's the team player in you and the side that decides which groups are your peers. It also shows the causes and social activities you hold near and dear.

The Twelfth House

This is the side of you that comes out when you're alone and in the mood to retreat or draw back. Here's where the secret side of you lives and where secret affairs and dealings take place. Here, too, is where matters like hospital stays are handled. Most importantly, though, this is the room where you keep all traits and behaviors you were taught early on to stifle, avoid, or deny—especially in public. This side of you is very fond of fantasy, illusion, and playing pretend.

The Fourth Building Block: Aspects and Transits
Aspects

As the planets move through the heavens, they form angles to one another. Planets in aspect have a 24-hour hotline. The particular angle that separates any two planets describes the nature of their conversation. For example, two planets that are 180 degrees apart are in opposition. Planets in this type of relationship are "hot-wired" to one another and connected in a very powerful way. Astrologers use nine angles most often, each producing a different type of relationship or conversation between the planets they join. Let's go over the meaning of each of the aspects.

The Conjunction: (0–8 degrees)

When two things, such as planets, are operating "in conjunction," it means they're operating together. Therefore, two (or more) planets conjoined are a team. They're fused together, so one or the other can't act alone. Some planets pair up more easily than others—Venus and the Moon, for example, since both are feminine and receptive; the Sun and Mars, each pretty feisty by nature. Planets in conjunction are usually sharing a "room" (a house) in your chart. They live together, so it's important to give them pursuits that will allow them to act together.

The Semisextile: (30 degrees)

The semisextile connects two planets in such a way so they are having a quiet conversation of sorts. The strength of this aspect is not monumental, ordinarily, and it seems to indicate that the two energies it links affect each other indirectly.

The Semisquare: (45 degrees)

This aspect denotes a minor irritation somewhat like the 90-degree angle (square) but with less awareness or concern. Many astrologers use this in personal astrology, but it should be noted that it can play a major role in mundane work such as research.

The Sextile: (60 degrees)

The sextile links planets in compatible elements. That is, planets in sextile are either in fire/air or earth/water signs, and since these pairs of elements get along so splendidly, so do two planets in this relationship. These planets are having an exciting conversation. The sextile encourages an active exchange between the two planets involved, so these "pieces of you" will be eager and anxious to work together.

The Square: (90 degrees)

Rub two sticks together at a right angle, and you're practicing the age-old technique of striking fire. The friction causes sparks and the sparks create flames. This is how squares work. Planets in this sign relationship are at cross-purposes—in essence, they're having a nonstop argument. Neither gives the other space to move, and there's constant friction between them. You can see squares operating in someone who's fidgety, nervous, or restless. Although they're uncomfortable and even aggravating at times, your squares point to places where tremendous growth is possible. They require constant movement to burn up that energy.

The Trine: (120 degrees)

Trines are formed between planets of the same element, so they're kindred spirits. They understand each other without having to finish the sentence. They show an ease of communication not found in any of the other aspects, and they're traditionally thought to have a favorable relationship. Of course, as with all else, there is a downside to trines. Planets in this relationship are getting along so well and so comfortably that they can get lazy and spoiled. Planets in trine show urges or needs that automatically support each other. The catch is that you've got to get them up off the couch to get them operating.

The Sesquiquadrate: (135 degrees)

This aspect is a combination of the square (90 degrees) and the semisquare (45 degrees) and denotes the area of the chart in which there is a conscious need to take action—a strong need to express oneself in activity and to make decisions.

The Quincunx: (150 degrees)

This aspect joins two signs that are completely different—they don't share a quality, element, or gender, and it's very difficult for them to communicate with each other. It's as if two strangers who speak different languages try to tell each other a story in a noisy room. For that reason, this aspect always insists on adjustment in the way the two planets are used. Planets in quincunx often feel pushed, forced, or obligated to perform. They also seem to correspond with health issues or disease.

The Opposition: (180 degrees)

When two forces are in opposition, they're working against each other—and that's the situation with planets in opposition to one another. They have the same mission, but their techniques are very different and neither is willing to concede. The only way to break their standoff is by becoming aware of one another and then compromising. This aspect is the least difficult of the traditionally known hard aspects—planets at odds with one another have a middle point to come to.

Transits

Transits are inarguably the favorite way to predict. They're easy to use and offer a lot of quick information—immediate astrological gratification. To use transits, you have to compare what's happening today to your own chart by penciling in the transiting planets on your natal chart and then looking at the houses and planets they affect. A good rule of thumb is that transiting planets represent incoming influences and events that your natal planet will be asked to handle. The nature of the transiting planets describes the types of situations that will arise, and the nature of your planet tells which piece of you you're working on at the moment. Transits are periods of change. Your natal planet will be very different after the transit has passed, especially if the transit was from an outer planet. Every transit you experience adds knowledge to your personality. That's why maturity and age naturally bring wisdom, and why it's true that life is the greatest teacher.

Sun

Sun transits point to the places in your chart where you'll want special attention and appreciation. Here's where you're the star of the show and where you want to shine. These often are times of public acclaim when we're recognized and applauded for what we've done. Of course, the ultimate Sun transit is our birthday, the day when we should be treated like royalty.

Moon

When the Moon touches our chart, the subject is feelings. When she touches one of our planets, we react from an emotional point of view. Moon transits often point to changing moods, gut feelings, and passing highs and lows. Our instincts are sharp during Moon transits. We're more likely to sense what's going on around us than to consciously know.

Mercury

Mercury transits are usually busy periods. The subject is communication of all kinds. Conversation, letters, quick errands, and short trips take up our time now. Often, because of Mercury's love of duality, events arrive in twos—as if Hermes the trickster were having fun with us. We often have to do at least two things at once during Mercury transits.

Venus

Venus transits are times when the universe gives us a small token of warmth or affection, a symbolic peck on the cheek, or a well-deserved break. These are sociable, friendly periods when we mingle and are more interested in good food and cushy conditions than anything resembling work. During Venus transits others will give us gifts, and since the planet rules money we may receive financial rewards as well.

Mars

Mars transits are times when your energy level runs on high. At best, you're stronger, restless, and active, but at worst, you're angry, accident-prone, and violent—you angrily stomp around the office for no good reason. When Mars happens along, it's best to feed him by working or exercising hard to use up this considerable energy. These are super times to initiate projects requiring a hard push of energy to begin.

Jupiter

Jupiter transits are *Star Trek* transits—you're in the mood to boldly go where you've never gone before. You get the urge to travel, take a class, or learn something new about the house or planet Jupiter touches. You ponder big questions and you grow—sometimes even physically. It's the time to take chances or risk a shot at the title. During Jupiter transits you're a bit bolder and more likely to succeed. Be sure to take the opportunities that come up.

Saturn

When Saturn comes along, it's time to wake up and see things as they truly are. This is often not the best thing for us, but opportunites for reward do occur. Saturn transits test the house or planet he touches to see if the structure will hold up. If we pass, we receive a symbolic "certificate"—often a real one, such as a diploma. Firming up our lives is Saturn's mission. These are great times to tap into Saturn's willpower and self-discipline to quit harmful activities. They are not good times to begin new ventures.

Uranus

What's the last thing in the world you'd ever expect to happen right now? This is exactly what you can expect under a Uranus transit. This planet revels in sudden and last-minute changes in plan, complete reversals, and shock effect. The subject is 100 percent freedom, so if you're feeling at all stuck in your present circumstances when a Uranus transit happens along, don't worry—you won't be stuck for long. "Temporary people" often enter your life at these times, folks whose only purpose is to jolt you out of your present circumstances by providing exactly what you were sorely missing. That done, they disappear and leave you in a shambles. Enjoy these visitors and allow them to break you out of your rut—just don't get comfortable.

Neptune

Neptune transits are times when the universe asks that you dream and nothing more. Your sensitivity heightens so much that harsh sounds can actually make you wince. Your compassion deepens and you often have truly psychic moments. Neptune transits inspire divine discontent. You sigh, feel nostalgic, and are unable to see things clearly. At the end of the transit, everything about you is different and the reality you were living at the beginning of the transit is eroded or erased right from under your feet.

Pluto

During a Pluto transit, the subject is obsession, regeneration, and inevitable change. Whatever has gone past the point of no return will pass from our lives now. Like Saturn transits, these are not wonderful times, but they are times when we learn just how strong we are and we are forced to see our true selves. Power struggles often accompany Pluto's visits, but being empowered is the end result of a positive Pluto transit. The secret is to let go, accept the losses or changes, and make plans for the future.

Retrogrades of Mercury and Other Planets

Retrograde literally means "backward," though none of the planets throw their engines in reverse and move backward. Rather, all of the planets except for the Sun and Moon appear periodically to move backward from the perspective of the Earth. What's happening is that we're moving either faster or slower than the planet that's retrograde, and since we have to look over our shoulder to see it, we think they are moving backward.

Mercury Retrograde: A Communication Breakdown

The way retrograde movement seems to affect our affairs is a bit involved. Every three months, Mercury goes through a retrograde period of three weeks. When this happens, it means the head of the Communications Department isn't paying close attention to where he's going because he's watching where he came from. Mercury doesn't tend to details as carefully as usual. And because Mercury correlates with Hermes, the original trickster, some of these errors can be very cleverly disguised.

All types of communications become confused, delayed, or misunderstood during Mercury retrograde. Letters are lost, sent to Auckland instead of Oakland, or stuffed under the car seat for three weeks. We sign a contract or agreement and find out later that our information was incorrect or what we signed was misleading in some way. We try repeatedly to reach someone via telephone but can never catch them, or our communications devices themselves break down or garble information in some way. The written word falls victim to Mercury's retrograde via constant errors. Our timing is off and short trips become difficult. We forget directions at home or write them incorrectly. We're late for or completely forget about our appointments.

A Good Time for Review

So, is there a constructive use to this time period? Aren't all planetary energies good for something? Astrologer Erin Sullivan has noted that the ratio of time Mercury spends moving retrograde to direct, or forward, corresponds with the amount of time humans spend awake and asleep—about a third of the time. So this period can be a time to take stock of what's happened and to assimilate our experiences just as we do when we sleep. New plans don't go forward well during Mercury retrograde because we're not supposed to be moving forward, just reviewing the past in preparation for our next stage of activity. A good rule of thumb with Mercury retrograde is to try to undertake activities that have "re" attached to the beginning of a word: reschedule, repair, return, rewrite, redecorate, restore, replace, renew, renovate.

Retrogrades of the Other Planets

As for the other planets, their retrogrades seem to work the same way. With Venus retrograde, relationships and money matters are delayed or muddled. With Mars, aggressors or initiators of battle are defeated, and new activities are confused or end up at cross-purposes to original intentions.

The Influence of the Moon

As the Moon goes along her way, she magically appears and disappears, waxing to Full from the barest sliver of a crescent just after she's New, then waning back to her invisible New phase again. The four quarters—the New Moon, the second quarter, the Full Moon, and the fourth quarter—correspond to the growth cycle of living things.

The Quarters

The First Quarter/New Moon

This phase begins when the Moon and Sun are together in the sky or conjunct to one another. At the beginning of the phase, the Moon is invisible, hidden by the brightness of the Sun as they travel the sky together. The Moon is often said to be in her "dark phase" when she is New, and toward the end of this phase, the Moon pulls farther away from the Sun and begins to wax or grow toward the second quarter stage, when a delicate silver crescent will appear. The first quarter corresponds with all new beginnings; this is the time to begin a project.

The Second Quarter

The second quarter begins when the Moon has moved 90 degrees away from the Sun. At this point, the waxing Moon rises at about noon and sets at about midnight. She can be seen in the western sky during the early evening hours as she grows from a crescent to her full beauty. This period corresponds with the development of life, and with projects that are coming close to fruition.

The Third Quarter/Full Moon

This phase begins with the Full Moon, which is when the Sun and Moon are opposite to one another in the sky—literally in opposition—and the Moon is reflecting all of the Sun's light. She is perfectly round at this point and well able to light the night—so well, in fact, that she casts Moon-shadows. It's now that she can be seen rising in the east at sunset, a bit later each night as this phase progresses. This is a time that corresponds with the culmination of plans, with maturity and completion. As she begins now to wane—or decrease—our plans come to bear, and we see the concrete results of the actions we initiated with the New Moon.

The Fourth Quarter

This phase occurs when the Moon has moved 90 degrees past the Full phase. At this time, she decreases in light and rises at midnight. She can be seen now in the eastern sky during the late evening hours and doesn't reach her highest point in the sky until early in the morning. This period in her journey corresponds with "disintegration," or a symbolic drawing back to reflect on accomplishments. It's now time to reorganize, clear the boards, and plan for the next New Moon stage.

The Moon through the Signs

Planets relate to urges or needs we have as a result of living inside human bodies. The signs say how we'll do things; they're a costume that shows the style of behavior a planet will display as it goes about its business. Since the Moon changes signs once every two-and-a-half days or so, she changes her symbolic "costume" more often than even the fastest of planets, Mercury.

Since the Moon rules the emotional tone of the day, it's good to know what type of mood she's in at any moment. The following thumbnail sketch should help you navigate through every day by cooperating with the Moon.

Moon in Aries

Here's the Moon at her fiery best, strutting around in red, feeling bold and energetic. Since this is Mars' favorite sign, you won't need to check your calendar to know when the Moon is here. For two days everyone is feisty and argumentative, nobody will let you step on their blue suede shoes, and even the meek will take a stand in their own defense. Since Aries is the first sign and a natural starting point for projects, it's also a wonderful time to channel all that "me-first" energy to initiate change and make new beginnings. Just watch out for a tendency to be too impulsive and stress oriented.

Moon in Taurus

The Moon in Taurus is dressed in her earthy finery of rich greens and browns. This Moon-ruled sign is the Lady at her most solid and sensual, feeling secure and well rooted in her sister Venus' sign. There's no need to hurry or change anything. You'll feel that all is quite well in your world when the Moon is in this sign, and there's no need to rock the boat. You'd rather sit still, have a wonderful dinner, and listen to good music. You're into appreciating the beauty of this Earth-planet—a truly Venusian activity—and into watching a sunset, viewing some good art, and taking care of money and other resources.

Moon in Gemini

Gemini Moons are active. This is a mutable air sign, so it likes to move quickly, and when the Moon is here we all tend to rush. The Moon's costume is now a coat of many colors and variety becomes the spice of life. Since Gemini is ruled by Mercury, we're suddenly in the mood for conversation, puzzles, and word games. We want at least two of everything, and we're more restless than usual. Now is a great time for letter-writing, phone calls, or short trips. We'll find the short cuts, but we should watch for a tendency to become a bit scattered under this fun, fickle Moon.

Moon in Cancer

Here's the Moon at her most emotional and nurturing. The Moon rules Cancer, so when she's here, she's home, lounging casually in her sea-greens and blues. Concerns turn to home, family, children, and our mothers, and we become more likely to express our emotions, or to be sympathetic and understanding to others. Now, too, is when we often find ourselves in the mood to take care of someone, to cook for or cuddle our dear ones. During this highly emotional sign, feelings run high, so it's important to watch out for becoming oversensitive, dependent, or needy. In all, now is a great time to putter around the house, have family over, and tend to domestic concerns.

Moon in Leo

When the Moon is in Leo, it's time for Drama with a capital "D." This theatrical sign is known for its big entrances, its love of display, and its need for attention. Leo is ruled by the Sun, the center of the universe, so when the Moon is in this sign, we're all feeling a need to be recognized and appreciated. After all, this is the Moon in royal robes, and someone ought to stop, bow, and ask which country she's queen of. Of course, this excitement and emotion can turn to histrionics or melodrama, so it's best not to overreact or overprimp during this period. It's a great time to take in a show (or star in one), be romantic, or express your feelings for someone in royal, regal style.

Moon in Virgo

Here's the Moon at her most discriminating. Wearing an efficient, tailored outfit that's specially designed for work, she's ready to take care of whatever needs taking care of. This is the most detail oriented sign out there, the sign most concerned with fixing and tending to. This Moon sign puts us in the mood to clean, scour, sort, and trouble-shoot. Virgo is the most helpful of all the signs, ready to take up a tool and offer her assistance. Now is when we're more health conscious, work oriented, and duty bound, too, so this is a great period to pay attention to our diet, our hygiene, and our daily schedules.

Moon in Libra

Libra is the second Venus-ruled sign, and the Moon is at her most other-oriented here. She's dressed in Venusian pastels and in the mood for attraction. Relationships and partnerships are important now. Since Libra's job is to restore balance, however, you may find yourself emotionally imbalanced and requiring a delicate tip of the scales to set yourself right; fortunately, you will be capable of doing just that. This is also a friendly Moon-time, when others will be cooperative and will more readily compromise. After all, Libra loves people. You will also be prompted by Libra Moons to make your surroundings beautiful or to take yourself to places of great beauty, so now is a great time to decorate, shop for the home, or visit places of elegant beauty.

Moon in Scorpio

Scorpio is a fixed, feminine water sign coruled by Mars and Pluto, so this Moon doesn't mess around. She's dressed up in formal black, looking so good she knows we can't take our eyes off her. Scorpio is the most intense of signs, so when the Moon is here, she feels everything to the absolute nth degree. Needless to say, we do, too. Passion, joy, jealousy, betrayal, love, and desire—they take center stage in our lives, and all our emotions deepen to the point of obsession. Be careful of a tendency to become secretive, suspicious, or to brood over an offense that was not intended. It's a great time to play detective and do research, or to allow ourselves to become intimate with someone.

Moon in Sagittarius

Here's the Moon at her most optimistic and nonjudgmental. Sagittarius is ruled by benevolent Jupiter, so it's time to shrug things off and laugh. Of course, Jupiter's also the planet of long-distance travel and educating the higher mind, so it's a great time to take off for a two-day adventure or to take a seminar on a new topic—say, philosophy or religion. Expect your intuitive abilities to run on high now, too—this is the sign with the gift of prophecy. Sag loves to collect knowledge, experiences, and wisdom, so when the Moon's in this sign she's dressed for adventure with a backpack and world atlas. Spend time outdoors, be spontaneous, and laugh much too loudly when the Moon is here. Enjoy life, but watch for a tendency toward excess.

Moon in Capricorn

Here's the Moon at her most organized and businesslike, wearing her best three-piece suit. Capricorn Moons bring out the dutiful, cautious, and pessimistic side in us, so for the time we suddenly prefer work over play. Our career goals become all-important now, and the right thing to do becomes the only thing to do. No sign is more concerned with conforming to set rules, touching the bases, and following orders. Now is the time to tend to the family business, to act responsibly, and to organize any part of our lives that's become scattered or disrupted. Now, too, is the time to set down rules and guidelines, to sit patiently and listen. Be careful of acting in too businesslike a way, at the expense of the emotions.

Moon in Aquarius

The Moon in Aquarius brings out the rebel in us, for better or worse. Dressed in something outrageous, eccentric, and electric blue, this Moon is ready to break free from the past. Now is when we escape our ruts and make sure everyone sees us for the unique individuals we are. It's a time of extreme and sudden actions—when we surprise even ourselves at what we say and when we're prone to complete reversals at the last minute. This sign is ruled by Uranus, so personal freedom and individuality are more important than anything. Our schedules are topsy-turvy, and our causes are urgent, but watch for a tendency to become fanatical or break tradition just for the sake of breaking it.

Moon in Pisces

This sign belongs to the planet Neptune, the ruler of altered states of reality. When the Moon slips into this sign, we crave something to help us escape from reality—sleep, meditation, prayer, drugs, or alcohol. Pisces Moon dresses in her most ethereal flowing pink gown, picks up her pink smoke machine and sparkling bucket of pink dust, and sets out to woo us and convince us everything's all right. Now is when we're most susceptible to emotional assaults of any kind, when we're feeling vague, dreamy, wistful, and impressionable. Now, too, is when we're at our most spiritual and when we're more compassionate and intuitive—a good time to attend a spiritual group or religious gathering.

The Void-of-Course Moon

The Moon makes a loop around the Earth every twenty-eight days, moving through each of the signs in two and a half days or so. As she passes through the 30 degrees of each sign, she "visits" with the planets in numerical order by forming angles or aspects with them. Because she moves one degree in just two to two-and-a-half hours, her influence on each planet lasts only a few hours, then she moves along. As she approaches the late degrees of the sign she's passing through, she eventually reaches the planet that's in the highest degree of any sign, and forms what will be her final aspect before leaving her own sign. From this point until she actually enters the new sign, she is referred to as void-of-course, or v/c.

Think of it this way: The Moon is the emotional "tone" of the day, carrying feelings with her particular to the sign she's wearing at the moment. She rules instinct, that way of knowing without really knowing. After she has contacted each of the planets, she symbolically rests before changing her costume, so her instinct is temporarily on hold. It's during this time that many people feel fuzzy, vague, or even scattered. Plans or decisions we make now will usually not pan out. Without the instinctual "knowing" the Moon provides as she touches each planet, we tend to be unrealistic or exercise poor judgment. The traditional description of the v/c Moon is that "nothing will come of this." And it is true that actions initiated under a v/c Moon are often wasted, irrelevant, or incorrect—usually because information needed to make a sound decision is hidden or missing or has been overlooked.

Although it's not a good time to initiate plans, routine tasks seem to go just fine during v/c Moon. This period is ideal for what the Moon does best: reflection. We are able to assimilate what the world has tossed at us over the past few days as the Moon transited through the current sign. Any planet changing signs signals a change in mass consciousness, and although the Moon changes signs more quickly than other planets she does not have any less impact on us. In fact, we should use this time to meditate, ponder, and imagine—let our conscious minds rest and allow ourselves to feel.

On the lighter side, remember that there are other good uses for the v/c Moon. This is the time when the universe seems to be most open to loopholes. It's a great time to make plans you don't want to fulfill or schedule things you don't want to do. In other words, like the song says, "to everything, there is a season." Even v/c Moons....

2001 Eclipses

Eclipse times in plain typeface are Eastern Standard; bold typeface times are Pacific Standard. Times are rounded off to the nearest minute. The exact time of an eclipse generally differs from the exact time of a New or Full Moon. For solar eclipses, "greatest eclipse" represents the time (converted from Local Mean Time) of the Moon's maximum obscuration of the Sun as viewed from the Earth. For lunar eclipses, "middle eclipse" represents the time at which the Moon rests at the centermost point of its journey through the shadow cast by the Earth passing between it and the Sun. Data is from *Astronomical Phenomena for the Year 2001,* prepared jointly by the United States Naval Observatory and the Royal Greenwich Observatory.

January 9
Total Eclipse of the Moon: 19° ♋ 39'

			Long.	Lat.
Moon enters penumbra	12:44 pm	**9:44 am**	80°W	22°N
Middle of eclipse	3:21 pm	**12:21 pm**		
Moon leaves penumbra	5:58 pm	**2:58 pm**	33°W	22°N

June 21
Total Eclipse of the Sun: 0° ♋ 10'

			Long.	Lat.
Eclipse begins	4:33 am	**1:33 am**	41°E	25°S
Greatest eclipse	6:58 am	**3:58 am**	1°W	11°S
Eclipse ends	9:34 am	**6:34 am**	45°W	15°S

July 5
Partial Eclipse of the Moon: 13° ♑ 39'

			Long.	Lat.
Moon enters penumbra	7:11 am	**4:11 am**	157°W	23°S
Middle of eclipse	9:55 am	**6:55 am**		
Moon leaves penumbra	12:40 pm	**9:40 am**	118°W	23°S

December 14
Annular Eclipse of the Sun: 22° ♐ 56'

			Long.	Lat.
Eclipse begins	1:03 pm	**10:03 am**	172°E	22°N
Greatest eclipse	3:45 pm	**12:45 pm**	132°E	1°N
Eclipse ends	6:41 pm	**3:41 pm**	89°E	6°N

December 30
Penumbral Eclipse of the Moon: 8° ♋ 48'

			Long.	Lat.
Eclipse begins	3:25 am	**12:25 am**	127°E	24°N
Middle of eclipse	5:29 am	**2:29 am**		
Eclipse ends	7:33 am	**4:33 am**	173°W	24°N

Astronomical Phenomena 2001
Visibility of Planets

The planets below are referenced to the constellations (astronomical or sidereal zodiac placements), not to the zodiac signs (tropical zodiac). Information on Uranus and Neptune assumes the use of a telescope.

Resource: *Astronomical Phenomena for the Year 2001*, prepared by the U.S. Naval Observatory and the Royal Greenwich Observatory.

Mercury can only be seen low in the east before sunrise, or low in the west after sunset (about the time of beginning or end of civil twilight). It is visible in the mornings between the following approximate dates: February 19 to April 15, June 26 to July 29, and October 21 to November 18. The planet is brighter at the end of each period; the best conditions in northern latitudes occur from late October to early November, and in southern latitudes in mid-March. It is visible in the evenings between the following approximate dates: January 10 to February 7, May 1 to June 7, August 15 to October 8, and from December 21 into the next year. The planet is brighter at the beginning of each period; the best conditions in northern latitudes occur from late January to early February and in mid-May, and in southern latitudes in September.

Venus is a brilliant object in the morning sky from the beginning of the year until late March when it becomes too close to the Sun for observation. Early in April it reappears in the morning sky, where it can be seen until a few days after the beginning of December, which it again becomes too close to the Sun for observation. Venus is in conjunction with Mercury on April 6, with Saturn on July 15, and with Jupiter on August 6.

Mars can be seen in the morning sky in Virgo shortly after midnight, moving into Libra after the first week of January and then into Scorpio from the last week of February. Its westward elongation gradually increases, moving into Ophiuchus from early March (passing 5°N of Antares on March 4), Sagittarius in the second half of April and back into Ophiuchus from early June. Mars is at opposition on June 13 when it is visible throughout the night. It passes into Sagittarius from early September, and can only be seen in the evening sky after mid-October, moving into Capricorn in late October and Aquarius in early December.

Jupiter is in Taurus at the beginning of the year, and can be seen for more than half the night until around the last week in February after which it can only be seen in the evening sky (passing 5°N of Aldebaran on April 16).

From the beginning of June it becomes too close to the Sun for observation. It reappears in the morning sky in late June moving into Gemini in mid-July in which constellation it remains throughout the rest of the year. Jupiter is in conjunction with Mercury on May 16 and July 12, and with Venus on August 6.

Saturn is in Taurus throughout the year. It can be seen for more than half the night until around mid-February, after which period it can only be seen in the evening sky. Its eastward elongation gradually decreases and from the start of the second week in May it becomes too close to the Sun for observation. It reappears in the morning sky in mid-June (passing 4°N of Aldebaran on July 13 and December 17). It is at opposition on December 3, when it can be seen throughout the night. For the remainder of the year its eastward elongation gradually decreases being visible for the greater part of the night. Saturn is in conjunction with Mercury on May 7 and with Venus on July 15.

Uranus is visible in the evening sky until a few days after mid-January in Capricorn and remains in this constellation throughout the year. It then becomes too close to the Sun for observation until early March, when it reappears in the morning sky. It is at opposition on August 15 when it can be seen throughout the night, after which its eastward elongation gradually decreases and from mid-November can only be seen in the evening sky.

Neptune is visible as an evening star in Capricorn at the beginning of January and remains in this constellation throughout the year. It then becomes too close to the Sun for observation until mid-February when it reappears in the morning sky. Its westward elongation gradually increases until July 30 when it is at opposition. From early November it can only be seen in the evening sky.

Do not confuse (1) Saturn with Mercury in the first week of May when Mercury is the brighter object. (2) Jupiter with Mercury in mid-May and again around mid-July; on both occasions Jupiter is brighter object. (3) Venus with Jupiter in the first half of August, and with Mercury from the end of the third week of October to mid-November; on both occasions Venus is the brighter object.

Time Zone Conversions

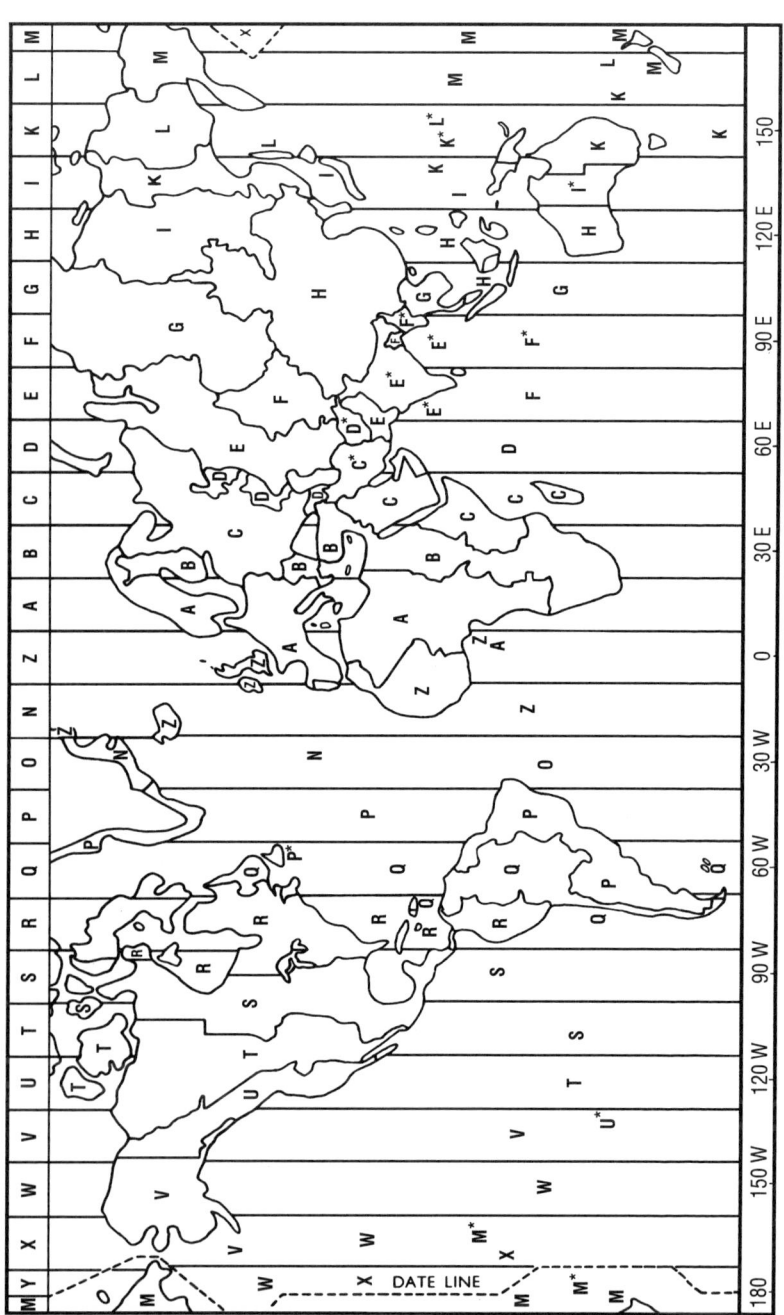

World Time Zones
Compared to Eastern Standard Time

( ) From Map
(S) Subtract 1 hour
(R) EST (Used in Guide)
(Q) Add 1 hour
(P) Add 2 hours
(O) Add 3 hours
(N) Add 4 hours
(Z) Add 5 hours
(T) MST/Subtract 2 hours
(U) PST/Subtract 3 hours
(V) Subtract 4 hours
(W) Subtract 5 hours
(X) Subtract 6 hours

(Y) Subtract 7 hours
(A) Add 6 hours
(B) Add 7 hours
(C) Add 8 hours
(D) Add 9 hours
(E) Add 10 hours
(F) Add 11 hours
(G) Add 12 hours
(H) Add 13 hours
(I) Add 14 hours
(K) Add 15 hours
(L) Add 16 hours
(M) Add 17 hours

(C*) Add 8.5 hours
(D*) Add 9.5 hours
(E*) Add 10.5 hours
(F*) Add 11.5 hours
(I*) Add 14.5 hours
(K*) Add 15.5 hours
(L*) Add 16.5 hours
(M*) Add 18 hours
(P*) Add 2.5 hours
(V*) Subtract 4.5 hours

Standard Time =
Universal Time (Greenwich Mean Time) + Value from Table

Planetary Stations for 2001

Planet	Begin	EST	PST	End	EST	PST	Planet	Begin	EST	PST	End	EST	PST
Saturn	09/12/00	6:35 am	3:35 am	1/24/01	7:24 pm	4:24 pm	Ceres	5/16/01	7:37 pm	4:37 pm	8/27/01	7:48 pm	4:48 pm
Jupiter	09/29/00	7:53 am	4:53 am	1/25/01	3:39 am	12:39 am	Uranus	5/29/01	10:11 am	7:11 am	10/30/01	5:55 pm	2:55 pm
Mercury	2/03/01	8:55 pm	5:55 pm	2/25/01	10:42 pm	7:42 pm	Mercury	6/04/01	12:21 am	(6/03) 9:21 pm	6/28/01	12:48 pm	(6/27) 9:48 pm
Venus	3/08/01	8:06 pm	5:06 pm	4/19/01	11:34 pm	8:34 pm	Saturn	9/26/01	7:04 pm	4:04 pm	2/07/02	8:33 pm	5:33 pm
Pluto	3/17/01	9:36 pm	6:36 pm	8/23/01	11:06 am	8:06 am	Vesta	10/01/01	2:24 pm	11:24 am	10/22/01	7:24 pm	4:24 pm
Pallas	4/05/01	9:05 pm	6:05 pm	7/18/01	7:45 am	4:45 am	Jupiter	10/09/01	6:20 am	3:20 am	1/14/02	3:45 pm	12:45 pm
Chiron	4/07/01	1:02 pm	10:02 am	8/26/01	4:19 pm	1:19 am	Juno	11/02/01	10:35 am	7:35 am	3/01/02	10:16 pm	7:16 pm
Neptune	5/10/01	8:13 pm	5:13 pm	10/17/01	8:48 pm	5:48 pm	Juno	12/25/01	6:09 pm	3:09 pm	3/27/02	10:27 pm	7:27 pm
Mars	5/11/01	11:08 am	8:08 am	7/19/01	5:45 pm	2:45 pm	Mercury	1/18/02	3:51 pm	12:51 pm	2/08/02	12:29 pm	9:29 am

	2000 DEC	2001 JAN	FEB	MAR	APR	MAY	JUN	JUL	AUG	SEP	OCT	NOV	DEC	2002 JAN	2002 FEB
♄															
♃															
☿															
♀															
⚴															
⚶															
⚵															
♇															
⚷															
⛢															
♆															
♂															

Eastern Standard Time in regular typeface, Pacific Standard Time in **bold typeface**.

2001 Weekly Forecasts

by Kim Rogers-Gallagher

January 1–7

This is a legendary year to be alive on our wonderful planet. And your chance to make it legendary begins on the morning of January 1, when the emotional Moon is in Aries. A veritable bullet, this lovely lady in silver rules the impatient mood of the day and is perfect for getting your New Year's resolutions off and running. Mars, the planet of initiation and fresh beginnings, meanwhile, will be in transformative Scorpio, eager for drastic change. This red-hot Rambo will charge off into the millennium in a square to woozy Neptune, creating an energy that's capable of turning dreams into reality. Just be sure you're not aiming too high, or being unrealistic. On Tuesday, the Moon will meet up with deep, penetrating Pluto. Examine your feelings and put plans into action now. By the time loving Venus tiptoes into tender Pisces on Wednesday afternoon, you'll feel brand new—and you might be in the company of someone new, too. This dreamy, romantic lady loves being in love, and on Friday morning she'll form an active square with daring Jupiter. This combination is never shy about stepping right up to someone new and saying, "Hello," but it also tends to be a bit on the excessive side. Try not to overdo it if you're out partying. Saturday and Sunday are perfect days to spend taking care of business, tending to paperwork, and considering the details of any major decision, as Mercury, the god of thought, will be in a cooperative trine with sturdy, practical Saturn.

January 8–14

Vesta is the astrological goddess that bestows an awareness of the sacred aspects of life. No matter how mundane or trivial the event, this asteroid allows us to see the spiritual reasons for its occurrence. On Monday, this reverential energy will enter Pisces, which is known for its psychic abilities. Take a moment to meditate and ponder where you are in the scheme of things—both personally and professionally. Tuesday's lunar eclipse in Cancer will illuminate an emotional issue and bring you closer to your dear ones. Wednesday's collection of energies asks that you let the real you shine. Show off your talents and say what's on your mind. That morning, the Moon will strut proudly into Leo, the sign of the performer, and communicative Mercury will begin an especially long stint in uncompromising Aquarius. For the next nine weeks, we'll all be pretty darned set in our ways, and changing each other's minds will be next to impossible. The idea behind the Messenger's trek through this sign is acceptance. and everyone's opinions are valid now. Granted, that's easier said than done, but gentle Venus will lend a hand by moving into unconditionally accepting Pisces for the rest of the month. By Saturday evening, when Mercury trines understanding Neptune, we'll have a chance to gain some insight into what makes others tick. The Sun and grounded Saturn will trine, too, making this another perfect evening to sit quietly and reflect, or share a dream with someone.

January 15–21

The week begins with the possibility of sudden, drastic changes in financial and relationship matters. Venus, the goddess of love, will team up Monday night with Juno, the goddess of commitment. What makes this situation interesting is that at just about that exact same time, the emotional Moon will connect with Uranus, who specializes in reversals and eye-openings. The fourth quarter Moon on Tuesday morning will be in relationship-oriented Libra, calling for you to finish things up and move on. And that night, Venus will square off with intense Pluto as she's trining Mars, giving us impetus to get to the heart of the matter in relationship issues. This cosmic mixture brings together sensuality and sexuality, so this would be a good night to stay home with your mate, rekindling the spark that brought you together. Single folks should expect new encounters to be exciting, as passion will linger through Wednesday and into Thursday when thoughtful Mercury will get up close and personal with seductive Pluto to share a secret—or uncover the truth. Saturday morning's merry Sagittarius Moon will have her hands full keeping the situation lighthearted, since passionate Pluto will meet up with her as chatty Mercury enters into a square with assertive Mars. If you wake up a bit testy, use this combination to dig in, either literally or figuratively. There's going to be a strong tone of competition in the air, so try to find a constructive outlet for your urge to win.

January 22–28

On Monday, Mercury will connect with startling Uranus in Aquarius, and when the messenger meets up with Mr. Unpredictable, you should expect surprises. For several days, be ready for a call or e-mail announcing the last thing on earth you ever expected. The New Moon on Wednesday morning will be in Aquarius, too, a sign of unexpected starts. The really big cosmic headline of the week, however, concerns Jupiter and Saturn, both of whom will stop in their tracks to turn forward after several months of going retrograde. Saturn's about-face will happen first, on Wednesday evening. Expect delays and traffic jams, and be patient. Look around and see if there are not any lessons to learn while you're siting still. Saturn is absolutely insisting you learn lessons—he didn't earn his nickname, "the Cosmic Schoolmaster," by accident, after all. Jupiter will station next, on Thursday morning. Since he's the heaven's version of Santa Claus, such times often point to sudden release. This time out, he'll punch that release button just as Saturn loosens his grip on the steering wheel, and it's going to feel like the lid has blown off the pressure cooker. In short, there's going to be a gush of energy, so step aside and let it go. A pensive Sun-Neptune conjunction that evening will help settle things, but the fireworks won't be over just yet. Late Friday, Venus will meet Saturn to make a solid promise concerning love, possessions, or money. And on Saturday morning, fiery Mars will square off with erratic Uranus, making the most volatile combination in the heavens. Don't take chances driving, and stay away from anyone with a history of violent or unstable behavior. Use this pair is to do something impulsive. Just be careful!

January 29–February 4

Your week begins with a burst of energy, brought to you courtesy of a lady who doesn't take "no" for an answer, the Moon in assertive Aries. She's famous for her impatience, too, so you may find yourself rushing through these days. By Wednesday, however, the Universe will provide a stable Taurus Moon to settle things down and put you in touch with creature comforts like chocolate, pillows, and fine wine. Indulge your senses. In the evening, Mercury, the god of the five senses, will ease his way into Pisces, and you'll find your taste in music changing to something more mellow—Mozart, Enya, Windham Hill—even as your stress level lightens. You may woo someone on Friday when loving Venus will storm into Aries, a passionate energy that's not at all shy on the approach. Don't be surprised if she and the Moon in Gemini put you in contact with someone from far away who's delightfully interesting and bold. No matter who you're seeing Saturday evening, be ready for delays. Mercury turns backwards late that night for one of his thrice-yearly retrograde periods and causes miscommunications and misunderstandings. Since active Mars will also oppose unwavering Saturn, you'll need to double-check directions, schedules, and all detailed paperwork with an extra careful eye. All's well that ends well, however, and it will, on Sunday. Venus and Jupiter, the easiest planets in the heavens to get along with, will form a stimulating sextile, giving you a chance to laugh over recent mishaps. These two are the stuff luck is made of, by the way, so you may want to pick up a lottery ticket....

February 5–11

Monday's Cancer Moon will mellow you out after a hectic weekend, so be sure to kick back and relax a bit in the comfort of your nest. Don't get too comfortable, however, as the Universe has another high-energy week scheduled. Starting Tuesday, communicative Mercury will back up into high-tech

Aquarius, prompting you to review all your personal causes—especially those you became involved with back in January. Group issues may also need to be reconsidered, since new information will turn up when you least expect it. Wednesday's menu, meanwhile, calls for a showy, dramatic Leo Moon to cast her bright light on a matter of romance. With Mercury in the mood to bring back voices from the past, you shouldn't be surprised if your hear one, especially with Friday's Sun/Uranus conjunction acting as a trigger. This combination will be more than enough excuse to do something that's totally out of character. Think of something you've always been afraid of pursuing, close your eyes, and go for it—and expect others to do the very same thing. A gentle Libra Moon will combine forces with her sister, Venus, and with Neptune, the planet of romance and unconditional love, to bring you a tender moment and a nostalgic daydream. If you're attached, it's prime time to get to know your partner again by offering up a rose or asking the band to play your song. Single folks could bump into someone new under chance circumstances—which, as any astrologer knows, aren't "chance" at all....

February 12–18

On Monday night, the Moon will sidle off into Scorpio, casting the shadow of a detective with instinctive insight. Trust your antennae now, and proof of your rightness will arrive. That evening, thoughtful Mercury will combine with the Sun and research-oriented Saturn to unearth hidden information that you must act on. Also, if you have to put in a few hours of overtime at work, now is a good time. Saturn represents authority figures who'll be watching you closely. On Wednesday afternoon, impetuous Mars will charge into fiery Sagittarius, the sign of generosity, daring, and excess. Be especially aware of speaking or acting overimpulsively when fleet-footed Mercury, the god of transportation and communication, connects with startling Uranus on Thursday afternoon. Friday morning's Sagittarius Moon will bring you the pat on the back you deserve—with an added bonus, raise, or promotion. This lovely lady in silver loves to laugh, exchange hugs, and meet folks from far away, so expect visitors from distant shores this weekend. The Sun sets up shop in Pisces on Sunday morning, a dreamy sign that activates creativity, spirituality, and the need to connect with like-minded others. Pisces also likes to escape every now and then, so be careful with substances, especially drugs or alcohol, on Sunday evening. Mars will touch base with Jupiter, who exaggerates every impulse. These two are famous for never knowing when to quit, so it's useless to tell yourself not to "just do it." You'll need to do something now, so make sure it's something positive and reasonable. The best use for this energy is intellectual competition, so get together with a group of friends and debate the virtues of your political party or your favorite team.

February 19–25

There's a sturdy Capricorn Moon holding court as the week begins, making this the perfect time to deal with responsibilities and details of all kinds. Remember too that Mercury is still retrograde and primed to help you review the facts and redo things right. An easy trine between the Moon and Saturn Monday evening means it's a good time to consult with experts and older relatives. Don't let your imagination carry you away Tuesday evening, however, when there will be a lot of sparkly pink stuff in the air as the Moon meets with romantic Neptune and the Sun squares off with exaggerating Jupiter in woozy Pisces. Make use of this cosmic mixture by tapping into your creative potential with a pen, paintbrush, or musical instrument. By Thursday, the Moon will square off with serious Saturn just as the Sun and Mars move into a square. If you have a tough mission, use this time to get you through the last of it. Restless or anxious feelings could arrive Friday, when the New Moon in Pisces will bring both luminaries into an assertive square with Mars. An impulsive Aries Moon will be in the building when you wake up Sunday, and since she'll arrive just a few hours before Mercury finally turns direct, fast-paced communications will be the order of the day. That trend will last for several days, since Mercury's station will put him in a long-winded sextile with intense Pluto. Add in Venus's loving touch and sweet words, and passion will suddenly be on Sunday evening's menu. Enjoy the closeness, and don't be afraid to be completely honest about your needs.

February 26–March 4

This is a wonderful week for learning, making positive changes in relationship and financial matters, and concentrating on difficult mental tasks. Mercury is barely moving and will be well within range of a sextile to Pluto all week, giving your perception a boost. At the same time, Venus, goddess of love, is slowing down to go retrograde, putting her in an easy, exciting trine with seductive Pluto for most of the month. Pluto just loves to dig, so if you've got to do a bit of detective work, and if it's a relationship matter you're investigating, your search for clues will yield results. And speaking of love, any romance that begins around this time will be deeply passionate and amazingly intimate, physically and intellectually. All your encounters will carry a tone of close understanding, especially if you happen to meet someone new on Thursday morning. Fiery Mars and intuitive Neptune will allow you to tune in to the thoughts and feelings of others and make connections with soul mates over the weekend. So don't be shy—introduce yourself!

March 5–11

Around lunchtime Monday, the Sun will square off with Pluto, a planet who knows exactly how to push buttons—especially power buttons. Since the

Sun often brings up issues concerning authority, this testy, argumentative aspect with Pluto may mean there's a power struggle brewing. However, this pair's potent energy can also bring closure to situations that have gone past the point of no return. Use this team wisely, and you'll effect positive change in your own life and in the lives of those around you. On Tuesday, a theatrical, showy Leo Moon will spend an easy day passing out trines and sextiles to every planet she encounters, making all your meetings feisty ones. By Wednesday, this proud, persuasive energy will oppose both chatty Mercury and unpredictable Uranus, possibly producing a bit of melodrama. Lovely Venus will shift into reverse on Thursday evening, bringing back memories for the next six weeks of past loves, and increasingly the likelihood that one will reappear. Friday's New Moon will raise health and work-related issues, inspiring you to change your habits. Communicative Mercury will collide with unpredictable Uranus, too, bringing unexpected missives, coincidental meetings, and flashes of brilliance.

March 12–18

Vesta will pass into Aries late Monday night into this most fiery of signs. She'll therefore become a goddess with a temper, inspiring you to defend your cause with a vengeance. You may have to stand your ground and speak your mind, too, regarding something that's near and dear to your heart, since Mercury, the communicator, will square off with Saturn. Expect delays in your travel plans, and be patient with dear ones who show up a bit late. If you've got an apology to offer up or accept, do it graciously on Thursday, when Mercury will combine forces with Chiron, the wise centaur. Words will hold powerful healing potential. On Friday, the Sun will enter into a stimulating sextile with Saturn, bringing together pride and experience. Don't be afraid to show higher-ups exactly what you can do. Late that same night, Mercury will leave electrifying Aquarius behind for two weeks in Pisces, turning his ordinarily intellectual nature into something much more psychic. Don't be surprised at how easy it becomes to know answers to pressing questions, and be sure to trust your intuition. Meanwhile, the weekend will arrive with a bang, as Pluto's retrograde station on Saturday will put him right smack dab in a tight conjunction with red-hot Mars. Any changes you've been putting off just won't wait any longer. Be as gentle as possible, but do make those changes now.

March 19–25

An early morning trine between Venus and Mars, the ancient lovers, will start your Monday off with a dose of passion. Her gentle touch will take the edge off whatever last weekend brought and will soothe any troubled waters. She'll also be in trine with seductive Pluto that evening. Add Venus, goddess of love, and Mars, god of fire and planet in charge of sexuality, to the mix and you'll have quite the passionate evening ahead. Tuesday and Wednesday stand to be every bit as exciting, too. The Sun will storm into Aries on Tuesday morning just as Neptune touches the Moon with her magic wand. This, friends, is the perfect astrological formula for love at first sight. If you see someone you're drawn to, then, don't hesitate to introduce yourself. There's no such thing as a coincidence—at least, not in the eyes of the Universe. Around lunch Wednesday a second dose of passion will arrive when the Moon connects with spontaneous Uranus as conversational Mercury forms an action-oriented square with Jupiter. This pair loves to elaborate, exaggerate, and turn molehills into mountains. Pluto will conjoin with Pallas Athena on Thursday evening, conjuring up the image of a wise, shrewd defender who's absolutely unstoppable. Choose a cause to champion, and have at! The New Moon on Saturday will occur in Aries, an impatient cosmic bullet just looking for a target. Fire when ready, just be sure you aim first.

March 26–April 1

An earthy Taurus Moon will put creature comforts at the top of your priority list Monday night, making physical pleasures, sensual encounters, and total hedonism the only way to go. That same touch-loving lady will be in the neighborhood on Tuesday, when the Sun in bold, daring Aries will team up with expansive Jupiter, old Santa Claus himself, to bring you luck. Expect to be in the right place at the right time and grab hold of any opportunities that come along with gusto. You'll be privy to secret information—or you'll feel the urge to confide in someone—that night, when thoughtful Mercury will connect with dark, secretive Pluto. You might want to begin your weekend early, and head out to have some fun on Thursday night, when the Sun will conjoin with Venus, both of whom will be wearing their Aries red. This team adds up to fiesty fun encounters and brand new beginnings in relationships. If you've been working something out with your partner, now is the time to put the changes into action. If you meet someone new, you'll be hard-pressed to resist hopping on a plane to Vegas within a few hours. Either way, the weekend will be equally invigorating, since lovely Venus will form sextiles with both Neptune—the goddess of harlequin romance—and Jupiter, the planet who loves to stomp on the accelerator.

April 2–8

The Leo Moon will start your week off with a dramatic flourish that's bound to have you wishing the weekend were longer. Her love of romance, of big entrances and exits, and of spoiling her loved ones will combine with tender Venus in impetuous Aries, Jupiter in witty Gemini, and dreamy, nostalgic Neptune. Yes, it's the perfect combination of energies for falling in love, so if you're single and you've got sick days coming, take one on Tuesday, and head out to play Monday night. You'll be more than able to make up for whatever you missed when you get back to your desk on Wednesday. Hardworking Saturn will connect with thoughtful Mercury to help you concentrate on the job at hand. The Sun will form an easy trine with Pluto on Wednesday, too, smoothing your dealings with superiors. Mercury will dash into Aries late Thursday night, adding a competitive edge to your conversations for the next two weeks. If you're feeling cranky or argumentative, treat your brain to a puzzle or get a good workout routine started. Saturday's lovely Full Moon will be in Libra, the sign that specializes in relationships. Now's the time to make commitments, especially since Mercury and Venus will get together Sunday to create beautiful words, pretty music, and poetry. This is the combination that inspires us to say, "I love you."

April 9–15

The Scorpio Moon starts your week off on a note of intrigue, inspiring you to make inquiries. On Tuesday, you may be quite surprised at what you find. Pushy Mars teams with that mad scientist, Uranus, to urge you to try a new technique to get what you're after. That same day, Mercury's natural talent for communicating will blend with Neptune's ability to infiltrate the ranks of any group, and you'll be able to mingle, ask all the right questions, and arrive at a decision based on what you've discovered. By Wednesday, you'll have the urge to chat at length about what you've been up to behind the scenes. Mercury, the cosmic microphone, will meet up in a fun, exciting sextile with Jupiter, who does not know how to keep a secret. On Friday, the asteroid goddess of relationships, Jupiter's faithful wife, Juno, will switch costumes and emerge from the galactic phone booth wearing her earthy Taurus green. This solid, commitment-oriented lady will give your new relationships her most earnest blessing. Surprises will be in the air later that evening when the Sun will form a sextile with startling Uranus. Use the weekend to take care of chores and tend to unfinished projects with the help of a hard-working Capricorn Moon, and a sky full of energetic fire-planets who'll be revved up and ready to get things accomplished.

April 16–22

There'll be a touch of rebellion in the air as you make your coffee Monday morning. The Moon will be on duty in eccentric, unconventional Aquarius, becoming a wild-eyed lady who believes in freedom and self-expression. You may even find that you're out to deliberately raise a few eyebrows on Tuesday evening, when the Moon connects with Uranus, the original radical himself. Wednesday's astrological weather calls for more of the same, when Mercury, the bringer of messages, will be jump-started by Uranus' electric touch. Fasten your seat belt, and prepare for something impossible to happen now. Get all that energy out of your system early in the week, by the way, because by Thursday, things will settle down considerably. The Sun will step into responsible Taurus, a sign that operates at a pace about ten light years slower than Aries. This doesn't mean your love life will be boring, however. The lady Venus will see that there's some action on the agenda that same day, when she turns forward after six weeks. It's time to move forward with as much speed as her red-hot Aries frame of mind will allow. In other words, when it comes to relationships, this will be the day to "go for it!" On Friday, Saturn will shift gears, crossing over the cosmic state line from Taurus—an outfit he was a little too comfortable in—to Gemini, the most mercurial of all the signs. As he shifts out of his fixed Taurean suit, you'll find it a bit easier to move. But you'll have to be sure to follow all the road-signs carefully. Mercury will set off for Taurus on Saturday, slowing his winged feet a bit and turning his attention towards speaking, writing, and driving carefully. Make sure you've got the right directions this weekend.

April 23–April 29

Bright and early Monday morning, the New Moon will plant a seed in fertile Taurus, asking that you begin anew in the department of money, possessions, and valuables. And yes, this includes valuable people. If you're out to woo someone, make your approach early this day, when both the Sun and Moon will connect with Mercury, and tender words of love will come easily and be well received. Tuesday's conjunction between Mercury and Juno, who loves making long-term vows, will solidify all existing bonds and prompt you to consider new ones. The romance continues throughout Wednesday, when conversational Mercury will join up with Neptune. Extend your hand, a promise or an apology, and accept a warm hug in return. On Thursday, the emotional Moon will meet generous Jupiter, and your heart will be wide open. These two specialize in blessing new relationships. If you're not looking for a love relationship at the moment, it'll be a wonderful time to visit the animal shelter to find a soulmate. The Moon will nest comfortably in Cancer all day Sunday, giving you a chance to stay home with the kids, your sweetie, or your new furry friend.

April 30–May 6

The Leo Moon arrived with her entourage on Sunday evening, sparking the perfect energy to begin this lively week. On Monday morning, she'll hook up with Neptune and create situations that will seem like Hallmark cards or Harlequin romances. On Tuesday, meanwhile, a caring Virgo Moon will combine with the initiative of Mars and the healing touch of Chiron to make all types of remedies and healings—including surgeries—go well. If you're up for an herbal cleansing or a juice fast, now is definitely the time to do it, as long as you consult with a holistic practitioner first. By Thursday, when thoughtful Mercury forms a quick-moving square with shocking Uranus, you'll feel like a new person. The emotional Moon will tiptoe into delicate Libra late Thursday evening, where she'll stay until the wee hours of Sunday morning. One-to-one relationships will be a priority now, while on Saturday Mercury will dash off happily into his favorite sign, fleet-footed Gemini, where he'll remain until mid-July. Use this lighthearted, witty energy to its fullest by enjoying conversation with friends over the next two months, by taking classes and working on intellectual matters, and by remembering the punchlines to your favorite jokes. Wind down, meanwhile, on Sunday, as the Moon retreats into Scorpio, a water-sign that loves privacy. Expansive Jupiter will step into a tug-of-war with powerful Pluto also on Sunday, which could mean that power struggles will be in the air. Be brave, however, and use this pair to make positive changes in your relationships.

May 7–13

Full Moons always mean there are revelations coming, and when one occurs in Scorpio, you can bet there's going to be a hot time in the old town tonight. We're talking passion, intrigue, and change. So fasten your seatbelt and be ready for anything early this week. After an initial period of intensity, however, you'll enjoy Tuesday and Wednesday, when the merry Sagittarius Moon will hold court, asking only that you get deep and philosophical on Wednesday morning before you have a good time. On Thursday, it's back to business with a dutiful Capricorn Moon, but expect your imagination to be running on high, too. Thoughtful Mercury, affectionate Venus, and dreamy Neptune will join hands for a three-way conference on saying, "I love you." On Friday, Mr. Mars will turn retrograde, and from now until July, you'll need to be careful when you issue challenges. Classically, when Mars is in reverse, the aggressor in any battle doesn't do too well—unless it's a battle you're fighting for the second or third time…. The weekend looks like great fun, but you'll have to do your homework before that Capricorn Moon and the Sun in hard-working Taurus will let you go out to play. By Sunday, however, a wild-eyed Aquarius Moon will roll in, looking for something "different" to do with her time. If you're bored or restless, try something new, or get out there and socialize with a whole new group of friends.

May 14–20

There's rebellion in the air as the week begins. The emotional Moon in Aquarius is the first culprit, a lady who considers the word "no" to be a personal challenge. She'll be in the vicinity on Monday, as chatty Mercury and potent Pluto are in opposition, and this will put you at odds with someone who's trying to manipulate or control you. It's okay to say, "I won't have it," just be sure you're not arguing for the sake of it. This testy mood could last through Tuesday, when the Moon and Sun both will form hard angles to shocking Uranus. Expect to be awakened with a start this morning, and to run up against unpredictable things for the rest of the day. Tuesday night's square between the emotional Moon in Pisces and strict Saturn in Gemini could mean it's going to be tough to express your feelings. On the other hand, it's a great time to lay down new rules for relationships, and an even better time to quit something, cut back on a habit, or begin budgeting your resources or energy. Vesta, the goddess of the hearth, will enter earthy Taurus on Wednesday evening, putting home and family at the top of your priority list. Expect fireworks on Friday morning, when the emotional Moon will square off with red-hot Mars before she storms off into feisty Aries. If you've got something to say, do it now, but try to be gentle. That same evening, loving Venus and seductive Pluto will fall into an easy trine, thus making strong affections easy to express. On Sunday, the Sun will set off for Gemini and create a burst of navigation energy that's bound to have you thinking about taking off for at least a short time.

May 21–27

There's a New Moon set for Tuesday, and it's going to be all dressed up in lively, fun Gemini. If you're thinking of starting classes, learning a new skill, or studying a foreign language, now is the perfect time. Be prepared to change your mind at least once that day, however, and it may happen suddenly, as thoughtful Mercury will connect with Uranus, who just loves to cause last-minute changes. Thursday, meanwhile, looks absolutely wonderful for relationship issues of all kinds. The emotional Moon, affectionate Venus, and generous Jupiter will join hands in the heavens, creating the time for love at first sight. It's also a great time to extend or accept an apology, tell someone how very much you care, and make plans for the future with your mate. Saturday and Sunday will host a showy, dramatic Leo Moon, long known for her love of turning ordinary life events into theater. Since conversational Mercury will oppose assertive Mars late Saturday night, you might expect some rather exciting words around that time. If arguments come up, don't try to avoid them. It may be time to clear the air.

May 28–June 3

A regal Leo Moon will start the week off with a burst of playful fire, so don't think for a minute that Monday will be boring. In fact, when the Moon meets up with communicative Mercury this evening, exciting news is due. Be sure to check your answering machine and e-mail. Meanwhile, on Tuesday Uranus will stop to turn retrograde, and as the mad scientist of the heavens, he will likely be watching over a lot of unusual situations. Since the Sun and nostalgic Neptune will form an easy trine that same day, chances are good you'll hear from someone out of the blue, and you will rejoice. On Wednesday, Venus will begin approaching a sextile to Uranus. From Thursday, when the aspect is exact, until Saturday, love and money issues are apt to change at a moment's notice. Fortunately, a sextile is an easy aspect, so these changes will be positive and invigorating. It's a great time to move, accept a proposal, or plan a most unusual outing with a most unusual companion. Just don't get too attached to a schedule of any kind as the weekend draws near. Mercury will stop Sunday to turn backwards for several weeks, promoting a kind of "Murphy's Law" effect. If anything can possibly go wrong, it will, and at the worst possible time. But rather than getting upset over broken plans and unexpected delays, relax and let the universe drive. For the next three weeks, you'll need to go over and redo anything that wasn't done right the first time, so be ready to make corrections and repairs, and to play phone tag with friends.

June 4–10

Mercury will still be in reverse on Monday morning, so allow a bit of extra time to get where you're going. Chances are good now that short trips will be challenging, but be patient. The Sun and demanding Pluto will be in opposition, too, so power struggles with authority figures could come up if you're not careful. If you feel a burst of energy coming on, there's good reason for it. The Full Moon is due Tuesday night, and it's happening while the emotional Moon is in Sagittarius, the sign that most loves to exaggerate. Needless to say, your feelings will be running on high, but it might be for a wonderful reason. On Wednesday morning, Venus will step firmly into Taurus, one of her very favorite signs. For the next four weeks, the goddess of love will inspire you to pursue creature comforts of the most sensual kind. Money will be no object, just don't forget that there are lots of lovely, and free, experiences to be had on the planet. Enjoy a sunrise, a hike in the woods, or a walk on the beach while this elegant energy is with us. On Wednesday evening, plans could come up rather suddenly, as chatty Mercury will connect with Venus just as action-oriented Mars meets up with startling Uranus. If you're single, that could change now. For the remainder of the week and throughout the weekend, keep in mind that assertive Mars will be edging up to an opposition with expansive Jupiter, creating a high-energy time. Use this combination to tackle tough physical tasks.

June 11–17

Monday night, the emotional Moon in Pisces will touch base with both shocking Uranus and chatty Mercury, making a time for lively conversation and new experiences. So if you're getting together with friends, it's going to be great fun. On Tuesday, the opposition between energetic Mars and Jupiter, the king of exaggeration, will be exact. Hold on tight, then, because it's time for a jolt. If you've been in a rut of any kind, don't worry. Wednesday's Sun/Mars opposition will create more energy for change; though there may also be a dispute to settle. These two cosmic fireballs are the ultimate masculine energies and known for being red-hot, impulsive, and ego-driven; once in opposition, there's likely to be confrontation in the air. Needless to say, if you meet someone new around this time, it's going to be a fiery relationship. Thursday's Aries Moon will hold court while a Sun/Jupiter conjunction becomes exact, and there'll be even more assertion, aggression, and possibly anger, in the air. However, look to Thursday night's square between loving Venus and sympathetic Neptune to put an end to the battle. And on Friday, Mercury will oppose Chiron, the Great Healer, so words can be used to heal now. Take care with what you say, and how you say it, especially when the Sun connects with Mercury the next morning. Saturday will be busy, and a good time to do lots of errands. The week will end on an easy note, but there'll still be change in the air, as Mercury, the messenger, forms an easy trine with surprising Uranus Sunday night.

June 18–24

Bright and early Monday morning, Mercury and Jupiter will combine forces in a conjunction. Since both will be wearing sociable, conversational Gemini clothing at the time, you can expect to receive all kinds of communiques, some from very distant places. These two in cahoots create a cosmic shout, so be ready for someone to make a very strong statement. On Tuesday, Jupiter and Uranus will form a trine and create prime conditions for the arrival of windfalls. If you're feeling lucky, invest in a lottery ticket before lunch. Thursday will be a very emotional day for all of us, especially for the water sign folks. The Sun and Moon will enter sensitive Cancer just minutes before they set up a total Solar Eclipse in that sign, so it'll be a good time to nest, spend time with the kids, and tend to family matters. At the same time, Pallas Athena, the warrior Goddess, will step into focused, determined Scorpio and create a force to be reckoned with; if you've got a cause to champion, you'll be just about unstoppable now. By Sunday, a trine between realistic Saturn and dreamy Neptune will be exact, giving you a rare opportunity to make your fantasies come true. If there's a long-held wish you've been putting off pursuing, don't wait any longer. Make it happen.

June 25–July 1

The trine between serious Saturn and romantic Neptune will be just a few hours old when you wake up Monday morning, which means it'll be a great time to go off to work, especially if you're in the healing profession. These two in an easy aspect allow us to dream impossible dreams and to create better circumstances. Furthermore, Mercury's direct station on Wednesday will assist us in this. After three weeks in reverse, the fleet-footed messenger finally turns forward and lets us go on our merry way at last. Also, since he'll be close to long-distance Jupiter for a time, you can expect a week's worth of catching up with anyone you've been trying to contact. This includes friends from far away, some of whom will either be arriving or asking you to come visit. Now's the time to do it—you'll learn a lot from new surroundings. And speaking of learning, Mercury and Jupiter are the two planets most concerned with education. If you're up for a few night classes this summer, sign up now. All kinds of communications will go easily over the course of the week, and well into the weekend. On Saturday morning, you single folks will want to be up and about early. Loving Venus will square off with Uranus, the planet of coincidence, and the someone you've been looking for could be right across the room.

July 2–8

If you're currently attached, you could find your mate in a rather cranky mood as you pour your coffee Monday morning. Impatient Mars will be in an opposition with Juno, the goddess of commitment, and relationship issues will undoubtedly be on the agenda. With the Moon in optimistic Sagittarius, however, there's really nothing to worry about. In fact, these energies may conjure up a sudden trip with your partner, possibly to a far-off shore. If you're so inclined, then, make plans for that much needed weekend away. A lunar eclipse will arrive Thursday, meanwhile, just as Venus slips off into Gemini. With so much heavenly activity, you should expect the same from your own day. In fact, we'll all be feeling sky-high with energy, but maybe a little bit fickle, too, since Venus loves to flirt when in this sign. If you've been mulling over a decision lately and thought you'd arrived at the answer, don't be too sure until after Friday morning. Mercury, the great communicator, will form a cooperative trine with changeable Uranus, and you might switch sides before all is said and done. The emotional Moon will hover above you in changeable Aquarius all weekend, too, so don't be afraid of getting bored. It's time to stretch your mind a bit, whether by reading the latest issue of *Discover* or attending a UFO conference. Odd and unusual activities are in the air. Try everything you never thought you would.

July 9–15

A nice, peaceful Pisces Moon will arrive Monday morning and put you in a sympathetic, compassionate frame of mind all day. Your psychic abilities will also be running on high, so don't be surprised if you find you can read someone's thoughts, or if you know who's on the telephone before you answer. This tender energy will reign in the heavens until Wednesday night, when she'll suddenly be in the mood to act, courtesy of her costume-change into red-hot Aries. From that point on, the pace of the week will pick up dramatically, and when both Mercury and Jupiter get together in emotional Cancer Thursday night, there'll be lots of contact with dear ones. If you're off for a family reunion or a spontaneous visit back home, you've chosen the perfect time to do it. If you're home-bound, however, stay with your mate and kids. A sensitive trine between Venus and Neptune will put us all in the mood to accept our loved ones unconditionally, and perhaps to open our hearts to a new family member or fur-person. You'll need to be realistic and practical with regard to relationship issues come Saturday and Sunday, when loving Venus and serious Saturn will come together to make plans for the future. Pay attention to the advice of elders at this time, and be sure you're being totally honest with yourself and others.

July 16–22

There could be a bit of intrigue on the menu at the beginning of the week, but you'll be in the mood for it. The emotional Moon will be in curious Gemini straight through Wednesday afternoon, putting you in mind to make calls, look through files, and ask lots of questions. At the same time, relationship-oriented Venus will face off with secretive Pluto on Tuesday, the perfect astrological formula for clandestine encounters, private meetings, and passion. If you've just recently begun seeing someone, now may be the time you take the relationship a step closer to intimacy. On Wednesday, Pallas Athena, a goddess on a mission, will stop in her tracks and force you to get passionate about a cause. She's also a mistress of strategy, so if you've got research to do, her station will certainly help. Fiery Mars will also station this week, right after dinner on Thursday. And since he'll be so close to Pluto at the time, there's going to be lots of simmering, subtle investigation, and secret plotting going on. If there's a money or love issue that's due, expect it that morning as Venus and Mars face off just as the emotional Moon steps up to Mercury's microphone. Make new starts in the department of home and family matters on Friday, when a New Moon in Cancer will arrive. Do it quickly, however, since both the Moon and the Sun will step into the cosmic phone booth to change costumes over the weekend and emerge in fiery and recreation-loving Leo. It's a prime time to have the family or go for a visit.

July 23–29

As the Sun continues on his path through playful Leo, your week will start with the urge to create something that reflects who you are. Give in to that prompting, and let your inner child out to play. It's time to see yourself in your creations, and revel in the joy of just being you. Come Tuesday, you're also going to be quite happy with others, as commitment-oriented Juno, the mythical wife of Jupiter, will enter nurturing Cancer. Expect family duties and home responsibilities to arrive, and expect to enjoy tending to them. On Thursday, the emotional Moon will set off for seductive Scorpio just as loving Venus and surprising Uranus step into a trine and make sudden passion the order of the day. This seductive Scorpio Moon will stay in the neighborhood all weekend—or at least up until Sunday—so if you're happily attached, you may not be venturing out much. This is a wonderful time to watch a mystery movie, participate in a murder mystery weekend, or just do some research. By Sunday, you'll likely be chilling out and having a few laughs with friends during the emotional Moon's passage into irrepressible Sagittarius, the sign that insists on having fun with others.

July 30–August 5

Speaking of fun, Mercury moves into entertaining Leo just in time for an upbeat Monday. This dramatic stellar voice will arrive early in the morning, adding his gift of charming chatter to a dreamy, romantic Sun/Neptune opposition. It's perfect astrological weather for wooing and being wooed, so allow yourself to be sentimental, emotional, and playfully flirtatious. Jupiter and Juno will conjoin on Tuesday morning, bringing the ancient king and queen of the gods together in loving Cancer. When these two meet up peacefully, marriage vows, promises of love, and decisions about family matters are favored. Lovely Venus will also step delicately into Cancer on Wednesday and edge closer to the famous Olympian couple over the coming week. She will be adding her gifts of compromise and cooperation to an already tender time. Thursday's opposition between psychic Neptune and mental Mercury will turn your antennae up, so don't be surprised if you're amazingly intuitive about the feelings of others. The Full Moon will arrive Friday evening, just in time to keep the romantic mood going. The fact that's she's going to activate the axis of flamboyant Leo and spontaneous Aquarius with her lovely silver beams is just the beginning. On Saturday, the Sun sextiles responsible Saturn and trines deep Pluto, and on Sunday thoughtful Mercury will do the same thing. All your meetings with friends and lovers will carry a meaningful tone now. Finally, the Universe seems to have saved the very best for last. On Sunday evening, just as you're winding down from a busy weekend, loving Venus will come together with Mr. Generous himself, Uncle Jupiter. Expect gifts of all shapes, sizes, and flavors.

August 6–12

Venus and Jupiter will still be locked in each other's arms as the week begins, a wonderful bonding of astrology's two favorite planets. Known classically as "the Benefics," these two like to see us happy. As a result, most anything begun under this loving influence—a new relationship, a new job, a long trip—is guaranteed to be successful, prosperous, and lasting. These two are also representative of money and wealth, by the way, so investments at this time aren't a bad idea. Just be careful of the temptation to go overboard on impulsive spending from Tuesday night through Friday afternoon, when the Moon's mood will be impatient, courtesy of her trek through Aries. Happy reunions with long-lost loved ones are possible on Thursday, when loving Venus will meet up with Juno. These two make us feel closer to our dear ones and more content. If your plans for the weekend are up in the air on Friday morning, sit tight. Mercury and Uranus will form an edgy opposition, creating tension and anxiety where it might not really be called for. Use these two to experiment with a new way to express your creativity. By Friday evening, the Sun and Mars—two powerful, assertive energies—will come together in an easy trine and provide inspiration for peaceful resolutions and swift decisions. A sensual Taurus Moon will flavor your Saturday and Sunday with a taste the finest things, so don't go second-class, no matter what you do. Spend the extra cash and do it up right.

August 13–19

Meticulous, detailed work is en route for Monday and Tuesday, as Mercury, the planet of communication, enters Virgo, the sign of lists, agendas, and plans. At the same time, the emotional Moon will be in Gemini, a sign that considers every detail as important as the day is long. Make plans early in the week, but don't be surprised if disruptions arrive on Wednesday, when the Sun will oppose Uranus. These two create the perfect astrological atmosphere for rebellion. Pallas Athena, the defender-goddess, will set off for Sagittarius Thursday afternoon, bringing environmental issues and animal rights to the forefront of our collective consciousness. If there's a critter cause that's near and dear to your heart, volunteer now. Stories, travel, and learning will color your Friday evening and Saturday morning, as Mercury and Jupiter, the planets of communication and movement, come together in a stimulating sextile. These two just love a good idea, so if you're remodeling, adding a room, or planning a family, you'll have their blessing. To add to the fun, a New Moon in Leo will make her splashy way across the heavens and plant a subtle seed of change. If you need to have a serious talk with your mate or spouse, do it Sunday night, when the Moon in practical Virgo will touch chatty Mercury, sedate Saturn, and penetrating Pluto.

August 20–26

Early this week, communicative Mercury will stalk off into the same squares with Pluto and Saturn that the Moon made Sunday evening, conjuring a deja vu of sorts. If you feel as if you're reliving the events of Sunday night on Monday and Tuesday, there may be something you missed that really needs to be resolved. On the other hand, you may have made a tough emotional decision that you now must act upon. Either way, there's serious stuff coming, so be ready to concentrate on solutions. On Wednesday, however, the Sun will set off for Virgo, a detail-oriented and very focused sign. This energy will work with Thursday's Pluto station to help you make a new start with a positive, grounded attitude. Active Mars and shocking Uranus will set off a string of changes that same day when they come together in an exciting sextile. You'll have Friday to recover, but don't even think about sitting still over the weekend. The Moon will set off for Sagittarius on Saturday morning, ready for some excessive fun, and on Sunday afternoon Venus will make a grand entrance into fiery Leo. With both feminines in the mood to party, I'll bet you'll be up late Sunday night—but for only the best of reasons.

August 27–September 2

With Venus decorated in her finest Leo outfit, we'll all be doing a bit of strutting and preening as the week begins, which means we'll be attracting the attention of others, and thriving on the romance in the air. Passionate words will also be arriving, on Tuesday morning, when Mercury is prodded into action by a square from feisty Mars. Fortunately, the emotional Moon will be in refined, elegant Capricorn at the moment, turning all that drama into a royal parade, rather than a melodramatic soap opera. You'll have lots of chances to make new friends and meet prospective lovers over the next three weeks, as conversational Mercury enters other-oriented Libra on Friday. If you're out socializing, better be ready to chat up a storm. On Saturday, meanwhile, loving Venus will oppose dreamy Neptune, and you may feel as if a loved one is sending you mixed signals. If that's the case, use Sunday's Full Moon to bring everything out into the open. Talk it out, make decisions, and let it rest.

September 3–9

Monday's peaceful Pisces Moon will start your week off on a sensitive note, bringing compassion and intuition to every encounter. On Tuesday evening, the Sun and Pluto square conjures the astrological spell for intense meetings with powerful people. This combination could point to power struggles, but it's also a perfect formula for persuasion. If you've got to convince someone of your inner strength and determination, you'll be well armed to pull it off. On Thursday, expect more intense energy, but with pleasant undertones, as loving Venus forms an easy trine with sexy Pluto and urges us towards intimacy on all levels. You may choose to spend an evening alone with your partner or make a call to remind someone how much you care. Later that evening, serious Saturn will form an action-oriented square to the Sun, conjuring up a stern authority figure. Put your foot down if you must, and let the world know you're in charge of your life. Solid earth-energies will hover overhead for the rest of the week, keeping your resolution strong. The Moon will be wearing her most luscious Taurus outfit from Thursday through Sunday, creating a stable emotional foundation. Then, on Saturday, fiery Mars will step into Capricorn, blowing a military horn. Added responsibilities and hard work are ahead, but so too are rewards. Pay attention to how you perceive others on Sunday evening, when thoughtful Mercury will sextile Pluto, making a potent combination that's equal parts detective, analyst, and assassin. If you've got to track someone or something down, now's the time.

September 10–16

Talk of commitments and responsibilities will continue as the week begins, and by Tuesday evening, when Mercury and Saturn come together in an easy trine, it may be time to announce a decision. Expect a warm reception, as these two create thoughtful appreciation in all of us. The heavens will shift into high drama on Thursday, when the Moon will strut off into proud, theatrical Leo. That same day, loving Venus will oppose Uranus, adding a strong dose of unpredictability to the evening. Don't be surprised if your plans for the weekend change abruptly. There are healing touches and soothing words on the menu for Saturday courtesy of a powerful combination of energies. The emotional Moon will enter Virgo, conjuring up a physician with a huge heart. At the same time, both tender Venus and the Sun will visit with Dr. Chiron, the great centaur and healer. Mend your fences, and be sure to offer or accept apologies graciously.

September 17–23

The New Moon in Virgo will arrive on Monday and offer up a great burst of energy that's perfect for concentrating on health and other detailed projects. Tackle your to-do list, and go after the hardest things first. This "taking care of business" tone will continue right through the week, too, as Mercury, the cosmic communicator, steps into a stimulating sextile with Chiron on Wednesday. This is a team that offers great new solutions for any problem. Take a moment to reflect on anything that's been a sore spot in your life recently, then get to work on fixing it. On Thursday evening, a lovely lady in pristine white will extend a hand, as loving Venus enters helpful Virgo. By the time the weekend rolls around complete with an optimistic Sagittarius Moon, you'll be ready to forgive, forget, and move along with a happy heart. Between this cheerful energy and the Sun's entry into Libra, the sign of balance, all will certainly end well by Sunday. Take a deep breath, pat yourself on the back, and relax with lighthearted friends.

September 24–30

A hard-working Capricorn Moon will be on hand when you open your eyes on Monday, inspiring you to get to work on time and take care of business meticulously. She'll be on duty until Wednesday afternoon, when a brilliant Aquarius Moon will arrive with her emotional insight. Be sure to keep a pen and paper handy over the next few days, and jot down your thoughts and feelings. Meanwhile, serious Saturn will station on Wednesday, creating an immovable energy that demands we fulfill every one of our responsibilities. Don't give him—or the authority figures in your life—a chance to point out the flaws in your performance. Tend to every detail, touch every base, and follow all the rules. Saturn is tough enough to start with, and when he's standing still with his arms folded, there's really nothing you can do. Besides, Mercury will be slowing to a stop as the week progresses, and it'll be primetime for delays. By Friday evening, however, a lovely touch of magic will be in the air, and we'll be ready to kick back and dream a little as the Sun in cooperative Libra forms an easy trine with woozy Neptune. This unhurried energy will lend a harmonious, insightful tone to the rest of the weekend, with an assist from the Moon, who'll be in Pisces, Neptune's own soft sign.

October 1–October 7

If you're a bit impatient as the week begins, it's no wonder. The Moon is stepping into impulsive Aries on Monday, and pushing us to take action. It may not be possible, however, since a few minutes later, Mercury will stop in his tracks and turn retrograde, bringing a time when all kinds of details get muddled. Since Venus will also square off with manipulative Pluto right around noon, it could be a rather frustrating afternoon. Try to be patient until the evening, when Venus and Mars will combine their talents in a peaceful trine, ensuring that partnership issues will end well and arguments will be resolved. Your energy will be running on high when you wake up on Tuesday, as the Full Moon in Libra arrives and directs your attention towards a partner. And since Libra loves to rebalance the scales, compromise and negotiation will be in the air. Venus and Jupiter will form a harmonious sextile that morning, bringing a promise of blessings and affection. Meanwhile, late that night, Venus will move into aspect with Saturn, the kind of planet that loves to make and keep promises. You'll find yourself thinking about settling down now, just be sure all financial details are taken care of. Remember, Venus also rules money, and Saturn will be in the mood to restrict any money flow. There's impulsive ventures on the agenda for Wednesday, however, when red-hot Mars will oppose Jupiter, expanding the urge to act. Be sure to look before you leap for the rest of the week, but don't be afraid of taking well-calculated risks. Meaningful encounters will be in the air on Friday night, and well into Saturday, too, when penetrating Pluto will touch base with the Sun.

Tend to chores on Sunday, as the Sun connects with both Jupiter and Saturn, a team that promises quick returns on the time you invest.

October 8–14

Last weekend's hectic energy will smooth out nicely as Monday arrives, courtesy of an easy-going Cancer Moon. She'll stay in the neighborhood until Wednesday night, when a Leo Moon will take her place. Once again, it's going to be time for entertainment, emotional drama, and risky business. Go ahead and indulge yourself in all those departments, but be sure to give your creativity an outlet, too. You'll be amazed at what both you and others dare to say out loud on Saturday and Sunday, when chatty Mercury and the Sun will team up with startling Uranus and spontaneous Mars. Talk about a surprising weekend! This combination fuels interesting conversations, sudden change of plans, and independent thinking, but it's also been known to spark an argument. Keep your mind occupied with tough projects that require innovative new solutions, and you'll be fine. Besides, the Moon and Venus will blend affection and emotional warmth when they form a trine Sunday night—just the right energy to end the week on a happy note.

October 15–21

Both personal feminines, the Moon and Venus, are happily trekking through compromising Libra as the week begins, settling any disputes on the job that started up Friday. Do your part to encourage a healthy solution, and enjoy the good and harmonious feelings brought by Tuesday's New Moon in Libra. Confusion, illusion, idealism and romance are possible on Wednesday, when vague, dreamy Neptune will stop before turning direct. It can be tough to see straight when the pink goddess is this focused, so don't even try. Pay attention to your intuition, and keep your eyes open. A perceptive Scorpio Moon will help you pick up on clues you might otherwise miss. There's an easy and optimistic weekend ahead, brought to you by a frivolous Sag Moon beginning Friday morning. Mercury and Jupiter will also get together and make a team that's primed for long-distance conversation, travel, and intellectual exchanges. If you're thinking of returning to school, investigate it now. Meanwhile, loving Venus and woozy Neptune will combine forces to make Saturday a lovely dream. If you're attached, spend some time alone together in beautiful surroundings. If you're single, be prepared for love at first sight. Finally, your dreams can become real if you make plans on Sunday, when a practical and realistic pair, Mercury and Saturn, connect.

October 22–28

Monday will arrive with a much-needed dose of clarity, as Mercury will turn forward after three long weeks of moving retrograde. Since he's all done up in Libra, it may be time to make a decision, especially with regard to a relationship. The Sun will enter seductive Scorpio on Tuesday, meanwhile, and for the next month you'll want depth and intimacy in all your encounters. Your thoughts will be sensible and reasonable for the next two days, too, since Mercury and staid Saturn will merge in an easy trine. The Moon in Aquarius, an unbiased emotional energy, will hold court for the next few days and inspire fair, unprejudiced dealings with others. Take a moment to get to know someone who's different, and open your heart to them. Over Friday and Saturday, the lovely lady Venus will connect with stable Saturn and powerful Pluto, creating a time to let go of negative influences. Pursue only those relationships that are well balanced, and give the gift of intimacy only where it's deserved. If you must make changes in a current partnership, you can do it guiltlessly on Saturday morning, when action-loving Mars will streak off into Aquarius, a sign that never looks back.

October 29–November 4

Mercury and Venus will be in partner-loving Libra as the week begins, and both will form sextiles to Juno, the asteroid goddess of commitment. Needless to say, last weekend's focus on relating will continue, and there may be some tender words on the agenda for Tuesday afternoon. An earthy, fertile Full Moon in Taurus will start November off with a touch of the sensual. This solid emotional energy will come in time to help you adapt to a surprise announcement, due Thursday morning, when loving Venus and chatty Mercury will turn their combined attention to Uranus, the planetary shockmeister. Whatever the news is, it could be final, by the way, so be prepared. Saturn and Pluto, the two most difficult planets, will be edging closer to an opposition on Friday morning—and these two play for keeps. If you're about to put the finishing touches on a project, this is a great energy to have on hand. When it comes to relationships, however, this combination can lead to power struggles. Keep a cool head, no matter what the world tosses your way, and try not to be overbearing or easily influenced.

November 5–11

This could well be a week of reunions and second tries at old relationships. A cosmic collection will assemble Monday morning that's the perfect formula for healing old wounds with honest words. Tender, forgiving Venus and Mercury, the ancient messenger, will meet up with Chiron, the healer, and so put ancient issues to rest. At the same time, Neptune will conjoin with Mars, nicely turning the red god's fury into passion and creating a romantic pink mist. If you're attached, be sure not to waste this energy. Spend quality time with your mate as Mercury and Venus move into sensual Scorpio on Wednesday and Thursday. On Sunday, the emotional Moon will enter peace-loving Libra, prompting cooperation in all dealings, and conversational Mercury will enter an active square with compassionate Neptune. If you're called on to mediate a situation, you'll be well equipped to do it fairly.

November 12–18

Monday evening will be a surprising one, so be ready for anything. The Sun and Moon will hook up with unpredictable Uranus, stirring sudden change. And since the Moon will also be in contact with lovely Venus and woozy Neptune on Tuesday, these changes certainly could involve relationships or money matters. Be careful not to be confused or misled. If you need advice, place your trust in an elder on Wednesday when Mars and Saturn will combine forces to help point you in the right direction via the advice of someone more experienced. The New Moon in Scorpio late Wednesday evening marks a time of new beginnings on the deepest emotional level, and you may see some changes as soon as Friday morning. Chatty Mercury will square off with Mars, creating the potential for quick actions, and transformative Pluto will be involved. Whatever you've absolutely got to do—no matter how personally difficult—you can do it swiftly now. By Saturday morning, you'll be optimistic about the future, as Mercury forms a trine with upbeat Jupiter.

November 19–25

There's sudden news due Tuesday, when the Moon in startling Aquarius will join up with a square between chatty Mercury and unpredictable Uranus. These two are a very surprising combination, so be prepared. On Wednesday, a dose of energy will get you revved up to fight for a cause. Pallas Athena, patron of heroes, will step foot into Capricorn and don her armor. At the same time, the Sun will enter Sagittarius, a sign that's adamant about its beliefs. Be careful not to overdo your defense of dear ones, but don't back down if you know you're right. Don't aggravate anyone who shows the potential for violent behavior, as the Moon collides with impulsive Mars and shocking Uranus that evening. On Friday, Venus and Mars will be in square, creating an astrological fighting stance pitting what we love against our urge to act on impulse. If you have to settle for less than you want, consider the alternatives. Tender Pisces Moon will hold court over the weekend, making this a great time to pursue spiritual, metaphysical, or psychic interests.

November 26–December 2

A fiery Aries Moon will welcome Mercury in Sagittarius on Monday afternoon, creating a lively start to your week that promises lots of long-distance talk with loved ones. These two will add their energies to a Mars/Uranus conjunction, astrology's most volatile combination. Take care driving, and don't use dangerous machinery. From Tuesday evening through Friday morning, the Moon in Taurus will be in charge of our emotions and offer relief after the week's early shakeups. She'll be joined on Wednesday by a peaceful sextile between the Sun and Neptune. Take time out from your schedule to do what you love. By Friday, the Full Moon in Gemini will teach you something new—concentrate on your communication skills and detail management. Venus will join Mercury and the Sun in Sagittarius on Sunday morning, putting us in the mood to travel with a loved one. If you've ever wanted to tour Europe, see the pyramids, or visit a rain forest, do it now. You owe it to yourself to see as much of the world as possible.

December 3–9

There could be serious news or conversations on your agenda for Monday, when both the Sun and Mercury, the cosmic microphone, will oppose Saturn, the bringer of reality. Accept whatever comes along, and try to see the need for it. This sedate, somber tone will last through Thursday, when both the Sun and Mercury will turn to Pluto, adding a heavy dose of intensity and depth to all your communications. Be prepared to make inevitable decisions now. Friday's sextile between loving Venus and dreamy Neptune, meanwhile, will bring a touch of magic and romance to the weekend and sooth the troubled waters of the early week. Take time to flip through old scrapbooks with a dear one and reminisce about the experiences you've shared.

December 10–16

You may need to consider budgeting, cutting back on expenses, or acquiring a second source of income on Monday, when Venus, the goddess of checkbooks, opposes Saturn. This frugal planet in hard aspect to Venus often puts us in the mood to consider our lifestyle, too, and to limit unhealthy habits. Why not start your New Year's resolutions early? You'll have plenty of help from Chiron, the Wounded Healer, who'll enter Capricorn Tuesday with a well-organized health plan. Happy surprises are possible on Thursday, when the Sun connects with startling Uranus. Intense feelings of love, passion, or jealousy are possible on Friday and Saturday, when loving Venus connects with deep Pluto. Don't jump to conclusions, however. If you've got a decision to make, wait until after Saturday afternoon, when thoughtful Mercury will enter Capricorn, a sign that never let emotions interfere with the facts. You'll be prepared to do something you don't want to do.

December 16–23

Fasten your seat-belts, folks, and get ready for emotional changes on Monday, Tuesday, and Wednesday. The emotional Moon will be in Aquarius, setting a backdrop of unpredictability that could turn the most carefully laid plans topsy-turvy—even as Venus, the goddess of relationships, touches base with erratic Uranus on Wednesday. If things get crazy, don't fight it. Loosen up and go with the flow, at least until a more stable pack of energies takes over for the weekend. On Friday, the Sun will enter Capricorn, donning his most official business suit. Mercury will form an easy sextile with energetic Mars that same day, inspiring lighthearted conversations. And speaking of conversation, there's going to be plenty in the air this weekend. Mercury will oppose Jupiter on Saturday and Sunday. Jupiter, of course, is an expert at making everything bigger, so expect a chatty evening, full of fun and long-distance talks. Don't be afraid to run up the phone bill just a bit, for 'tis the season, after all. Happy winter solstice!

December 24–30

No matter where you are on Christmas day, you're sure to have a wonderful time. On Christmas night, Venus will enter Capricorn, the sign that's loyal to loved ones, respectful of elders, and appreciative of good friends. Spread these good feelings around if you can. And if you have to repair a relationship, restore someone's faith in you, or just lay a soothing hand on an old wound, Thursday is the perfect time to do it. Tender Venus will come together with Chiron, the healer, making a warm, comforting combination that's all about loving. Late Friday night, Juno, the wife, will enter lavish Leo, creating the potential for happy commitments that will last and stay romantic. So if you're thinking of signing up permanently, these two will give you powerful assistance. You may not have a chance to relax much on Sunday, when Mars and Pluto will square off, and create an urgent need to act quickly in lieu of of a highly charged situation. The Moon will also be Full that day, and since she'll be in her own sign, Cancer, everyone's feelings will be larger than life. Don't be surprised if you don't sleep much, either.

December 31

This last day of the year will carry a dramatic tone, brought to you courtesy of the Moon in fiery Leo, the sign of the performer. She'll have an assist from the Sun and expansive, generous Jupiter, primed and ready to overdo things. Since it's New Year's Eve, you'll be best off making plans to stay over wherever you happen to land. Celebrate the New Year safely, and have a prosperous 2002!!!

Planetary Business Guide

Collections

Try to make collections on days when your Sun is well aspected. Avoid days when Mars or Saturn are aspected. If possible, the Moon should be in a Cardinal sign: Aries, Cancer, Libra, or Capricorn. It is more difficult to collect when the Moon is in Taurus or Scorpio.

Employment, Promotion

Choose a day when your Sun is favorably aspected or Moon is in your 10th house. Good aspects of Venus or Jupiter to your 10th house are beneficial.

Loans

Moon in the first and second quarters favors the lender, in the third and fourth it favors the borrower. Good aspects of Jupiter or Venus to the Moon are favorable to both, as is Moon in Leo, Sagittarius, Aquarius, or Pisces.

New Ventures

Things usually get off to a better start during the increase of the Moon. If there is impatience, anxiety, or deadlock, it can often be broken at the Full Moon. Agreements can be reached then.

Partnerships

Agreements and partnerships should be made on a day that is favorable to both parties. Mars, Neptune, Pluto, and Saturn should not be square or opposite the Moon. It is best to make an agreement or partnership when the Moon is in a mutable sign, especially Gemini or Virgo. The other signs are not favorable, with the possible exception of Leo or Capricorn. Begin partnerships when the Moon is increasing in light, as this is a favorable time for starting new ventures.

Public Relations

The Moon rules the public, so this must be well aspected, particularly by the Sun, Mercury, Uranus, or Neptune.

Selling

In general, selling is favored by good aspects of Venus, Jupiter, or Mercury to the Moon. Afflictions of Saturn retard. If you know the planetary ruler of your product, try to get this well aspected by Venus, Jupiter, or the Moon. Your product will be more highly valued then.

Signing Important Papers

Sign contracts or agreements when the Moon is increasing in a fruitful sign. Avoid days when Mars, Saturn, Neptune, or Pluto are afflicting the Moon. Don't sign anything if your Sun is badly afflicted.

How to Use Your Daily Planetary Guide

Both Eastern and Pacific times are given in the datebook. The Eastern times are listed in the left-hand column in medium typeface. The Pacific times are in the right-hand column in bold typeface. Adjustments have not been made for Daylight Saving Time. You need to add one hour to the time given if your locale uses Daylight Saving Time. The void-of-course Moon is listed to the right of the daily aspect at the exact time that it occurs. It is indicated by "v/c." On days on which it occurs for only one time zone and not the other, it is indicated next to the appropriate column and then repeated on the next day for the other time zone. The ephemeris is shown for midnight, Greenwich Mean Time (GMT). The handy flap on the back cover can help you use this guide on a daily basis.

Symbol Key

Planets				
	☉	Sun	⚶	Vesta
	☽	Moon	♃	Jupiter
	☿	Mercury	♄	Saturn
	♀	Venus	⚷	Chiron
	♂	Mars	♅	Uranus
	⚳	Ceres	♆	Neptune
	⚴	Pallas	♇	Pluto
	⚵	Juno		

Signs				
	♈	Aries	♎	Libra
	♉	Taurus	♏	Scorpio
	♊	Gemini	♐	Sagittarius
	♋	Cancer	♑	Capricorn
	♌	Leo	♒	Aquarius
	♍	Virgo	♓	Pisces

Aspects				
	☌	Conjunction (0°)	△	Trine (120°)
	⚺	Semisextile (30°)	⚼	Sesquiquadrate (135°)
	∠	Semisquare (45°)	⚻	Quincunx (150°)
	✶	Sextile (60°)	☍	Opposition (180°)
	□	Square (90°)		

Motion	℞	Retrograde	D	Direct

2001   **JANUARY**   **2001**

3rd ♍

CAPRICORN ♑
Duality: Feminine
Quality: Cardinal
Element: Earth
House: 10th
Planetary Ruler: Saturn
Rules: Knees, Bones, Joints
Keyword: Ambition
Keynote: I use.

1 MONDAY

☽ □ ♂	2:39 am					
☽ △ ♀	3:00 am	**12:00 am**				
☽ ✶ ♄	6:36 am	**3:36 am**	☽ v/c			
☽ ⊻ ⚹	10:41 am	**7:41 am**				
♂ □ ♆	12:01 pm	**9:01 am**				
☽ ⊻ ♀	12:55 pm	**9:55 am**				
☽ ✶ ♃	9:20 pm	**6:20 pm**				
☽ ⊼ ♅		**9:27 pm**				
☉ ⊼ ⚹		**10:51 pm**				

1st ♓
☽ enters ♈   5:14 pm   **2:14 pm**

NEW YEAR'S DAY • KWANZAA ENDS

2 TUESDAY

☽ ⊼ ♅	12:27 am		
☉ ⊼ ⚹	1:51 am		
☽ ✶ ♆	3:40 am	**12:40 am**	
☽ ⊼ ♂	4:23 am	**1:23 am**	
☽ ⊻ ⚹	6:23 am	**3:23 am**	
☽ ⚻ ♀	9:10 am	**6:10 am**	
☽ ⊼ ♄	11:38 am	**8:38 am**	
☿ ⚻ ♃	12:06 pm	**9:06 am**	
☿ ⊻ ?	2:10 pm	**11:10 am**	
☽ ⊼ ⚹	4:48 pm	**1:48 pm**	
☽ □ ☉	5:31 pm	**2:31 pm**	
☽ △ ♇	7:52 pm	**4:52 pm**	
☽ ⊼ ♀	8:37 pm	**5:37 pm**	
☽ ⊼ ♃		**10:52 pm**	
☽ △ ?		**11:36 pm**	

1st ♈
2nd Quarter   5:31 pm   **2:31 pm**

3 WEDNESDAY

☽ ⊼ ♃	1:52 am			
☽ △ ?	2:36 am			
☽ □ ☿	3:58 am	**12:58 am**		
☽ ✶ ♅	5:09 am	**2:09 am**	☽ v/c	
☽ ⊼ ⚹	11:49 am	**8:49 am**		
☽ △ ♂	12:45 pm	**9:45 am**		
☿ ⊻ ♅	1:30 pm	**10:30 am**		
☽ ⊼ ♀	2:22 pm	**11:22 am**		
☽ ⊻ ♄	3:47 pm	**12:47 pm**		
☽ ✶ ⚹	9:53 pm	**6:53 pm**		
☉ ⊻ ♇	11:25 pm	**8:25 pm**		
☽ ⚻ ♇	11:54 pm	**8:54 pm**		

2nd ♈
♀ enters ♓   1:14 pm   **10:14 am**
☽ enters ♉   **10:57 pm**

Eastern Standard Time in medium type
Pacific Standard Time in bold type

JANUARY 2001

4 THURSDAY

☽	✶	♀	3:06 am	**12:06 am**	
☽	⊻	♃	5:28 am	**2:28 am**	
☽	⚻	♄	7:12 am	**4:12 am**	
☽	☐	♆	11:51 am	**8:51 am**	
☽	☍	♂	2:55 pm	**11:55 am**	
☽	✶	♅	4:10 pm	**1:10 pm**	
☽	⚻	⚷	4:21 pm	**1:21 pm**	
☽	⚼	♇		**11:55 pm**	

2nd ♈

☽ enters ♉ 1:57 am **1:37 am**

5 FRIDAY

☽	⚼	♇	2:55 am		
☽	△	☉	5:04 am	**2:04 am**	
♀	☐	♃	6:14 am	**3:14 am**	
♄	☍	♀	9:52 am	**6:52 am**	
☽	⚼	♄	10:42 am	**7:42 am**	
☽	☐	♅	11:37 am	**8:37 am**	
☽	△	☿	5:38 pm	**2:38 pm**	
☽	⚼	⚷	6:55 pm	**3:55 pm**	
☽	☌	♄	9:09 pm	**6:09 pm**	☽ v/c
☽	☍	♀	9:30 pm	**6:30 pm**	

2nd ♉

6 SATURDAY

☽	☐	⚳	4:45 am	**1:45 am**	
☿	⊻	⚷	5:02 am	**2:02 am**	
♂	⚼	⚷	7:12 am	**4:12 am**	
☽	⚻	☉	8:58 am	**5:58 am**	
☽	☌	♃	9:45 am	**6:45 am**	
☽	☐	♀	12:09 pm	**9:09 am**	
☿	⚼	⚳	1:33 pm	**10:33 am**	
☽	△	♆	4:04 pm	**1:04 pm**	
☉	⚻	♃	7:19 pm	**4:19 pm**	
☽	⚼	♂	8:59 pm	**5:59 pm**	
☽	☐	♅	9:39 pm	**6:39 pm**	
♅	✶	♄	10:21 pm	**7:21 pm**	
☽	⚻	☿	10:24 pm	**7:24 pm**	
☿	△	♄	10:46 pm	**7:46 pm**	

2nd ♉

☽ enters ♊ 6:44 pm **3:44 pm**

7 SUNDAY

☽	☍	♇	6:07 am	**3:07 am**	
☿	✶	♀	10:51 am	**7:51 am**	
☽	⚼	☉	11:49 am	**8:49 am**	
☽	△	♅	2:19 pm	**11:19 am**	☽ v/c
☽	☍	♃	2:43 pm	**11:43 am**	
☽	⚻	♆	4:54 pm	**1:54 pm**	
☽	☍	⚷	9:22 pm	**6:22 pm**	
☽	⚻	♂	10:37 pm	**7:37 pm**	
☽	⊻	♄	10:59 pm	**7:59 pm**	
☽	⚼	♀		**9:45 pm**	
☽	⚼	☿		**11:05 pm**	

2nd ♊

Eastern Standard Time in medium type
Pacific Standard Time in bold type

JANUARY 2001

8 MONDAY
2nd ♊

☽	⊼	☿	12:45 am		
☽	⊼	☿	2:05 am		
☽	△	⚷	7:51 am	4:51 am	
☽	⊻	♃	10:49 am	7:49 am	
☽	⊓	♅	2:37 pm	11:37 am	
☽	△	♀	5:05 pm	2:05 pm	
☽	⊼	♆	5:08 pm	2:08 pm	
♀	⊻	♆	5:50 pm	2:50 pm	
☽	⌙	♄	11:00 pm	8:00 pm	
☽	△	♂	11:38 pm	8:38 pm	
☽	△	⚚	11:51 pm	8:51 pm	
☽	⊓	♀		10:23 pm	
☉	⊻	♅		10:37 pm	

☽ enters ♋ 8:09 am **5:09 am**
⚷ enters ♓ 5:10 pm **2:10 pm**

9 TUESDAY
2nd ♋

☽	⊓	♀	1:23 am		
☉	⊻	♅	1:37 am		
☽	⊼	♇	6:33 am	3:33 am	
☽	⊓	⚷	8:31 am	5:31 am	
☽	⌙	♃	10:36 am	7:36 am	
☽	⊼	♅	2:32 pm	11:32 am	
☽	☍	☉	3:24 pm	12:24 pm	
☽	⊼	♁	4:03 pm	1:03 pm	
☽	⊓	♀	6:40 pm	3:40 pm	
☿	⌙	♇	7:05 pm	4:05 pm	
☽	⊼	⚸	9:32 pm	6:32 pm	
☽	✶	♄	10:41 pm	7:41 pm	
☽	⊓	⚚		9:20 pm	
☽	△	♀		10:42 pm	

Full Moon 3:24 pm **12:24 pm**

LUNAR ECLIPSE ☍ (19° ♋ 39') 3:22 PM EST/12:22 AM PST

10 WEDNESDAY
3rd ♋

☽	⊓	⚚	12:20 am		
☽	△	♀	1:42 am		
♂	△	⚚	3:35 am	12:35 am	
☽	⊓	♇	6:18 am	3:18 am	
☉	⊻	♁	6:42 am	3:42 am	
☽	☍	☿	7:39 am	4:39 am	☽ v/c
☽	⊼	⚷	8:57 am	5:57 am	
☽	✶	♃	10:11 am	7:11 am	
☽	⊓	♁	4:21 pm	1:21 pm	
☽	☍	♆	4:42 pm	1:42 pm	
☽	⊼	♀	8:06 pm	5:06 pm	
☽	⊓	⚸	9:22 pm	6:22 pm	
☿	⊻	⚷	11:36 pm	8:36 pm	
☽	⊼	⚚		9:45 pm	
☽	□	♂		9:55 pm	

☽ enters ♌ 7:44 am **4:44 am**
☿ enters ♒ 8:26 am **5:26 am**

11 THURSDAY
3rd ♌

☽	⊼	⚚	12:45 am		
☽	□	♂	12:55 am		
☽	△	♇	6:03 am	3:03 am	
☿	△	♃	6:21 am	3:21 am	
♆	⌙	♁	7:05 am	4:05 am	
☽	☍	♅	2:07 pm	11:07 am	
☽	△	♁	4:47 pm	1:47 pm	
☽	⊼	☉	6:17 pm	3:17 pm	
☽	△	⚸	9:23 pm	6:23 pm	
☽	□	♄	10:08 pm	7:08 pm	☽ v/c
♃	□	⚷	10:11 pm	7:11 pm	
☽	□	♀		11:30 pm	

Eastern Standard Time in medium type
Pacific Standard Time in bold type

2001   **JANUARY**   **2001**

12 FRIDAY

☽	□	♀	2:30 am		
☽	□	♃	9:48 am	**6:48**	**am**
☽	☍	⚷	10:12 am	**7:12**	**am**
☽	⚻	☿	1:22 pm	**10:22**	**am**
☽	⚻	♆	4:45 pm	**1:45**	**pm**
☽	⚃	☉	8:16 pm	**5:16**	**pm**
☽	☌	♀	11:51 pm	**8:51**	**pm**
☽	☍	⚴		**11:33**	**pm**

3rd ♌
☽ enters ♍   7:26 am   **4:26 am**

13 SATURDAY

☽	☍	⚴	2:33 am		
☽	⚹	♂	3:06 am	**12:06**	**am**
☽	□	♇	6:34 am	**3:34**	**am**
☽	⚻	♅	3:04 pm	**12:04**	**pm**
☽	⚃	☿	5:13 pm	**2:13**	**pm**
☽	⚃	♆	5:33 pm	**2:33**	**pm**
☽	□	♃	7:04 pm	**4:04**	**pm**
☿	☌	♆	8:10 pm	**5:10**	**pm**
☉	⚺	⚷	8:53 pm	**5:53**	**pm**
☽	□	⚷	10:52 pm	**7:52**	**pm**
☽	△	☉	11:00 pm	**8:00**	**pm**
☽	△	♄	11:12 pm	**8:12**	**pm** ☽ v/c
☉	△	♄		**10:49**	**pm**

3rd ♍

14 SUNDAY

☉	△	♄	1:49 am		
☽	⚼	♂	5:11 am	**2:11**	**am**
☽	⚹	♀	5:13 am	**2:13**	**am**
☽	△	♃	11:27 am	**8:27**	**am**
☿	⚼	⚴	1:38 pm	**10:38**	**am**
☽	⚻	⚷	1:44 pm	**10:44**	**am**
☽	⚃	♅	4:34 pm	**1:34**	**pm**
☽	△	♆	7:06 pm	**4:06**	**pm**
☽	△	☿	10:09 pm	**7:09**	**pm**
☽	⚃	♄		**9:51**	**pm**

3rd ♍
☽ enters ♎   9:05 am   **6:05 am**

JANUARY

S	M	T	W	T	F	S
	1	2	3	4	5	6
7	8	9	10	11	12	13
14	15	16	17	18	19	20
21	22	23	24	25	26	27
28	29	30	31			

Eastern Standard Time in medium type
Pacific Standard Time in bold type

2001   **JANUARY**   **2001**

15 MONDAY
3rd ♎

☽	⚻	♄	12:51 am	
☽	⊼	♀	6:39 am	**3:39 am**
☽	⊼	⚹	7:13 am	**4:13 am**
☽	∟	♀	7:48 am	**4:48 am**
☽	⩗	♂	8:12 am	**5:12 am**
☽	✶	♇	9:47 am	**6:47 am**
☽	⚻	♃	1:29 pm	**10:29 am**
♄	⊼	⚴	2:25 pm	**11:25 am**
☽	⚻	⚷	4:51 pm	**1:51 pm**
☽	△	♅	6:57 pm	**3:57 pm**
♀	☌	⚹	7:48 pm	**4:48 pm**
☿	∟	⚴	9:02 pm	**6:02 pm**
☽	✶	⚴		**9:36 pm**

MARTIN LUTHER KING, JR.'S BIRTHDAY (OBSERVED)

16 TUESDAY
3rd ♎

☽	✶	⚴	12:36 am		
☽	⊼	♄	3:23 am	**12:23 am**	
☽	✶	⚴	3:30 am	**12:30 am**	
☽	☐	☉	7:35 am	**4:35 am**	☽ v/c
☽	⚻	⚹	11:01 am	**8:01 am**	
☽	⩗	♀	11:23 am	**8:23 am**	
☽	⚻	♀	11:42 am	**8:42 am**	
☽	∟	♇	12:44 pm	**9:44 am**	
☽	⊼	♃	4:26 pm	**1:26 pm**	
☽	△	⚷	9:00 pm	**6:00 pm**	
♂	⩗	♇		**9:26 pm**	
☽	☐	♆		**9:56 pm**	
♀	☐	♇		**10:35 pm**	
♀	△	♂		**11:58 pm**	

4th Quarter   7:35 am   **4:35 am**
☽ enters ♏   2:02 pm   **11:02 am**

17 WEDNESDAY
4th ♏

♂	⩗	♇	12:26 am		
☽	☐	♆	12:56 am		
♀	☐	♇	1:35 am		
♀	△	♂	2:58 am		
☽	∟	⚴	4:52 am	**1:52 am**	
☽	∟	⚴	7:14 am	**4:14 am**	
☽	☐	☿	11:55 am	**8:55 am**	
☽	△	⚹	3:51 pm	**12:51 pm**	
☽	⩗	♇	4:37 pm	**1:37 pm**	
☽	☌	♂	5:20 pm	**2:20 pm**	
☽	△	♀	5:53 pm	**2:53 pm**	
☽	☐	♅		**11:31 pm**	

18 THURSDAY
4th ♏

☽	☐	♅	2:31 am		
☽	⩗	⚴	10:06 am	**7:06 am**	
☽	☍	♄	11:12 am	**8:12 am**	
☽	⩗	⚴	11:51 am	**8:51 am**	
♇	☐	⚹	1:45 pm	**10:45 am**	
☽	✶	☉	8:44 pm	**5:44 pm**	☽ v/c
☽	☌	♀	9:28 pm	**6:28 pm**	
☽	☍	♃		**10:01 pm**	
☿	✶	♇		**10:53 pm**	

☽ enters ♐   10:35 pm   **7:35 pm**

Eastern Standard Time in medium type
Pacific Standard Time in bold type

2001   **JANUARY**   **2001**

19 FRIDAY

☽ ☍ ♃	1:01 am			
☿ ✶ ♇	1:53 am			
☉ ∟ ♇	4:25 am	**1:25 am**		
☿ ⊻ ⚳	6:49 am	**3:49 am**		
☽ ☐ ⚷	8:14 am	**5:14 am**		
☉ ✶ ♀	9:56 am	**6:56 am**		
☽ ✶ ♆	10:18 am	**7:18 am**		
☉ ∟ ⚳	4:48 pm	**1:48 pm**		
♄ ⊼ ⚴	8:23 pm	**5:23 pm**		
☽ ♂ ♇		**11:48 pm**		

☉ enters ♒   7:16 pm   **4:16 pm**

4th ♐

SUN ENTERS PISCES

20 SATURDAY

☽ ♂ ♇	2:48 am			
☿ ☐ ♂	4:05 am	**1:05 am**		
☽ ☐ ⚳	4:15 am	**1:15 am**		
☽ ∟ ☉	4:48 am	**1:48 am**		
☽ ⊻ ♂	6:16 am	**3:16 am**		
☽ ✶ ☿	6:28 am	**3:28 am**		
☽ ☐ ♀	9:15 am	**6:15 am**		
☽ ✶ ♅	1:18 pm	**10:18 am**	☽ v/c	
☽ ∟ ♆	4:02 pm	**1:02 pm**		
☽ ⊼ ♄	10:04 pm	**7:04 pm**		
☽ ♂ ⚴	10:56 pm	**7:56 pm**		
☽ ♂ ⚸	11:17 pm	**8:17 pm**		
☉ △ ♃	11:58 pm	**8:58 pm**		

♀ enters ♐   12:40 pm   **9:40 pm**

4th ♐

INAUGURATION DAY

21 SUNDAY

☽ ⊻ ♀	10:35 am	**7:35 am**	
☽ ⊼ ♃	12:23 pm	**9:23 am**	
⚸ ♂ ⚴	1:18 pm	**10:18 am**	
☽ ⊻ ☉	1:33 pm	**10:33 am**	
☽ ∟ ♂	1:44 pm	**10:44 am**	
☽ ∟ ☿	4:54 pm	**1:54 pm**	
♆ ⊻ ⚷	6:54 pm	**3:54 pm**	
☽ ∟ ♅	7:31 pm	**4:31 pm**	
☽ ⊻ ♆	10:15 pm	**7:15 pm**	
☽ ✶ ⚷	10:22 pm	**7:22 pm**	

☽ enters ♑   9:57 am   **6:57 am**

4th ♐

JANUARY

S	M	T	W	T	F	S
	1	2	3	4	5	6
7	8	9	10	11	12	13
14	15	16	17	18	19	20
21	22	23	24	25	26	27
28	29	30	31			

Eastern Standard Time in medium type
Pacific Standard Time in bold type

JANUARY 2001

22 MONDAY
4th ♑

☽ ⊡ ♄	4:13 am	**1:13 am**
♀ ⩗ ♅	1:36 pm	**10:36 am**
☿ ♂ ♅	2:35 pm	**11:35 am**
☽ ⩗ ♇	3:10 pm	**12:10 pm**
☿ ⩗ ♀	4:26 pm	**1:26 pm**
☽ ∟ ♀	5:49 pm	**2:49 pm**
☽ ⊡ ♃	6:40 pm	**3:40 pm**
☽ ✶ ※	7:05 pm	**4:05 pm**
☽ ✶ ♂	9:35 pm	**6:35 pm**
☽ ⩗ ♅		**11:02 pm**

23 TUESDAY
4th ♑

☽ enters ♒ 10:43 pm **7:43 pm**

☽ ⩗ ♅	2:02 am	
☽ ✶ ♀	3:06 am	**12:06 am**
☽ ⩗ ☿	3:35 am	**12:35 am**
☽ ∟ ⚷	6:01 am	**3:01 am**
☽ △ ♄	10:38 am	**7:38 am** ☽ v/c
☽ ⩗ ⚴	12:26 pm	**9:26 am**
☽ ⩗ ⚵	1:37 pm	**10:37 am**
☽ ∟ ♇	9:43 pm	**6:43 pm**
♃ ☍ ♀	10:12 pm	**7:12 pm**
♀ ∟ ♆	11:50 pm	**8:50 pm**
☽ △ ♃		**10:09 pm**
☽ ✶ ♀		**10:14 pm**
☽ ∟ ※		**11:54 pm**

24 WEDNESDAY
4th ♒

New Moon 8:07 am **5:07 pm**
♄ D 7:24 pm **4:24 pm**

☽ △ ♃	1:09 am	
☽ ✶ ♀	1:14 am	
☽ ∟ ※	2:54 am	
☽ ♂ ☉	8:07 am	**5:07 am**
☽ ♂ ♆	11:21 am	**8:21 am**
☽ ∟ ♀	12:20 pm	**9:20 am**
☽ ⩗ ⚷	1:49 pm	**10:49 am**
☽ ∟ ⚴	7:12 pm	**4:12 pm**
☽ ∟ ⚵	9:10 pm	**6:10 pm**

CHINESE NEW YEAR

25 THURSDAY
1st ♒

♃ D 3:38 am **12:38 am**

☽ ✶ ♇	4:18 am	**1:18 am**
☽ ⩗ ※	10:44 am	**7:44 am**
☽ □ ♂	1:37 pm	**10:37 am**
☽ ♂ ♅	3:20 pm	**12:20 pm**
☿ □ ♄	4:35 pm	**1:35 pm**
☽ ⩗ ♀	9:29 pm	**6:29 pm**
☉ ♂ ♆	10:55 pm	**7:55 pm**
☽ □ ♄	11:37 pm	**8:37 pm**
☽ ♂ ☿		**9:28 pm** ☽ v/c
☽ ✶ ⚴		**10:54 pm**

Eastern Standard Time in medium type
Pacific Standard Time in bold type

JANUARY 2001

26 FRIDAY

☽ ☌ ☿	12:28 am			☽ v/c
☽ ⚹ ♅	1:54 am			
☽ ⚹ ♀	4:38 am	**1:38 am**		
☽ ☐ ♃	2:03 pm	**11:03 am**		
☿ ⚹ ♅	3:34 pm	**12:34 pm**		
☽ ☐ ♀	3:57 pm	**12:57 pm**		
☽ ⚺ ♆		**9:21 pm**		
♀ ⚹ ♄		**9:25 pm**		
☽ ⚺ ☉		**11:38 pm**		

1st ♒
☽ enters ♓ 11:39 am **8:39 am**

27 SATURDAY

☽ ⚺ ♆	12:21 am		
♀ ⚹ ♄	12:25 am		
☽ ⚺ ☉	2:38 am		
☽ ☌ ⚳	5:06 am	**2:06 am**	
♂ ☐ ♅	6:09 am	**3:09 am**	
☽ ☐ ♇	5:01 pm	**2:01 pm**	
☽ ☌ ⚴		**10:49 pm**	

1st ♓

28 SUNDAY

☽ ☌ ⚴	1:49 am			
☽ ⚺ ♅	4:01 am	**1:01 am**		
☽ △ ♂	4:58 am	**1:58 am**		
☽ ⊔ ♆	6:28 am	**3:28 am**		
♀ ☐ ♅	11:15 am	**8:15 am**		
☽ ⊔ ☉	11:22 am	**8:22 am**		
☽ ⚹ ♄	11:52 am	**8:52 am**		
☽ ☐ ♅	2:33 pm	**11:33 am**		
☽ ☌ ♀	2:48 pm	**11:48 am**	☽ v/c	
☿ ⚹ ♀	5:13 pm	**2:13 pm**		
☽ ☐ ♃	6:41 pm	**3:41 pm**		
☽ ⚺ ☿	6:45 pm	**3:45 pm**		
☽ ⚹ ♃		**10:58 pm**		

1st ♓
☽ enters ♈ 11:35 pm **8:35 pm**

JANUARY

S	M	T	W	T	F	S
	1	2	3	4	5	6
7	8	9	10	11	12	13
14	15	16	17	18	19	20
21	22	23	24	25	26	27
28	29	30	31			

Eastern Standard Time in medium type
Pacific Standard Time in bold type

JANUARY 2001

29 MONDAY — 1st ♈

☽	✶	♃	1:58 am		
☽	△	♀	5:27 am	**2:27 am**	
☉	⊻	⚷	6:39 am	**3:39 am**	
☽	∟	♅	9:46 am	**6:46 am**	
☽	⊡	♂	11:57 am	**8:57 am**	
☽	✶	♆	12:07 pm	**9:07 am**	
☽	∟	♄	5:21 pm	**2:21 pm**	
☽	⊻	⚷	6:54 pm	**3:54 pm**	
☽	✶	☉	7:29 pm	**4:29 pm**	
☽	∟	☿		**11:20 pm**	

30 TUESDAY — 1st ♈

☽	∟	☿	2:20 am		
☽	△	♇	4:11 am	**1:11 am**	
☉	∟	⚸	4:50 am	**1:50 am**	
☽	∟	♃	7:11 am	**4:11 am**	
☽	⊡	♀	11:21 am	**8:21 am**	
♅	⊻	⚹	1:26 pm	**10:26 am**	
☽	✶	♅	2:54 pm	**11:54 am**	
☽	⊻	⚹	2:57 pm	**11:57 am**	
☽	⊼	♂	6:14 pm	**3:14 pm**	
☽	⊻	♄	10:12 pm	**7:12 pm**	
☽	∟	⚷		**9:49 pm**	
☽	△	⚸		**10:10 pm**	

31 WEDNESDAY — 1st ♈

☽	∟	⚷	12:49 am		
☽	△	⚸	1:10 am		
☽	⊻	♀	5:26 am	**2:26 am**	
☽	△	♇	6:26 am	**3:26 am**	
☽	✶	☿	8:36 am	**5:36 am**	☽ v/c
☽	⊡	♇	8:48 am	**5:48 am**	
☽	⊻	♃	11:43 am	**8:43 am**	
☽	⊼	♀	4:28 pm	**1:28 pm**	
☽	∟	⚹	8:22 pm	**5:22 pm**	
☽	□	♆	9:27 pm	**6:27 pm**	

☽ enters ♉ 9:21 am **6:21 am**
☿ enters ♓ **11:13 pm**

AQUARIUS ♒
Duality: Masculine
Quality: Fixed
Element: Air
House: 11th
Planetary Ruler: Uranus
Rules: Circulation, Shins, Ankles
Keyword: Truth
Keynote: I know.

Eastern Standard Time in medium type
Pacific Standard Time in bold type

2001 FEBRUARY 2001

1 THURSDAY

☽ ⛢ ♂	5:20 am	**2:20 am**		
♀ □ ♃	5:33 am	**2:33 am**		
☽ ✶ ♆	5:51 am	**2:51 am**		
☽ □ ☉	9:02 am	**6:02 am**		
☽ ⛢ ♃	11:04 am	**8:04 am**		
☽ ∟ ♀	11:18 am	**8:18 am**		
☽ ⊼ ♇	12:35 pm	**9:35 am**		
☽ □ ♅	10:50 pm	**7:50 pm**		
☽ ✶ ⚸		**9:50 pm**		
♆ ∟ ⚸		**11:06 pm**		

☿ enters ♓ 2:13 am
2nd Quarter 9:02 am **6:02 am**

1st ♉

2 FRIDAY

☽ ✶ ⚸	12:50 am			
♆ ∟ ⚸	2:06 am			
☽ ☍ ♂	4:05 am	**1:05 am**		
☽ ☌ ♄	5:31 am	**2:31 am**	☽ v/c	
☽ ⊼ ♂	8:36 am	**5:36 am**		
☽ ⊼ ♃	2:44 pm	**11:44 am**		
☽ ✶ ♀	4:02 pm	**1:02 pm**		
☽ □ ☿	4:56 pm	**1:56 pm**		
☽ ☌ ♃	6:14 pm	**3:14 pm**		
☽ ☍ ♀	11:53 pm	**8:53 pm**		
☉ ∟ ♃		**10:26 pm**		

♀ enters ♈ 2:14 pm **11:14 am**
☽ enters ♊ 3:56 pm **12:56 pm**

2nd ♉

IMBOLC • GROUNDHOG DAY

3 SATURDAY

☉ ∟ ♃	1:26 am		
☽ △ ♆	3:24 am	**12:24 am**	
☉ ✶ ♇	8:05 am	**5:05 am**	
☿ ⊻ ♀	8:59 am	**5:59 am**	
☽ □ ⚸	12:59 pm	**9:59 am**	
♂ ☍ ♄	4:33 pm	**1:33 pm**	
☽ ☍ ♇	5:30 pm	**2:30 pm**	
☽ △ ☉	6:13 pm	**3:13 pm**	

☿ ℞ 8:55 pm **5:55 pm**

2nd ♊

4 SUNDAY

☽ △ ♅	3:12 am	**12:12 am**	☽ v/c	
♀ ✶ ♃	4:26 am	**1:26 am**		
☽ ⛢ ♆	5:03 am	**2:03 am**		
☽ □ ⚸	6:47 am	**3:47 am**		
☽ ⊻ ♄	9:19 am	**6:19 am**		
☽ ⊼ ♂	9:57 am	**6:57 am**		
☽ ☍ ♂	12:28 pm	**9:28 am**		
☽ ☍ ♃	7:13 pm	**4:13 pm**		
☽ △ ☿	8:00 pm	**5:00 pm**		
☽ ⛢ ☉	9:13 pm	**6:13 pm**		
☽ ⊻ ♃	9:17 pm	**6:17 pm**		
☽ □ ♀	10:16 pm	**7:16 pm**		

♃ enters ♑ 10:31 am **7:31 am**
☽ enters ♋ 7:00 pm **4:00 pm**

2nd ♊

Eastern Standard Time in medium type
Pacific Standard Time in bold type

2001 FEBRUARY 2001

5 MONDAY
2nd ♋

☽	⊼	♀	3:35 am	**12:35 am**
☽	⚻	♅	4:09 am	**1:09 am**
☽	⊼	♆	5:54 am	**2:54 am**
☽	⦞	♄	10:02 am	**7:02 am**
☽	⚻	♂	11:33 am	**8:33 am**
☿	⚹	⚷	2:08 pm	**11:08 am**
☽	△	⚹	4:27 pm	**1:27 pm**
☽	⊼	♇	7:09 pm	**4:09 pm**
☽	⚻	☿	7:59 pm	**4:59 pm**
☽	⦞	♃	9:43 pm	**6:43 pm**
☽	⊼	☉	11:21 pm	**8:21 pm**

6 TUESDAY
2nd ♋

☽	⚻	♀	4:19 am	**1:19 am**	
☽	⊼	♅	4:28 am	**1:28 am**	
☽	△	⚹	9:23 am	**6:23 am**	
☽	⚹	♄	10:10 am	**7:10 am**	
☽	△	♂	12:30 pm	**9:30 am**	☽ v/c
☽	⊼	⚷	1:22 pm	**10:22 am**	
☽	⚻	⚹	5:12 pm	**2:12 pm**	
☽	⚻	♇	7:07 pm	**4:07 pm**	
☽	⊼	☿	7:12 pm	**4:12 pm**	
☽	⊼	⚷	8:45 pm	**5:45 pm**	
☽	⚹	♃	9:40 pm	**6:40 pm**	
☽	△	♀		**10:14 pm**	

☿ enters ♒ 2:57 pm **11:57 am**
☽ enters ♌ 7:21 pm **4:21 pm**

7 WEDNESDAY
2nd ♌
Full Moon **11:12 pm**

☽	△	♀	1:14 am		
☽	△	♀	4:36 am	**1:36 am**	
☽	☍	♆	5:58 am	**2:58 am**	
♄	⚹	⚹	9:02 am	**6:02 am**	
☽	⚻	⚹	9:57 am	**6:57 am**	
☽	⚻	⚷	1:11 pm	**10:11 am**	
♂	⚼	⚷	4:52 pm	**1:52 pm**	
☽	⊼	⚹	5:36 pm	**2:36 pm**	
☽	△	♇	6:47 pm	**3:47 pm**	
☽	⚻	♃	8:57 pm	**5:57 pm**	
☉	⦞	♀	9:57 pm	**6:57 pm**	
☽	⚻	♀		**11:08 pm**	
☽	☍	☉		**11:12 pm**	

8 THURSDAY
2nd ♌
Full Moon 2:12 am
☽ enters ♍ 6:35 pm **3:35 pm**

☽	⚻	♀	2:08 am		
☽	☍	☉	2:12 am		
☽	☍	♅	4:01 am	**1:01 am**	
☽	□	♄	9:32 am	**6:32 am**	
☽	⊼	⚹	10:21 am	**7:21 am**	
☽	△	⚷	12:54 pm	**9:54 am**	
☽	□	♂	1:31 pm	**10:31 am**	
♃	⊼	⚹	4:13 pm	**1:13 pm**	
☽	☍	☿	4:25 pm	**1:25 pm**	☽ v/c
☽	□	♃	9:03 pm	**6:03 pm**	
☽	△	⚹	9:09 pm	**6:09 pm**	

Eastern Standard Time in medium type
Pacific Standard Time in bold type

FEBRUARY 2001

9 FRIDAY
3rd ♍

☽	⊼	♀	3:04 am	**12:04 am**
☽	□	♀	4:49 am	**1:49 am**
☽	⊼	♆	5:21 am	**2:21 am**
☉	☌	♅	7:19 am	**4:19 am**
♇	□	⚷	8:50 am	**5:50 am**
☽	□	♇	6:17 pm	**3:17 pm**
♀	⊥	♅	6:19 pm	**3:19 pm**
☽	☍	⚷	6:35 pm	**3:35 pm**
☿	□	♂	9:58 pm	**6:58 pm**

10 SATURDAY
3rd ♍

☽ enters ♎ 6:46 pm **3:46 pm**

☽	⊼	♅	3:52 am	**12:52 am**	
☽	⊼	☉	5:17 am	**2:17 am**	
☽	⚹	♆	5:26 am	**2:26 am**	
☽	△	♄	9:28 am	**6:28 am**	
♆	⚹	♀	11:04 am	**8:04 am**	
☽	☍	⚸	11:58 am	**8:58 am**	
☽	□	⚴	1:07 pm	**10:07 am**	
☽	⊼	☿	1:36 pm	**10:36 am**	
☽	⚹	♂	3:18 pm	**12:18 pm**	☽ v/c
☿	⚹	⚴	7:47 pm	**4:47 pm**	
☽	△	♃	9:30 pm	**6:30 pm**	
☽	□	⚵	10:39 pm	**7:39 pm**	

11 SUNDAY
3rd ♎

♀	⚹	♆	3:08 am	**12:08 am**
☿	⚼	⚸	4:11 am	**1:11 am**
☽	⊥	♅	4:34 am	**1:34 am**
☽	△	♆	6:09 am	**3:09 am**
☽	☍	♀	6:18 am	**3:18 am**
☽	⚹	⚴	6:30 am	**3:30 am**
☽	⊥	☉	7:48 am	**4:48 am**
☽	⊥	♄	10:18 am	**7:18 am**
♀	△	⚴	12:32 pm	**9:32 am**
☽	⊥	☿	12:45 pm	**9:45 am**
☽	⊥	♂	5:14 pm	**2:14 pm**
☽	⚹	♇	7:45 pm	**4:45 pm**
☽	⊼	⚷	9:44 pm	**6:44 pm**
☽	⊥	♃	10:47 pm	**7:47 pm**
⚴	□	⚸		**11:09 pm**

FEBRUARY

S	M	T	W	T	F	S
				1	2	3
4	5	6	7	8	9	10
11	12	13	14	15	16	17
18	19	20	21	22	23	24
25	26	27	28			

Eastern Standard Time in medium type
Pacific Standard Time in bold type

2001 FEBRUARY 2001

12 MONDAY

♂ □ ⚹	2:09 am			
☽ △ ♅	6:06 am	**3:06 am**		
☽ ⊥ ♀	8:33 am	**5:33 am**		
☽ △ ☉	11:22 am	**8:22 am**		
☽ ⊼ ♄	12:00 pm	**9:00 am**		
☽ △ ☿	12:31 pm	**9:31 am**	☽ v/c	
☽ ⚹ ♂	4:05 pm	**1:05 pm**		
☽ ⊼ ⚹	4:33 pm	**1:33 pm**		
☿ □ ♄	6:25 pm	**3:25 pm**		
☉ ☌ ☿	7:17 pm	**4:17 pm**		
☽ ⊻ ♂	8:11 pm	**5:11 pm**		
☉ □ ♄	8:21 pm	**5:21 pm**		
☽ ⊥ ♇	9:48 pm	**6:48 pm**		
☽ ⊼ ♆		**9:46 pm**		
☽ ⊼ ♃		**10:01 pm**		

☽ enters ♏ 9:51 pm **6:51 pm**

3rd ♎ → **6:51 pm**

13 TUESDAY

☽ ⊡ ♆	12:46 am			
☽ ⊼ ♃	1:01 am			
☽ ⚹ ?	3:26 am	**12:26 am**		
☽ □ ♅	10:16 am	**7:16 am**		
☽ ⊻ ♀	11:39 am	**8:39 am**		
☿ ⊥ ♀	11:43 am	**8:43 am**		
☽ ⊼ ♀	1:14 pm	**10:14 am**		
☽ ⊥ ♂	7:04 pm	**4:04 pm**		
☽ ⊡ ⚹	8:31 pm	**5:31 pm**		
☽ ⊻ ♇		**9:54 pm**		

3rd ♏

14 WEDNESDAY

☽ ⊻ ♇	12:54 am			
☽ △ ♆	4:59 am	**1:59 am**		
☽ ⊥ ?	7:29 am	**4:29 am**		
☽ □ ♅	12:15 pm	**9:15 am**		
☽ □ ☿	2:24 pm	**11:24 am**		
☽ ⊡ ♀	6:28 pm	**3:28 pm**		
☽ ☍ ♄	6:33 pm	**3:33 pm**		
♀ ⊥ ♄	7:59 pm	**4:59 pm**		
☽ □ ☉	10:23 pm	**7:23 pm**	☽ v/c	
☽ ⊻ ♂	11:08 pm	**8:08 pm**		
☽ △ ⚹		**10:41 pm**		

♂ enters ♐ 3:06 pm **12:06 pm**
4th Quarter 10:23 pm **7:23 pm**

3rd ♏

VALENTINE'S DAY

15 THURSDAY

☽ △ ⚹	1:41 am		
☽ ☌ ♂	5:38 am	**2:38 am**	
☉ ⚹ ♂	8:24 am	**5:24 am**	
☽ ☍ ♃	8:45 am	**5:45 am**	
☽ ⊻ ?	12:40 pm	**9:40 am**	
☿ ☌ ♅	1:38 pm	**10:38 am**	
☽ ⚹ ♆	6:34 pm	**3:34 pm**	
☽ ☌ ♀	9:13 pm	**6:13 pm**	
☽ △ ♀		**9:51 pm**	

☽ enters ♐ 5:02 am **2:02 am**

4th ♏ → ♐

Eastern Standard Time in medium type
Pacific Standard Time in bold type

FEBRUARY 2001

16 FRIDAY
4th ♐

☽ △ ♀	12:51 am		
☽ ☌ ♇	10:11 am	**7:11 am**
☽ □ ⚷	4:50 pm	**1:50 pm**
☽ ✶ ☿	7:43 pm	**4:43 pm**
☽ ✶ ♅	10:30 pm	**7:30 pm**
☽ ⊥ ♆		**9:08 pm**

17 SATURDAY
4th ♐

☽ enters ♑   3:59 pm   **12:59 pm**

☽ ⊥ ♆	12:08 am		
☿ ⊥ ⚵	3:20 am	**12:20 am**
☽ ⊼ ♄	5:06 am	**2:06 am**
☽ ☌ ⚷	10:07 am	**7:07 am**
☽ ✶ ☉	2:22 pm	**11:22 am**	☽ v/c
☽ □ ⚹	3:09 pm	**12:09 pm**
☿ ⊻ ⚵	7:08 pm	**4:08 pm**
☽ ⊻ ♂	7:18 pm	**4:18 pm**
☽ ⊼ ♃	8:15 pm	**5:15 pm**
☽ ⊥ ☿	11:32 pm	**8:32 pm**
☽ ☌ ⚵		**10:47 pm**

18 SUNDAY
4th ♑

☉ enters ♓   9:27 am   **6:27 am**
⚹ enters ♈   9:38 am   **6:38 am**

☽ ☌ ⚵	1:47 am		
☽ ⊥ ♅	4:45 am	**1:45 am**
☽ ⊻ ♆	6:21 am	**3:21 am**
☉ ⊻ ⚹	9:15 am	**6:15 am**
☽ ⊻ ♀	10:20 am	**7:20 am**
☽ ⚻ ♄	11:25 am	**8:25 am**
☽ □ ♀	4:00 pm	**1:00 pm**
♂ ☍ ♃	8:57 pm	**5:57 pm**
☽ ⊻ ♇	10:28 pm	**7:28 pm**
☽ ⊥ ☉	11:32 pm	**8:32 pm**
☽ ⚻ ♃		**11:51 pm**

SUN ENTERS PISCES

FEBRUARY

S	M	T	W	T	F	S
				1	2	3
4	5	6	7	8	9	10
11	12	13	14	15	16	17
18	19	20	21	22	23	24
25	26	27	28			

Eastern Standard Time in medium type
Pacific Standard Time in bold type

2001 FEBRUARY 2001

19 MONDAY

4th ♑

☽	⛢	♃	2:51 am		
☽	⊥	♂	3:05 am	12:05 am
☽	⊻	☿	3:58 am	12:58 am
☽	✱	♆	7:47 am	4:47 am
☽	⊻	♅	11:22 am	8:22 am
☽	⊥	♀	5:33 pm	2:33 pm
☽	△	♄	6:03 pm	3:03 pm	☽ v/c
☽	⊻	⚷	11:18 pm	8:18 pm

PRESIDENT'S DAY (OBSERVED)

20 TUESDAY

4th ♑

☽ enters ♒   4:53 am   **1:53 am**

☽	⊥	♇	5:05 am	**2:05 am**
☽	✱	⚸	6:56 am	**3:56 am**
☽	⊻	☉	8:58 am	**5:58 am**
☽	△	♃	9:39 am	**6:39 am**
☽	✱	♂	11:03 am	**8:03 am**
☽	⊥	♆	3:40 pm	**12:40 pm**
☽	⊻	⚴	4:38 pm	**1:38 pm**
☉	□	♃	5:39 pm	**2:39 pm**
☽	☌	♇	7:36 pm	**4:36 pm**
☽	✱	♀		**9:48 pm**

21 WEDNESDAY

4th ♒

☽	✱	♀	12:48 am	
☿	⊥	⚸	4:28 am	**1:28 am**
☽	⊥	⚷	6:02 am	**3:02 am**
☽	✱	♀	8:06 am	**5:06 am**
☽	✱	♇	11:39 am	**8:39 am**
☽	☌	☿	2:02 pm	**11:02 am**
☽	⊥	⚸	2:54 pm	**11:54 am**
☽	⊻	♆	11:25 pm	**8:25 pm**
☽	⊥	⚴	12:00 pm	**9:00 pm**
☽	☌	♅		**9:42 pm**

22 THURSDAY

4th ♒

☽ enters ♓   5:45 pm   **2:45 pm**

☽	☌	♅	12:42 am	
☽	□	♄	7:18 am	**4:18 am**	☽ v/c
☉	□	♂	8:11 am	**5:11 am**
☽	✱	⚷	12:35 pm	**9:35 am**
☽	⊥	♀	3:48 pm	**12:48 pm**
☽	⊻	⚸	10:37 pm	**7:37 pm**
☽	□	♃	10:53 pm	**7:53 pm**
☽	□	♂		**11:31 pm**

Eastern Standard Time in medium type
Pacific Standard Time in bold type

FEBRUARY 2001

23 FRIDAY
4th ♓

☽ □ ♂	2:31 am			
☽ ☌ ☉	3:21 am	**12:21 am**		
♅ ∟ ♄	5:50 am	**2:50 am**		
♃ ⚹ ⚴	5:51 am	**2:51 am**		
☽ ⚹ ♄	7:04 am	**4:04 am**		
☽ ⚼ ♆	8:24 am	**5:24 am**		
♅ ⚼ ⚳	11:31 am	**8:31 am**		
☽ □ ♀	2:38 pm	**11:38 am**		
☽ ⚼ ♀	11:02 pm	**8:02 pm**		
☽ □ ♇		**9:01 pm**		
☽ ⚼ ☿		**9:47 pm**		

New Moon 3:21 am **12:21 am**

24 SATURDAY
1st ♓

☽ □ ♇	12:01 am			
☽ ⚼ ☿	12:47 am			
☽ ⚼ ♅	1:00 pm	**10:00 am**		
☽ ☌ ⚳	1:55 pm	**10:55 am**		
☽ ∟ ♆	2:17 pm	**11:17 am**		
☽ ⚹ ♄	7:25 pm	**4:25 pm**	☽ v/c	
♆ ∟ ⚳		**9:07 pm**		
☽ □ ⚴		**9:36 pm**		

25 SUNDAY
1st ♓

♆ ∟ ⚳	12:07 am			
☽ □ ⚴	12:36 am			
♀ △ ♇	3:30 am	**12:30 am**		
☽ ∟ ☿	6:08 am	**3:08 am**		
☽ ⚹ ♃	10:48 am	**7:48 am**		
☽ ☌ ⚴	12:47 pm	**9:47 am**		
♆ ⚼ ⚳	12:51 pm	**9:51 am**		
☽ △ ♂	4:22 pm	**1:22 pm**		
☉ ⚼ ♆	5:28 pm	**2:28 pm**		
☽ ∟ ♅	6:31 pm	**3:31 pm**		
☿ ⚹ ♀	6:50 pm	**3:50 pm**		
☉ ⚹ ⚳	7:28 pm	**4:28 pm**		
☽ ⚹ ♆	7:44 pm	**4:44 pm**		
☽ □ ⚳	7:55 pm	**4:55 pm**		
☽ ⚼ ☉	7:56 pm	**4:56 pm**		

☽ enters ♈ 5:20 am **2:20 am**
☿ D 10:42 am **7:42 am**

☽ ∟ ♄   9:50 pm
☽ △ ♀   11:47 pm

FEBRUARY

S	M	T	W	T	F	S
				1	2	3
4	5	6	7	8	9	10
11	12	13	14	15	16	17
18	19	20	21	22	23	24
25	26	27	28			

Eastern Standard Time in medium type
Pacific Standard Time in bold type

2001　　　　　　　　　　**FEBRUARY**　　　　　　　　　　**2001**

26　MONDAY　　　　　　　　　　　　　　　　　1st ♈

☽	⊥	♄	12:50 am		
☽	△	♀	2:47 am		
☽	△	♇	10:47 am	**7:47 am**	
☽	✶	☿	11:22 am	**8:22 am**	
☽	☌	♀	11:47 am	**8:47 am**	
☽	⊥	♃	4:05 pm	**1:05 pm**	
☽	⚼	♂	10:31 pm	**7:31 pm**	
☽	✶	♅	11:34 pm	**8:34 pm**	☽ v/c
☽	⩛	♆		**11:30 pm**	

27　TUESDAY　　　　　　　　　　　　　　　　1st ♈
　　　　　　　　　　　　　　　☽ enters ♉　　3:06 pm　**12:06 pm**

☽	⩛	♆	2:30 am		
☽	⊥	☉	3:20 am	**12:20 am**	
☽	⩛	♄	5:47 am	**2:47 am**	
☽	⚼	♀	8:06 am	**5:06 am**	
☽	△	⚷	10:49 am	**7:49 am**	
☽	⚼	♇	3:26 pm	**12:26 pm**	
☽	⩛	♃	8:50 pm	**5:50 pm**	
☽	⩛	⚹		**9:50 pm**	

MARDI GRAS

28　WEDNESDAY　　　　　　　　　　　　　　　1st ♉

☽	⩛	⚹	12:50 am		
☽	⊼	♂	4:03 am	**1:03 am**	
☽	□	♆	5:09 am	**2:09 am**	
☽	△	♇	6:39 am	**3:39 am**	
☽	⊥	⚷	7:55 am	**4:55 am**	
☽	✶	☉	10:02 am	**7:02 am**	
☽	⊼	♀	12:49 pm	**9:49 am**	
☽	⚼	⚷	3:06 pm	**12:06 pm**	
☽	⊼	♇	7:31 pm	**4:31 pm**	
☽	□	☿	9:04 pm	**6:04 pm**	
☽	⩛	♀	9:57 pm	**6:57 pm**	

ASH WEDNESDAY

PISCES ♓
Duality: Feminine
Quality: Mutable
Element: Water
House: 12th
Planetary Ruler: Neptune
Rules: Feet, Lymph System
Keyword: Unity
Keynote: I believe.

Eastern Standard Time in medium type
Pacific Standard Time in bold type

2001   **MARCH**   **2001**

1 THURSDAY

☽	⊥	⚹	5:54 am	**2:54 am**	
☽	□	♅	7:59 am	**4:59 am**	
♂	✶	♆	10:32 am	**7:32 am**	
☽	⊡	♃	11:04 am	**8:04 am**	
☽	✶	⚵	12:39 pm	**9:39 am**	
☽	☌	♄	1:57 pm	**10:57 am**	☽ v/c
☽	⊼	⚸	6:45 pm	**3:45 pm**	
☽	⊥	♀		**10:55 pm**	

1st ♉
☽ enters ♊ 10:06 pm **7:06 pm**

2 FRIDAY

☽	⊥	♀	1:55 am		
☽	☌	♃	4:33 am	**1:33 am**	
☉	□	♀	6:57 am	**3:57 am**	
☽	✶	⚹	10:14 am	**7:14 am**	
☽	△	♆	12:09 pm	**9:09 am**	
☽	☍	♂	1:03 pm	**10:03 am**	
☽	⊼	♃	2:47 pm	**11:47 am**	
☽	☍	♀	8:13 pm	**5:13 pm**	
☽	□	☉	9:03 pm	**6:03 pm**	
☽	☍	♇		**10:44 pm**	

1st ♊
2nd Quarter 9:03 pm **6:03 pm**

3 SATURDAY

☽	☍	♇	1:44 am		
☽	△	☿	4:59 am	**1:59 am**	
☽	✶	♀	5:03 am	**2:03 am**	
♄	✶	⚵	5:50 am	**2:50 am**	
☿	✶	♀	7:36 am	**4:36 am**	
♅	⊥	⚹	1:10 pm	**10:10 am**	
☽	△	♅	1:45 pm	**10:45 am**	☽ v/c
☽	⊡	♆	2:37 pm	**11:37 am**	
☽	⊻	♄	7:27 pm	**4:27 pm**	
☽	□	⚵	7:52 pm	**4:52 pm**	
☽	☍	⚸	11:58 pm	**8:58 pm**	

2nd ♊

4 SUNDAY

☽	⊡	☿	8:03 am	**5:03 am**	
☽	⊻	♃	9:28 am	**6:28 am**	
♆	✶	⚹	12:12 pm	**9:12 am**	
☽	⊡	♅	3:34 pm	**12:34 pm**	
☽	⊼	♆	4:22 pm	**1:22 pm**	
☽	□	⚹	4:31 pm	**1:31 pm**	
☽	⊼	♂	6:55 pm	**3:55 pm**	
☽	☍	♃	7:54 pm	**4:54 pm**	
☽	⊥	♄	9:08 pm	**6:08 pm**	
☽	⊼	♀		**9:39 pm**	

2nd ♊
☽ enters ♋ 3:24 am **12:24 am**

Eastern Standard Time in medium type
Pacific Standard Time in bold type

2001 — MARCH — 2001

5 MONDAY
2nd ♋

☽ ⊼ ♀	12:39 am			
☽ △ ☉	4:33 am	**1:33 am**		
☽ ⊼ ♇	5:09 am	**2:09 am**		
☽ □ ♀	8:54 am	**5:54 am**		
☽ ⊼ ☿	10:30 am	**7:30 am**		
☽ ⊥ ♃	10:52 am	**7:52 am**		
☉ □ ♇	1:11 pm	**10:11 am**		
☽ ⊼ ♅	4:42 pm	**1:42 pm**		
☽ ⚻ ♂	8:43 pm	**5:43 pm**		
☽ ✶ ♄	10:10 pm	**7:10 pm**	☽ v/c
☽ △ ♆		**9:02 pm**		
☽ ⚻ ♀		**10:49 pm**		
☽ ⊼ ☿		**11:24 pm**		

6 TUESDAY
2nd ♋   ☽ enters ♌ 5:30 am **2:30 am**

☽ △ ♆	12:02 am			
☽ ⚻ ♀	1:49 am			
☽ ⊼ ☿	2:24 am			
☽ ⚻ ♇	5:53 am	**2:53 am**		
☽ ⚻ ☉	7:06 am	**4:06 am**		
☽ ✶ ♃	11:41 am	**8:41 am**		
☽ ☍ ♆	5:58 pm	**2:58 pm**		
☽ △ ♅	7:55 pm	**4:55 pm**		
☽ △ ♂	9:56 pm	**6:56 pm**		
☽ ⊼ ♄	10:18 pm	**7:18 pm**		
☽ ⚻ ♆		**10:11 pm**		
☽ △ ♀		**11:28 pm**		
☽ ⚻ ☿		**11:47 pm**		

7 WEDNESDAY
2nd ♌

☽ ⚻ ♆	1:11 am			
☽ △ ♀	2:28 am			
☽ ⚻ ☿	2:47 am			
☽ △ ♇	6:09 am	**3:09 am**		
☽ ⊼ ☉	9:04 am	**6:04 am**		
☽ △ ♀	10:04 am	**7:04 am**		
☽ ☍ ☿	1:55 pm	**10:55 am**		
☽ ☍ ♅	5:28 pm	**2:28 pm**		
☽ ⚻ ♂	8:54 pm	**5:54 pm**		
♄ ⚻ ♃	9:42 pm	**6:42 pm**		
☽ □ ♄	10:50 pm	**7:50 pm**	☽ v/c
☽ ⚻ ♃	10:51 pm	**7:51 pm**		
☉ ⚺ ♀		**9:42 pm**		
☽ ⊼ ♆		**10:59 pm**		
☽ △ ☿		**11:52 pm**		

8 THURSDAY
2nd ♌   ☽ enters ♍ 5:44 am **2:44 am**   ♀ ℞ 8:06 pm **5:06 pm**

☉ ⚺ ♀	12:42 am			
☽ ⊼ ♆	1:59 am			
☽ △ ☿	2:52 am			
♂ ⚺ ♃	6:40 am	**3:40 am**		
☽ ⚻ ♀	10:05 am	**7:05 am**		
☽ □ ♃	12:12 pm	**9:12 am**		
☽ ⊼ ♆	6:04 pm	**3:04 pm**		
☽ ⊼ ♅	9:43 pm	**6:43 pm**		
☽ △ ♃	11:15 pm	**8:15 pm**		
☽ □ ♂	11:26 pm	**8:26 pm**		
☽ □ ♀		**11:59 pm**		

Eastern Standard Time in medium type
Pacific Standard Time in bold type

2001   **MARCH**   **2001**

9 FRIDAY

☽	□	♀	2:59 am			
☽	□	♇	6:04 am	**3:04 am**		
⚷	□	⚵	8:43 am	**5:43 am**		
☽	⊼	♀	10:01 am	**7:01 am**		
☽	☍	☉	12:23 pm	**9:23 am**		
☽	⊼	☿	4:50 pm	**1:50 pm**		
☽	⊼	♅	5:33 pm	**2:33 pm**		
☽	⚻	♆	6:07 pm	**3:07 pm**		
☽	△	♄	11:01 pm	**8:01 pm**	☽ v/c	

Full Moon   12:23 pm   **9:23 pm**

2nd ♍

PURIM

10 SATURDAY

☽	□	⚵	3:01 am	**12:01 am**	
☽	☍	⚷	3:34 am	**12:34 am**	
☿	☌	♅	4:50 am	**1:50 am**	
♄	⊥	⚴	9:27 am	**6:27 am**	
☽	△	♃	12:49 pm	**9:49 am**	
☽	⚻	♅	5:58 pm	**2:58 pm**	
☽	△	♆	6:31 pm	**3:31 pm**	
☽	⚻	☿	6:51 pm	**3:51 pm**	
☽	⚻	♄	11:36 pm	**8:36 pm**	
☽	☍	⚴		**9:05 pm**	
☽	□	⚶		**9:46 pm**	
☽	✶	♂		**10:32 pm**	

☽ enters ♎   5:47 am   **2:47 am**

3rd ♍

11 SUNDAY

☽	☍	⚴	12:05 am		
☽	□	⚶	12:46 am		
☽	✶	♂	1:32 am		
☽	✶	♀	4:13 am	**1:13 am**	
☽	✶	♇	6:50 am	**3:50 am**	
☽	☍	♀	10:42 am	**7:42 am**	
☽	⚻	♃	1:50 pm	**10:50 am**	
☽	⊼	☉	5:05 pm	**2:05 pm**	
☽	△	♅	6:59 pm	**3:59 pm**	
☽	△	☿	9:44 pm	**6:44 pm**	☽ v/c
☽	⊼	♄		**9:50 pm**	

3rd ♎

MARCH

S	M	T	W	T	F	S
					1	2	3
4	5	6	7	8	9	10
11	12	13	14	15	16	17
18	19	20	21	22	23	24
25	26	27	28	29	30	31

Eastern Standard Time in medium type
Pacific Standard Time in bold type

2001 MARCH 2001

12 MONDAY

☽	⊼	♄	12:50 am		
☽	⌙	♂	3:32 am	**12:32 am**	
☽	⚹	⚷	4:56 am	**1:56 am**	
☽	⌙	♀	5:46 am	**2:46 am**	
☽	⊼	⚹	7:07 am	**4:07 am**	
☽	⌙	♇	8:10 am	**5:10 am**	
⚴	□	☿	1:21 pm	**10:21 am**	
☽	⊼	♃	3:40 pm	**12:40 pm**	
☽	⊡	☉	8:47 pm	**5:47 pm**	
☽	□	♆	9:21 pm	**6:21 pm**	
☉	⩗	♅	9:48 pm	**6:48 pm**	

☽ enters ♏ 7:43 am **4:43 am**
⚹ enters ♈ 9:34 pm

3rd ♎

13 TUESDAY

☉	⌙	♆	4:44 am	**1:44 am**	
☽	⚹	⚴	5:03 am	**2:03 am**	
☽	⊼	⚹	5:23 am	**2:23 am**	
☽	⩗	♂	6:32 am	**3:32 am**	
☽	⌙	⚷	7:09 am	**4:09 am**	
☽	⩗	♀	8:16 am	**5:16 am**	
☽	⊡	⚹	10:18 am	**7:18 am**	
☽	⩗	♇	10:27 am	**7:27 am**	
☽	⊼	♀	2:01 pm	**11:01 am**	
☿	□	♄	5:30 pm	**2:30 pm**	
☽	□	♅	11:45 pm	**8:45 pm**	
☽	△	☉		**10:46 pm**	

⚹ enters ♈ 2:34 am

3rd ♏

14 WEDNESDAY

☽	△	☉	1:46 am		
☽	☍	♄	6:10 am	**3:10 am**	
☽	□	☿	7:17 am	**4:17 am**	☽ v/c
☽	⌙	⚴	8:47 am	**5:47 am**	
☽	⊡	⚹	9:43 am	**6:43 am**	
☽	⩗	⚷	10:26 am	**7:26 am**	
☽	△	⚹	2:41 pm	**11:41 am**	
☽	⊡	♀	5:02 pm	**2:02 pm**	
☽	☍	♃	10:29 pm	**7:29 pm**	

☽ enters ♐ 1:17 pm **10:17 am**

3rd ♏

15 THURSDAY

☽	⚹	♆	4:10 am	**1:10 am**	
☿	⌙	⚴	5:24 am	**2:24 am**	
☽	⩗	⚴	1:40 pm	**10:40 am**	
☽	△	⚹	3:18 pm	**12:18 pm**	
☽	☌	♂	4:01 pm	**1:01 pm**	
☽	☌	♀	4:31 pm	**1:31 pm**	
☽	☌	♇	6:12 pm	**3:12 pm**	
☿	⚹	⚷	7:39 pm	**4:39 pm**	
☽	△	♀	8:58 pm	**5:58 pm**	

3rd ♐

Eastern Standard Time in medium type
Pacific Standard Time in bold type

2001   **MARCH**   **2001**

16 FRIDAY

☽	⚹	♅	8:46 am	**5:46 am**	
☿	∟	⚹	8:51 am	**5:51 am**	
☽	∟	♆	9:09 am	**6:09 am**	
♂	☌	♀	1:21 pm	**10:21 am**	
☽	□	☉	3:45 pm	**12:45 pm**	
☽	⚻	♄	3:49 pm	**12:49 pm**	
☉	⚹	♄	4:42 pm	**1:42 pm**	
☽	☌	⚷	8:10 pm	**5:10 pm**	
☽	⚹	☿	10:48 pm	**7:48 pm**	☽ v/c
☽	□	♇		**11:54 pm**	

3rd ♐

4th Quarter   3:45 pm   **12:45 pm**
☽ enters ♑   11:02 pm   **8:02 pm**
☿ enters ♓   **10:05 pm**

17 SATURDAY

☽	□	♇	2:54 am		
♀	△	⚹	3:25 am	**12:25 am**	
☽	⚻	♃	9:33 am	**6:33 am**	
☽	∟	♅	2:40 pm	**11:40 am**	
☽	⚺	♆	3:00 pm	**12:00 pm**	
☿	∟	♀	9:11 pm	**6:11 pm**	
☽	⚼	♄	9:59 pm	**6:59 pm**	
☽	☌	⚷		**11:20 pm**	

4th ♑

☿ enters ♓   1:05 am
♇ ℞   9:36 pm   **6:36 pm**

ST. PATRICK'S DAY

18 SUNDAY

☽	☌	⚷	2:20 am		
☽	⚺	♀	4:37 am	**1:37 am**	
☽	□	⚹	5:34 am	**2:34 am**	
☽	⚺	♂	5:38 am	**2:38 am**	
☽	⚺	♇	5:41 am	**2:41 am**	
♂	☌	♇	6:45 am	**3:45 am**	
☽	□	♀	6:55 am	**3:55 am**	
♇	△	⚹	8:01 am	**5:01 am**	
☽	∟	☿	8:25 am	**5:25 am**	
♂	△	⚹	12:11 pm	**9:11 am**	
☽	⚼	♃	4:13 pm	**1:13 pm**	
☽	⚺	♅	9:08 pm	**6:08 pm**	
♀	☌	⚹	10:49 pm	**7:49 pm**	
☉	□	⚷	11:16 pm	**8:16 pm**	
♀	△	♂		**9:30 pm**	

4th ♑

	MARCH					
S	M	T	W	T	F	S
				1	2	3
4	5	6	7	8	9	10
11	12	13	14	15	16	17
18	19	20	21	22	23	24
25	26	27	28	29	30	31

Eastern Standard Time in medium type
Pacific Standard Time in bold type

2001   **MARCH**   **2001**

19 MONDAY

4th ♑

☽ enters ♒   11:36 am   **8:36 am**

♀	△	♂	12:30 am		
☽	△	♄	4:38 am	**1:38 am**	
☽	⚹	⚷	8:49 am	**5:49 am**	
☽	⚹	☉	9:40 am	**6:40 am**	☽ v/c
☿	⚹	♆	11:05 am	**8:05 am**	
☽	⊥	♀	11:25 am	**8:25 am**	
☽	⊥	♇	12:10 pm	**9:10 am**	
☽	⊥	♂	1:17 pm	**10:17 am**	
☽	⚹	♆	6:07 pm	**3:07 pm**	
♀	△	♇	6:31 pm	**3:31 pm**	
☽	⚹	☿	6:41 pm	**3:41 pm**	
☽	△	♃	11:09 pm	**8:09 pm**	

20 TUESDAY

4th ♒

☉ enters ♈   8:31 am   **5:31 am**

☽	☌	♆	4:03 am	**1:03 am**	
♀	△	♀	8:31 am	**5:31 am**	
☽	⊥	⚷	3:27 pm	**12:27 pm**	
☽	⚹	♃	4:47 pm	**1:47 pm**	
☽	⚹	♀	5:49 pm	**2:49 pm**	
☽	⚹	♀	6:17 pm	**3:17 pm**	
☽	⚹	♇	6:43 pm	**3:43 pm**	
☽	⊥	☉	7:02 pm	**4:02 pm**	
☽	⚹	♂	8:57 pm	**5:57 pm**	
☽	⚹	❋	9:39 pm	**6:39 pm**	
☽	⊥	♆		**10:55 pm**	

SUN ENTERS ARIES
OSTARA (SPRING EQUINOX) 8:31 AM EST/5:31 AM PST

21 WEDNESDAY

4th ♒

☽ enters ♓   **9:28 pm**

☽	⊥	♆	1:55 am		
♀	□	♃	9:43 am	**6:43 am**	
☽	☌	♅	10:24 am	**7:24 am**	
☿	□	♃	2:41 pm	**11:41 am**	
☽	□	♄	6:03 pm	**3:03 pm**	☽ v/c
☽	⚹	⚷	9:52 pm	**6:52 pm**	
☽	⊥	♀	10:57 pm	**7:57 pm**	
☽	⊥	♃	11:49 pm	**8:49 pm**	

22 THURSDAY

4th ♒

☽ enters ♓   12:28 am

☽	⚹	☉	4:05 am	**1:05 am**	
☽	⊥	❋	5:25 am	**2:25 am**	
☽	⚹	♆	9:23 am	**6:23 am**	
☽	□	♃	12:37 pm	**9:37 am**	
☽	☌	☿	3:08 pm	**12:08 pm**	
☽	⚹	♆	4:44 pm	**1:44 pm**	
♇	☌	♀	4:47 pm	**1:47 pm**	

Eastern Standard Time in medium type
Pacific Standard Time in bold type

2001   **MARCH**   **2001**

23 FRIDAY   4th ♓

☽	⊻	♀	3:37 am	**12:37 am**
☿	⊻	♆	5:14 am	**2:14 am**
☽	✶	♄	6:22 am	**3:22 am**
☽	□	♇	6:53 am	**3:53 am**
☽	□	♀	7:01 am	**4:01 am**
☽	□	♂	11:12 am	**8:12 am**
☽	⊻	☄	12:41 pm	**9:41 am**
☽	⊻	♅	10:21 pm	**7:21 pm**
☽	⌐	♆	10:25 pm	**7:25 pm**

24 SATURDAY   4th ♓

☽	✶	♄	5:58 am	**2:58 am**	☽ v/c
♇	⊻	♄	6:35 am	**3:35 am**	
☽	□	⚷	9:20 am	**6:20 am**	
☽	☌	☉	8:21 pm	**5:21 pm**	
☽	☌	☄	10:39 pm	**7:39 pm**	
☽	✶	♃		9:13 pm	

☽ enters ♈   11:43 am   **8:43 am**
New Moon   8:21 pm   **5:21 pm**

25 SUNDAY   1st ♈

☽	✶	♃	12:13 am	
☽	⌐	♅	3:32 am	**12:32 am**
☽	✶	♆	3:32 am	**12:32 am**
♃	⊻	♀	5:04 am	**2:04 am**
☽	⊻	☿	9:25 am	**6:25 am**
☽	⌐	♄	11:07 am	**8:07 am**
☽	☌	♀	11:24 am	**8:24 am**
♀	⌐	♄	4:27 pm	**1:27 pm**
☽	△	♇	5:02 pm	**2:02 pm**
☽	△	♀	5:35 pm	**2:35 pm**
☽	□	♃	5:45 pm	**2:45 pm**
☿	⊻	♀	10:04 pm	**7:04 pm**
☽	△	♂	11:06 pm	**8:06 pm**
☽	☌	☄		10:21 pm

	MARCH					
S	M	T	W	T	F	S
				1	2	3
4	5	6	7	8	9	10
11	12	13	14	15	16	17
18	19	20	21	22	23	24
25	26	27	28	29	30	31

Eastern Standard Time in medium type
Pacific Standard Time in bold type

2001 MARCH 2001

26 MONDAY

☽	☌	♅	1:21 am		
☽	⊥	♃	5:11 am	2:11 am	
☽	✶	♆	8:10 am	5:10 am	☽ v/c
☽	⩗	♄	3:44 pm	12:44 pm	
☽	⊥	☿	5:33 pm	2:33 pm	
☽	△	⚷	6:37 pm	3:37 pm	
☽	⚼	♇	9:19 pm	6:19 pm	
☽	⚼	♀	10:02 pm	7:02 pm	
☉	☌	⚸		10:40 pm	

☽ enters ♉   8:50 pm   **5:50 pm**

1st ♈

27 TUESDAY

☉	☌	⚸	1:40 am		
☽	⚼	♂	4:10 am	1:10 am	
☉	✶	♃	5:57 am	2:57 am	
☽	⩗	⚸	9:32 am	6:32 am	
☽	⩗	♃	9:37 am	6:37 am	
☽	⩗	☉	9:53 am	6:53 am	
☽	□	♆	12:12 pm	9:12 am	
♃	✶	⚸	1:14 pm	10:14 am	
☽	⩗	♀	5:11 pm	2:11 pm	
☽	⚼	⚷	10:31 pm	7:31 pm	
☽	✶	☿		10:04 pm	
☽	⚻	♇		10:07 pm	
☿	□	♇		10:28 pm	
☽	⚻	♀		10:59 pm	
☽	△	♃		11:54 pm	

1st ♉

28 WEDNESDAY

☽	✶	☿	1:04 am		
☽	⚻	♇	1:07 am		
☿	□	♇	1:28 am		
☽	⚻	♀	1:59 am		
☽	△	♃	2:54 am		
☽	⚻	♂	8:42 am	5:42 am	
☿	□	♀	9:08 am	6:08 am	
☽	⩗	♅	11:41 am	8:41 am	
☽	⊥	⚸	2:10 pm	11:10 am	
☽	⊥	☉	3:43 pm	12:43 pm	
☽	□	♅	3:57 pm	12:57 pm	
☉	✶	♆	4:55 pm	1:55 pm	
☉	⊥	♅	6:55 pm	3:55 pm	
☿	✶	♃	7:19 pm	4:19 pm	
☽	⊥	♀	7:25 pm	4:25 pm	

☽	☌	♄	11:29 pm	8:29 pm	☽ v/c
☽	⚻	⚷		10:56 pm	

1st ♉

29 THURSDAY

☽	⚻	⚷	1:56 am		
☽	⚼	⚸	6:44 am	3:44 am	
☽	⊥	♅	4:05 pm	1:05 pm	
☽	☌	♃	5:05 pm	2:05 pm	
☽	✶	⚸	6:18 pm	3:18 pm	
☽	△	♆	6:58 pm	3:58 pm	
☽	✶	☉	9:00 pm	6:00 pm	
☽	✶	♀	9:15 pm	6:15 pm	
☉	☌	♀	11:16 pm	8:16 pm	

☽ enters ♊   4:01 am   **1:01 am**

1st ♉

Eastern Standard Time in medium type
Pacific Standard Time in bold type

2001 — MARCH/APRIL — 2001

30 FRIDAY

☽ ☍ ♇	7:21 am	**4:21 am**		
☽ ☍ ♀	8:26 am	**5:26 am**		
☽ ⊼ ♃	10:05 am	**7:05 am**		
♆ ✶ ⚴	2:07 pm	**11:07 am**		
☽ □ ☿	2:23 pm	**11:23 am**		
☽ ☍ ♂	4:16 pm	**1:16 pm**		
☽ ✶ ⚵	7:58 pm	**4:58 pm**		
♅ ∟ ⚴	8:55 pm	**5:55 pm**		
☽ ⚻ ♆	9:40 pm	**6:40 pm**		
☽ △ ♅	9:54 pm	**6:54 pm**	☽ v/c	
♃ ∟ ⚵		**10:16 pm**		

1st ♊

31 SATURDAY

♃ ∟ ⚵	1:16 am		
☽ ⚺ ♄	5:24 am	**2:24 am**	
☽ ☍ ⚳	7:26 am	**4:26 am**	
♀ ☌ ⚴	8:01 am	**5:01 am**	
☿ □ ♂	10:36 am	**7:36 am**	
♀ ∟ ♅	3:07 pm	**12:07 pm**	
♀ ✶ ♆	8:30 pm	**5:30 pm**	
☽ ⚺ ♃	10:41 pm	**7:41 pm**	
☽ □ ♀	11:45 pm	**8:45 pm**	
☽ ⊼ ♆	11:54 pm	**8:54 pm**	
☽ ⚻ ♅		**9:10 pm**	
☽ □ ⚴		**10:02 pm**	

1st ♊

☽ enters ♋ 9: 23 am **6:23 am**

ARIES ♈
Duality: Masculine
Quality: Cardinal
Element: Fire
House: 1st
Planetary Ruler: Mars
Rules: Head
Keyword: Action
Keynote: I am.

1 SUNDAY

☽ ⚻ ♅	12:10 am		
☽ □ ⚴	1:02 am		
☽ □ ☉	5:49 am	**2:49 am**	
☽ ∟ ♄	7:39 am	**4:39 am**	
☽ ⊼ ♇	11:45 am	**8:45 am**	
☽ ⊼ ♀	12:59 pm	**9:59 am**	
☽ ☍ ♃	3:17 pm	**12:17 pm**	
♀ ✶ ♃	6:18 pm	**3:18 pm**	
♅ ✶ ⚵	9:30 pm	**6:30 pm**	
☽ ⊼ ♂	9:46 pm	**6:46 pm**	
☽ ∟ ♃		**9:45 pm**	
☽ △ ☿		**10:19 pm**	
☽ ⊼ ♅		**10:58 pm**	
☽ □ ⚵		**11:09 pm**	

1st ♋
2nd Quarter 5:49 am **2:49 am**

APRIL FOOLS' DAY
DAYLIGHT SAVING TIME BEGINS AT 2 AM

Eastern Standard Time in medium type
Pacific Standard Time in bold type

2001   APRIL   2001

2 MONDAY

2nd ♋

☽	⊥	♃	12:45 am			
☽	△	☿	1:19 am			
☽	⊼	♅	1:58 am			
☽	□	※	2:09 am			
☿	⊥	♆	4:22 am	1:22 am		
☿	⋎	♅	7:01 am	4:01 am		
☽	✶	♄	9:26 am	6:26 am	☽ v/c	
☉	⊥	♄	10:34 am	7:34 am		
☽	⊼	⚷	11:03 am	8:03 am		
☿	⋎	※	11:42 am	8:42 am		
☽	⊡	♇	1:15 pm	10:15 am		
☽	⊡	♀	2:31 pm	11:31 am		
☽	⊡	♂	11:45 pm	8:45 pm		
☽	△	♀		9:42 pm		
☽	✶	♃		11:22 pm		
☽	☍	♆		11:59 pm		

☽ enters ♌   12:54 pm   **9:54 am**

3 TUESDAY

2nd ♌

☽	△	♀	12:42 am		
☽	✶	♃	2:22 am		
☽	☍	♆	2:59 am		
☽	△	⚸	5:44 am	2:44 am	
☽	⊡	☿	5:55 am	2:55 am	
☽	⊡	⚷	12:11 pm	9:11 am	
☽	△	☉	12:22 pm	9:22 am	
☽	△	♇	2:20 pm	11:20 am	
☽	△	♀	3:38 pm	12:38 pm	
☽	⊼	♄	6:35 pm	3:35 pm	
☽	⊡	♀		9:40 pm	
☽	△	♂		10:19 pm	

4 WEDNESDAY

2nd ♌

☽	⊡	♀	12:40 am		
☽	△	♂	1:19 am		
☽	☍	♅	4:18 am	1:18 am	
☽	△	※	6:23 am	3:23 am	
☽	⊡	⚸	7:26 am	4:26 am	
☽	⊼	☿	10:02 am	7:02 am	
☽	□	♄	11:46 am	8:46 am	☽ v/c
☽	△	⚷	1:00 pm	10:00 am	
☽	⊡	☉	2:57 pm	11:57 am	
☉	△	♇	5:02 pm	2:02 pm	
☽	⊡	♀	7:41 pm	4:41 pm	
☽	⊼	♀		9:25 pm	
☿	✶	♄		10:40 pm	

☽ enters ♍   2:46 pm   **11:46 am**

5 THURSDAY

2nd ♍

☽	⊼	♀	12:25 am		
☿	✶	♄	1:40 am		
☽	□	♃	4:33 am	1:33 am	
☽	⊼	♆	4:36 am	1:36 am	
☽	⊡	※	8:01 am	5:01 am	
☽	⊼	⚸	8:52 am	5:52 am	
♃	△	♆	9:26 am	6:26 am	
☿	□	⚷	11:17 am	8:17 am	
☉	△	♀	12:56 pm	9:56 am	
☽	□	♇	3:39 pm	12:39 pm	
☽	□	♀	5:00 pm	2:00 pm	
☽	⊼	☉	5:18 pm	2:18 pm	
☽	△	♄	8:36 pm	5:36 pm	

♀ ℞   9:05 pm   **6:05 pm**
☿ enters ♈   **11:14 pm**

Eastern Standard Time in medium type
Pacific Standard Time in bold type

2001 APRIL 2001

6 FRIDAY

2nd ♍

☽	□	♂	3:42 am	**12:42 am**	
☽	⚟	♆	5:12 am	**2:12 am**	
☽	⚻	♅	5:38 am	**2:38 am**	
☽	⚻	⚹	9:35 am	**6:35 am**	
☽	△	♄	1:18 pm	**10:18 am**	☽ v/c
☽	□	⚳	2:11 pm	**11:11 am**	
☽	☍	☿	5:49 pm	**2:49 pm**	
☽	☍	♀	11:54 pm	**8:54 pm**	

☿ enters ♈ 2:14 am
☽ enters ♍ 3:57 pm **12:57 pm**

7 SATURDAY

2nd ♎

☽	△	♆	5:55 am	**2:55 am**
☽	⚟	♅	6:24 am	**3:24 am**
☽	△	♃	6:26 am	**3:26 am**
☽	☍	⚸	11:49 am	**8:49 am**
☽	⚟	♄	2:16 pm	**11:16 am**
☽	⚹	♇	5:01 pm	**2:01 pm**
☽	⚹	♀	6:25 pm	**3:25 pm**
☽	☍	☉	10:22 pm	**7:22 pm**
☽	□	⚳	10:50 pm	**7:50 pm**

⚳ ℞ 1:02 pm **10:02 am**
Full Moon 10:22 pm **7:22 pm**

8 SUNDAY

3rd ♎

☽	⚹	♂	6:33 am	**3:33 am**	
☉	□	⚳	6:48 am	**3:48 am**	
☽	△	♅	7:31 am	**4:31 am**	☽ v/c
☽	⚟	♃	7:49 am	**4:49 am**	
☿	☌	♀	10:25 am	**7:25 am**	
☽	☍	⚸	1:33 pm	**10:33 am**	
☽	⚻	♄	3:40 pm	**12:40 pm**	
☽	⚹	♇	4:11 pm	**1:11 pm**	
☽	⚼	♇	6:16 pm	**3:16 pm**	
☽	⚼	♀	7:41 pm	**4:41 pm**	
☽	⚻	♀		**9:39 pm**	

☽ enters ♏ 6:01 pm **3:01 pm**

PALM SUNDAY • PASSOVER BEGINS

		APRIL				
S	M	T	W	T	F	S
1	2	3	4	5	6	7
8	9	10	11	12	13	14
15	16	17	18	19	20	21
22	23	24	25	26	27	28
29	30					

Eastern Standard Time in medium type
Pacific Standard Time in bold type

2001   **APRIL**   **2001**

9 MONDAY

3rd ♏

☽	⊼	♀	12:39 am	
☽	⊼	☿	3:18 am	**12:18 am**
♂	∟	♆	3:18 am	**12:18 am**
☽	□	♆	8:39 am	**5:39 am**
☽	∟	♂	8:46 am	**5:46 am**
☽	⊼	♃	9:49 am	**6:49 am**
☽	⊼	♅	4:34 pm	**1:34 pm**
☽	∟	⚷	6:04 pm	**3:04 pm**
☽	⊻	♇	8:12 pm	**5:12 pm**
☽	⊻	♀	9:38 pm	**6:38 pm**
☽	⚼	♀		**11:02 pm**

10 TUESDAY

3rd ♏

☽ enters ♐   10:47 pm   **7:47 pm**

☽	⚼	♀	2:02 am	
☽	⚹	⚷	3:09 am	**12:09 am**
☽	⊼	☉	5:56 am	**2:56 am**
♂	⚹	♅	8:27 am	**5:27 am**
☽	⚼	☿	9:40 am	**6:40 am**
☽	□	♅	11:44 am	**8:44 am**
☽	⊻	♂	11:48 am	**8:48 am**
☿	⚹	♆	8:02 pm	**5:02 pm**
☽	⚼	♃	8:14 pm	**5:14 pm**
☽	⊼	⚵	8:25 pm	**5:25 pm**
☽	☍	♄	8:43 pm	**5:43 pm** ☽ v/c
☽	⊻	⚷	8:49 pm	**5:49 pm**
☿	∟	♅		**9:51 pm**

11 WEDNESDAY

3rd ♐

☿	∟	♅	12:51 am	
☽	△	♀	4:19 am	**1:19 am**
♄	⊻	⚵	4:56 am	**1:56 am**
⚷	△	⚵	5:25 am	**2:25 am**
☽	∟	⚹	6:37 am	**3:37 am**
♄	⊼	⚷	7:20 am	**4:20 am**
☿	⚹	♃	9:13 am	**6:13 am**
☽	⚼	☉	11:19 am	**8:19 am**
♄	∟	⚷	2:24 pm	**11:24 am**
☽	⚹	♆	2:29 pm	**11:29 am**
☽	☍	♃	4:29 pm	**1:29 pm**
☽	△	☿	5:36 pm	**2:36 pm**
☽	△	⚷		**9:59 pm**
☽	⚼	⚵		**10:26 pm**
☽	☌	♇		**11:46 pm**

12 THURSDAY

3rd ♐

⚵ enters ♉   **11:24 pm**

☽	△	⚷	12:59 am	
☽	⚼	⚵	1:26 am	
☽	☌	♇	2:46 am	
☽	☌	♀	4:11 am	**1:11 am**
☽	⊻	⚹	11:07 am	**8:07 am**
☽	△	☉	5:58 pm	**2:58 pm**
☽	∟	♆	6:53 pm	**3:53 pm**
☽	⚹	♅	7:40 pm	**4:40 pm**
☽	☌	♂	8:56 pm	**5:56 pm** ☽ v/c

Eastern Standard Time in medium type
Pacific Standard Time in bold type

2001   **APRIL**   **2001**

13 FRIDAY

☽	☌	⚷	5:12 am	**2:12 am**	
☽	☍	♄	5:39 am	**2:39 am**	
♇	⚻	⚴	6:06 am	**3:06 am**	
☽	△	⚴	7:35 am	**4:35 am**	
☽	□	♀	11:51 am	**8:51 am**	
☉	✶	♅	4:24 pm	**1:24 pm**	
☿	⚼	♄	7:46 pm	**4:46 pm**	
☽	⚹	♆		**9:12 pm**	
♇	△	⚴		**9:47 pm**	
☽	⚼	♅		**10:03 pm**	

3rd ♐

♅ enters ♉   2:24 am
☽ enters ♑   7:21 am   **4:21 am**

GOOD FRIDAY • ORTHODOX GOOD FRIDAY

14 SATURDAY

☽	⚹	♆	12:12 am		
♇	△	⚴	12:47 am		
☽	⚼	♅	1:03 am		
☽	☍	♃	3:11 am	**12:11 am**	
☿	△	♇	6:37 am	**3:37 am**	
♀	⚻	⚴	8:29 am	**5:29 am**	
☿	☌	⚴	8:31 am	**5:31 am**	
☽	⚻	♄	11:31 am	**8:31 am**	
☽	⚹	♇	1:07 pm	**10:07 am**	
☽	□	⚴	1:37 pm	**10:37 am**	
☽	□	☿	2:22 pm	**11:22 am**	
☽	⚹	♀	2:23 pm	**11:23 am**	
☿	△	♀	2:27 pm	**11:27 am**	
☉	△	♂	9:31 pm	**6:31 pm**	
☽	☌	♃	10:53 pm	**7:53 pm**	
☉	⚼	♃	10:57 pm	**7:57 pm**	

3rd ♑

PASSOVER ENDS

15 SUNDAY

♀	△	⚴	6:56 am	**3:56 am**	
☽	⚹	♅	7:10 am	**4:10 am**	
☽	⚹	♂	9:43 am	**6:43 am**	
☽	⚻	♃	9:45 am	**6:45 am**	
☽	□	☉	10:31 am	**7:31 am**	
☽	⚹	⚷	4:54 pm	**1:54 pm**	
☽	△	♄	6:00 pm	**3:00 pm**	☽ v/c
☽	⚼	♇	7:17 pm	**4:17 pm**	
☽	⚼	♀	8:26 pm	**5:26 pm**	
☽	□	⚴	10:31 pm	**7:31 pm**	
☽	✶	♀	10:48 pm	**7:48 pm**	
♀	⚹	⚴		**11:57 pm**	

3rd ♑

4th Quarter   10:31 am   **7:31 am**
☽ enters ♒   7:11 pm   **4:11 pm**

EASTER • ORTHODOX EASTER

APRIL						
S	M	T	W	T	F	S
1	2	3	4	5	6	7
8	9	10	11	12	13	14
15	16	17	18	19	20	21
22	23	24	25	26	27	28
29	30					

Eastern Standard Time in medium type
Pacific Standard Time in bold type

2001 APRIL **2001**

16 MONDAY

4th ♒

☿	⚼	✴	2:57 am		
☽	☌	♆	12:40 pm	9:40 am
☽	△	♃	4:41 pm	1:41 pm
☽	⊥	♂	4:50 pm	1:50 pm
☿	□	⚷	9:44 pm	6:44 pm
☽	⊥	⚸	11:19 pm	8:19 pm
☽	✶	♇		10:43 pm
☽	✶	♀		11:41 pm

17 TUESDAY

4th ♒

☽	✶	♇	1:43 am	
☽	✶	♀	2:41 am	
☽	✶	⚼	4:47 am	1:47 am
☽	⊥	♀	4:55 am	1:55 am
☽	⚼	♃	12:33 pm	9:33 am
☽	✶	☿	3:20 pm	12:20 pm
☽	☌	♅	8:11 pm	5:11 pm
☽	✶	♂	11:55 pm	8:55 pm

18 WEDNESDAY

4th ♒

☽ enters ♓ 8:00 am **5:00 am**

☽	✶	☉	4:49 am	1:49 am
☽	✶	⚸	5:40 am	2:40 am
☽	□	♄	7:26 am	4:26 am ☽ v/c
☽	⚼	♀	11:02 am	8:02 am
☽	⊥	⚼	12:20 pm	9:20 am
☽	✶	✴	2:26 pm	11:26 am
☉	△	⚸	2:52 pm	11:52 am
☽	⊥	♃	7:11 pm	4:11 pm
☿	✶	♅	7:53 pm	4:53 pm
☽	⚼	♆		10:20 pm

19 THURSDAY

4th ♓

☉ enters ♉ 7:36 pm **4:36 pm**
♀ D 11:34 pm **8:34 pm**

☽	⚼	♆	1:20 am	
☽	⊥	☿	3:43 am	12:43 am
☽	□	♃	6:13 am	3:13 am
☽	⊥	☉	1:27 pm	10:27 am
☽	□	♇	1:56 pm	10:56 am
☽	□	♀	2:29 pm	11:29 am
☉	⚼	♄	4:39 pm	1:39 pm
☉	⚻	♇	7:19 pm	4:19 pm
☽	⚼	⚼	7:23 pm	4:23 pm
☿	⊥	♃	7:38 pm	4:38 pm
☽	⊥	✴	9:46 pm	6:46 pm
☿	△	♂	10:21 pm	7:21 pm
☉	⚻	♀		9:59 pm
☽	✶	♃		10:18 pm

SUN ENTERS TAURUS

Eastern Standard Time in medium type
Pacific Standard Time in bold type

2001 APRIL 2001

20 FRIDAY

☉	⊡	♀	12:59	am		
☽	✶	♄	1:18	am		
☽	∟	♆	6:59	am	3:59	am
☽	⊻	♅	8:04	am	5:04	am
☽	□	♂	12:40	pm	9:40	am ☽ v/c
☽	⊻	☿	3:15	pm	12:15	pm
☽	□	⚸	4:57	pm	1:57	pm
☽	✶	♄	7:19	pm	4:19	pm
☽	⊻	☉	9:19	pm	6:19	pm
☽	☌	♀	10:09	pm	7:09	pm
☿	△	⚸			10:14	pm

♄ enters ♊ 4:59 pm **1:59 pm**
☽ enters ♈ 7:18 pm **4:18 pm**

4th ♓

21 SATURDAY

☿	△	⚸	1:14	am		
☽	⊻	✷	4:22	am	1:22	am
☉	⊻	♀	8:18	am	5:18	am
☽	✶	♆	11:57	am	8:57	am
☽	∟	♅	1:04	pm	10:04	am
☿	⊡	♇	2:39	pm	11:39	am
☿	⊡	♀	3:28	pm	12:28	pm
☿	⊻	♄	4:28	pm	1:28	pm
☽	✶	♃	5:31	pm	2:31	pm
☽	△	♇	11:52	pm	8:52	pm
☽	△	♀	11:55	pm	8:55	pm
☽	∟	♄			9:15	pm

☿ enters ♉ 3:08 pm **12:08 pm**

4th ♈

22 SUNDAY

☽	∟	♄	12:15	am		
♇	☌	♀	7:09	am	4:09	am
☽	☌	✷	7:18	am	4:18	am
☿	⊻	♀	8:58	am	5:58	am
☽	□	♃	11:25	am	8:25	am
☽	✶	♅	5:22	pm	2:22	pm
☽	∟	♃	10:06	pm	7:06	pm
☽	△	♂	10:34	pm	7:34	pm ☽ v/c
☽	△	⚸			10:36	pm

4th ♈

EARTH DAY

APRIL

S	M	T	W	T	F	S
1	2	3	4	5	6	7
8	9	10	11	12	13	14
15	16	17	18	19	20	21
22	23	24	25	26	27	28
29	30					

Eastern Standard Time in medium type
Pacific Standard Time in bold type

2001 APRIL 2001

23 MONDAY

☽	△	⚷	1:36	am	
☽	⚼	♀	3:37	am	**12:37 am**
☽	⚼	♇	3:48	am	**12:48 am**
☉	☌	☿	4:24	am	**1:24 am**
☽	⊻	♄	4:29	am	**1:29 am**
☽	⊻	♀	7:00	am	**4:00 am**
☽	☌	☉	10:26	am	**7:26 am**
☽	☌	☿	11:04	am	**8:04 am**
☽	☌	⚹	3:12	pm	**12:12 pm**
☽	□	♆	7:53	pm	**4:53 pm**
☽	⊻	♃			**11:02 pm**
☽	⚼	♂			**11:28 pm**

4th ♈

☽ enters ♉ 3:56 am **12:56 am**
New Moon 10:26 am **7:26 am**

24 TUESDAY

☽	⊻	♃	2:02	am	
☽	⚼	♂	2:28	am	
☽	⚼	⚷	4:59	am	**1:59 am**
☽	⚻	♀	6:43	am	**3:43 am**
☽	⚻	♇	7:09	am	**4:09 am**
☽	∟	♀	10:38	am	**7:38 am**
☽	⊻	⚹	4:19	pm	**1:19 pm**
☽	△	♃	6:50	pm	**3:50 pm**
☿	☌	⚹	8:34	pm	**5:34 pm**
☽	□	♅			**9:08 pm** ☽ v/c

1st ♉

25 WEDNESDAY

☽	□	♅	12:08	am		☽ v/c
☽	⚻	♂	5:48	am	**2:48 am**	
☽	⚻	⚷	7:51	am	**4:51 am**	
☽	☌	♄	11:12	am	**8:12 am**	
☽	⚹	♀	1:50	pm	**10:50 am**	
☿	□	♆	5:23	pm	**2:23 pm**	
☽	∟	⚹	7:59	pm	**4:59 pm**	
☽	⊻	☉	8:38	pm	**5:38 pm**	
☽	⚼	♃	9:46	pm	**6:46 pm**	
☽	⊻	⚹	11:30	pm	**8:30 pm**	
☽	△	♆			**10:37 pm**	

1st ♉

☽ enters ♊ 10:11 am **7:11 am**

26 THURSDAY

☽	△	♆	1:37	am	
☽	⊻	☿	3:09	am	**12:09 am**
☽	☌	♃	8:22	am	**5:22 am**
☽	☍	♀	11:29	am	**8:29 am**
☽	☍	♇	12:26	pm	**9:26 am**
☽	⚹	⚷	11:14	pm	**8:14 pm**
☽	⚻	♃			**9:20 pm**
☽	∟	☉			**9:59 pm**
☽	∟	⚹			**11:58 pm**

1st ♊

Eastern Standard Time in medium type
Pacific Standard Time in bold type

2001 APRIL 2001

27 FRIDAY

1st ♊

☽	⊼	♃	12:20 am		
☽	∟	☉	12:59 am		
☽	∟	⚷	2:58 am		
☽	⛝	♆	3:55 am	**12:55 am**	
☽	△	♅	5:07 am	**2:07 am**	
☽	∟	☿	10:15 am	**7:15 am**	
☽	☍	♂	11:12 am	**8:12 am**	☽ v/c
☽	☍	⚸	12:26 pm	**9:26 am**	
☿	⊻	♃	3:23 pm	**12:23 pm**	
☽	⊻	♄	4:17 pm	**1:17 pm**	
☿	⛝	♂	4:45 pm	**1:45 pm**	
☽	□	♀	7:20 pm	**4:20 pm**	
☿	⛝	⚸		**9:09 pm**	
♆	□	⚷		**10:19 pm**	

☽ enters ♋   2:49 pm   **11:49 am**

28 SATURDAY

1st ♋

☿	⛝	⚸	12:09 am		
♆	□	⚷	1:19 am		
☽	✶	☉	4:58 am	**1:58 am**	
☿	⊼	♀	5:00 am	**2:00 am**	
☽	⊼	♆	5:56 am	**2:56 am**	
☽	✶	⚷	6:08 am	**3:08 am**	
☽	⛝	♅	7:09 am	**4:09 am**	
☽	⊻	♃	1:19 pm	**10:19 am**	
☿	⊼	♇	1:51 pm	**10:51 am**	
☽	⊼	♀	2:57 pm	**11:57 am**	
☽	⊼	♇	4:25 pm	**1:25 pm**	
☽	✶	☿	4:53 pm	**1:53 pm**	☽ v/c
♃	□	⚷	5:44 pm	**2:44 pm**	
☽	∟	♄	6:24 pm	**3:24 pm**	
☉	□	♆	6:49 pm	**3:49 pm**	

29 SUNDAY

1st ♋

☽	☍	♃	4:34 am	**1:34 am**	
☽	□	⚷	4:51 am	**1:51 am**	
☽	⊼	♅	8:58 am	**5:58 am**	
☽	⊼	♂	3:23 pm	**12:23 pm**	
☽	∟	♃	3:25 pm	**12:25 pm**	
☽	⊼	⚸	3:57 pm	**12:57 pm**	
☽	⛝	♀	4:19 pm	**1:19 pm**	
☽	⛝	♇	6:04 pm	**3:04 pm**	
☽	✶	♄	8:18 pm	**5:18 pm**	
☉	☌	⚷	9:18 pm	**6:18 pm**	
☽	△	♀		**9:02 pm**	

☽ enters ♌   6:25 pm   **3:25 pm**

	APRIL					
S	M	T	W	T	F	S
1	2	3	4	5	6	7
8	9	10	11	12	13	14
15	16	17	18	19	20	21
22	23	24	25	26	27	28
29	30					

Eastern Standard Time in medium type
Pacific Standard Time in bold type

2001 APRIL/MAY **2001**

30 MONDAY

☽ △ ♀	12:02 am			
☿ ⌑ ♀	6:07 am	**3:07 am**		
☽ ☍ ♆	9:18 am	**6:18 am**		
☽ □ ⛢	11:42 am	**8:42 am**		
☽ □ ☉	12:08 pm	**9:08 am**		
☽ ⚻ ♂	5:09 pm	**2:09 pm**		
☽ ⚹ ♃	5:20 pm	**2:20 pm**		
☽ ⚻ ⚷	5:24 pm	**2:24 pm**		
☽ △ ♀	5:30 pm	**2:30 pm**		
☽ △ ♇	7:32 pm	**4:32 pm**		
♃ ☍ ♀	11:05 pm	**8:05 pm**		
☽ ⚻ ♀		**11:10 pm**		

1st ♌
2nd Quarter   12:08 pm   **9:08 am**

TAURUS ♉
Duality: Feminine
Quality: Fixed
Element: Earth
House: 2nd
Planetary Ruler: Venus
Rules: Neck and Throat
Keyword: Stability
Keynote: I have.

1 TUESDAY

☽ ⚻ ♀	2:10 am			
☽ □ ☿	5:02 am	**2:02 am**		
☽ ⚻ ♃	7:56 am	**4:56 am**		
☽ △ ♆	9:34 am	**6:34 am**		
☽ ☍ ⛢	12:01 pm	**9:01 am**		
♂ ☌ ⚷	4:56 pm	**1:56 pm**		
☽ △ ⚷	6:42 pm	**3:42 pm**		
☽ △ ♂	6:43 pm	**3:43 pm**	☽ v/c	
☽ □ ♄	11:35 pm	**8:35 pm**		
☿ △ ♃		**10:41 pm**		

2nd ♌
☽ enters ♍   9:16 pm   **6:16 pm**

BELTANE

2 WEDNESDAY

☿ △ ♃	1:41 am		
☽ ⚻ ♀	4:13 am	**1:13 am**	
☽ ⚻ ♃	9:24 am	**6:24 am**	
☽ ⚻ ♆	11:42 am	**8:42 am**	
☽ ⚻ ♆	12:02 pm	**9:02 am**	
☽ △ ⛢	4:35 pm	**1:35 pm**	
☽ △ ☉	6:31 pm	**3:31 pm**	
☽ □ ♀	7:26 pm	**4:26 pm**	
☿ ⚺ ♆	7:44 pm	**4:44 pm**	
☽ □ ♃	8:45 pm	**5:45 pm**	
☽ □ ♇	10:06 pm	**7:06 pm**	

2nd ♍

Eastern Standard Time in medium type
Pacific Standard Time in bold type

2001   **MAY**   **2001**

3 THURSDAY

2nd ♍

☿ □ ♅	5:42 am	**2:42 am**		
☉ ⊼ ♀	5:46 am	**2:46 am**		
☽ △ ♃	10:49 am	**7:49 am**		
☽ ⊡ ♆	1:18 pm	**10:18 am**		
☽ ⊼ ⚷	1:48 pm	**10:48 am**		
☉ ⊡ ⚸	2:30 pm	**11:30 am**		
☽ ⊼ ♅	2:39 pm	**11:39 am**		
☽ △ ☿	4:07 pm	**1:07 pm**		
☽ ⊡ ⚹	6:57 pm	**3:57 pm**		
☽ □ ⚸	9:08 pm	**6:08 pm**		
☽ ⊡ ☉	9:38 pm	**6:38 pm**		
☽ □ ♂	9:39 pm	**6:39 pm**	☽ v/c	
☉ ⊡ ♂	9:43 pm	**6:43 pm**		
☽ △ ♄		**11:36 pm**		

☽ enters ♎   11:50 pm   **8:50 pm**

4 FRIDAY

2nd ♎

☽ △ ♄	2:36 am		
☽ ☍ ♀	8:26 am	**5:26 am**	
☉ ⚺ ♃	12:04 pm	**9:04 am**	
☽ △ ♆	2:40 pm	**11:40 am**	
☽ ⊡ ♅	4:04 pm	**1:04 pm**	
♅ ⚹ ⚸	6:09 pm	**3:09 pm**	
☿ ⊼ ⚹	7:53 pm	**4:53 pm**	
☽ ⚹ ♀	9:22 pm	**6:22 pm**	
☽ ⊼ ⚹	9:27 pm	**6:27 pm**	
☽ ⊡ ☿	9:39 pm	**6:39 pm**	
☉ ⊼ ♇	10:06 pm	**7:06 pm**	
☽ △ ♃		**9:14 pm**	
☽ ⚹ ♇		**9:44 pm**	
☽ ⊼ ☉		**9:56 pm**	

5 SATURDAY

2nd ♎

☽ △ ♃	12:14 am			
☽ ⚹ ♇	12:44 am			
☽ ⊼ ☉	12:56 am			
☿ ⊼ ⚸	3:29 am	**12:29 am**		
☽ ⊡ ♄	4:18 am	**1:18 am**		
☿ ⊼ ♂	9:17 am	**6:17 am**		
☽ □ ♃	1:59 pm	**10:59 am**		
☽ △ ♅	5:43 pm	**2:43 pm**		
☽ ☍ ⚷	6:28 pm	**3:28 pm**		
⚸ ⊡ ⚹	8:39 pm	**5:39 pm**		
☽ ⊥ ♀	10:38 pm	**7:38 pm**		
☽ ⚹ ⚸		**9:06 pm**		
☽ ⚹ ♂		**10:03 pm**	☽ v/c	
☽ ⊡ ♃		**11:22 pm**		
☽ ⊥ ♇		**11:26 pm**		

☿ enters ♊   11:53 pm   **8:53 pm**

CINCO DE MAYO

6 SUNDAY

2nd ♎

☽ ⚹ ⚸	12:06 am		
☽ ⚹ ♂	1:03 am		☽ v/c
☽ ⊡ ♃	2:22 am		
☽ ⊥ ♇	2:26 am		
☽ ⊼ ☿	3:30 am	**12:30 am**	
♃ ☍ ♇	5:40 am	**2:40 am**	
☽ ⊼ ♄	6:19 am	**3:19 am**	
☽ ⊼ ♀	1:46 pm	**10:46 am**	
☽ □ ♆	6:16 pm	**3:16 pm**	
♂ ⊡ ⚹	8:47 pm	**5:47 pm**	
☽ ⚺ ♀		**9:19 pm**	
☿ ☌ ♄		**10:26 pm**	
☽ ⊥ ⚸		**11:11 pm**	

☽ enters ♏   3:00 am   **12:00 am**

Eastern Standard Time in medium type
Pacific Standard Time in bold type

2001   **MAY**   **2001**

7 MONDAY

2nd ♏

☽ ⊻ ♀	12:19 am			
☿ ☌ ♄	1:26 am			
☽ ∟ ⚴	2:11 am			
☽ ∟ ♂	3:21 am	12:21 am		
☽ ☍ ♅	3:37 am	12:37 am		
☽ ⊻ ♇	4:35 am	1:35 am		
☽ ⊼ ♃	5:00 am	2:00 am		
☽ ☍ ☉	8:53 am	5:53 am		
☽ ⚼ ♀	5:20 pm	2:20 pm		
☽ ⚹ ⚴	6:41 pm	3:41 pm		
☽ □ ♁	10:25 pm	7:25 pm	☽ v/c	
☽ ⊼ ♆		9:59 pm		
♇ ⊼ ♅		10:13 pm		

Full Moon   8:53 am   **5:53 am**

8 TUESDAY

3rd ♏

☽ ⊼ ♆	12:59 am		
♇ ⊼ ♅	1:13 am		
☽ ⊻ ⚴	4:52 am	1:52 am	
☽ ⊻ ♂	6:15 am	3:15 am	
☽ ☍ ♄	12:05 pm	9:05 am	
☽ ☍ ☿	5:17 pm	2:17 pm	
☽ △ ♀	9:46 pm	6:46 pm	
☽ ∟ ♃	10:01 pm	7:01 pm	
☽ ⚹ ♆		9:09 pm	

☽ enters ♐   8:05 am   **5:05 am**

9 WEDNESDAY

3rd ♐

☽ ⚹ ♆	12:09 am		
☽ ⚼ ♅	5:23 am	2:23 am	
♃ ⊻ ♅	5:25 am	2:25 am	
☽ ☌ ♀	5:32 am	2:32 am	
♀ ⚼ ♅	8:14 am	5:14 am	
☽ ☌ ♇	10:56 am	7:56 am	
☽ ☍ ♃	12:25 pm	9:25 am	
☽ ⊼ ♅	12:38 pm	9:38 am	
☽ ⊼ ☉	8:03 pm	5:03 pm	
☽ ⊻ ⚴		11:10 pm	

10 THURSDAY

3rd ♐

☽ ⊻ ⚴	2:10 am		
☽ ∟ ♆	4:15 am	1:15 am	
☿ ⚼ ⚴	5:38 am	2:38 am	
☽ ⚹ ♅	5:59 am	2:59 am	
☽ △ ♆	10:42 am	7:42 am	
☽ ☌ ⚴	12:34 pm	9:34 am	
☽ ☌ ♂	2:20 pm	11:20 am	☽ v/c
☽ ⚼ ♅	6:32 pm	3:32 pm	
☿ ⚹ ♀	6:47 pm	3:47 pm	
☽ ⊼ ♄	8:59 pm	5:59 pm	
☿ △ ♆	9:15 pm	6:15 pm	
♀ ⚻ ♆		10:25 pm	

☽ enters ♑   4:10 pm   **1:10 pm**
♆ ℞   8:13 pm   **5:13 pm**

Eastern Standard Time in medium type
Pacific Standard Time in bold type

2001   MAY   2001

11 FRIDAY

3rd ♑

♀	⚹	♆	1:25 am	
☽	⚻	☉	3:11 am	**12:11 am**
☽	⚺	♆	9:12 am	**6:12 am**
☽	□	♀	9:37 am	**6:37 am**
☽	⚼	♅	11:00 am	**8:00 am**
☽	⚻	☿	11:03 am	**8:03 am**
☽	⚺	♀	1:43 pm	**10:43 am**
☽	⚺	♇	8:29 pm	**5:29 pm**
☽	⚻	♃	11:14 pm	**8:14 pm**
☽	△	✴		**10:21 pm**
☽	⚻	♄		**11:40 pm**

♂ ℞   11:08 am   **8:08 am**

12 SATURDAY

3rd ♑

☽	△	✴	1:21 am	
☽	⚻	♄	2:40 am	
☿	☍	♀	4:55 am	**1:55 am**
⚷	△	♆	10:12 am	**7:12 am**
☽	△	☉	11:17 am	**8:17 am** ☽ v/c
☽	♂	?	12:49 pm	**9:49 am**
♀	⚼	♅	12:56 pm	**9:56 am**
☽	⚺	♅	4:45 pm	**1:45 pm**
☽	⚼	♀	6:50 pm	**3:50 pm**
☽	⚻	☿	9:18 pm	**6:18 pm**
☽	⚺	⚷	11:20 pm	**8:20 pm**
☽	□	♆	11:54 pm	**8:54 pm**
☽	⚺	♂		**10:23 pm**
☽	⚼	♇		**11:19 pm**

13 SUNDAY

3rd ♑

☽	⚺	♂	1:23 am	
☽	⚼	♇	2:19 am	
☽	⚻	♃	5:45 am	**2:45 am**
☉	△	?	6:49 am	**3:49 am**
☽	△	♄	9:00 am	**6:00 am**
♀	△	♀	5:40 pm	**2:40 pm**
☽	♂	♆	9:02 pm	**6:02 pm**
☽	⚹	♀		**9:24 pm**
☽	⚹	♀		**9:58 pm**
☿	⚼	⚷		**10:22 pm**

☽ enters ♒   3:20 am   **12:20 am**

MOTHER'S DAY

MAY

S	M	T	W	T	F	S
		1	2	3	4	5
6	7	8	9	10	11	12
13	14	15	16	17	18	19
20	21	22	23	24	25	26
27	28	29	30	31		

Eastern Standard Time in medium type
Pacific Standard Time in bold type

2001   **MAY**   **2001**

14 MONDAY

3rd ♒

☽	⚹	♀	12:24 am			
☽	⚹	♀	12:58 am			
☿	⊥	♅	1:22 am			
☽	⊥	⚷	5:29 am	**2:29 am**		
☽	⊥	♂	7:37 am	**4:37 am**		
☽	△	☿	7:57 am	**4:57 am**		
☽	⚹	♇	8:34 am	**5:34 am**		
☽	△	♃	12:39 pm	**9:39 am**		
☿	☍	♇	12:52 pm	**9:52 am**		
♂	△	♅	1:30 pm	**10:30 am**		
☽	□	⚹	4:51 pm	**1:51 pm**		
☽	⊻	⚴		**10:28 pm**		

15 TUESDAY

3rd ♒   4th Quarter 5:11 am **2:11 am**
                 ☽ enters ♓ 4:01 pm **1:01 pm**

☽	⊻	⚴	1:28 am			
☽	□	☉	5:11 am	**2:11 am**		
☽	☌	♆	5:25 am	**2:25 am**		
☉	□	♅	8:06 am	**5:06 am**		
☽	⊥	♀	9:15 am	**6:15 am**		
☽	⚹	⚷	11:45 am	**8:45 am**		
♇	⚻	♅	1:47 pm	**10:47 am**		
☽	⚹	♂	1:53 pm	**10:53 am**	☽ v/c
☽	⚹	♅	2:56 pm	**11:56 am**		
☽	□	♄	10:22 pm	**7:22 pm**		

16 WEDNESDAY

4th ♓   ⚴ ℞ 7:37 pm **4:37 pm**
                 ♅ enters ♉ 8:08 pm **5:08 pm**

☿	☌	♃	6:15 am	**3:15 am**
☽	⊥	⚴	7:45 am	**4:45 am**
☽	⊻	♆	9:41 am	**6:41 am**
☽	□	♀	11:39 am	**8:39 am**
☽	⊻	♀	5:21 pm	**2:21 pm**
☽	□	♇	8:57 pm	**5:57 pm**
☽	⊥	♅	10:12 pm	**7:12 pm**
☽	□	♃		**11:14 pm**

17 THURSDAY

4th ♓

☽	□	♃	2:14 am			
☽	□	☿	4:15 am	**1:15 am**		
☽	⚹	⚹	8:18 am	**5:18 am**		
☽	⚹	⚴	1:36 pm	**10:36 am**		
☽	⊥	♆	3:29 pm	**12:29 pm**		
☽	⊻	♅	5:29 pm	**2:29 pm**		
☽	⚹	☉	10:20 pm	**7:20 pm**		
☽	□	⚷	11:18 pm	**8:18 pm**		
☽	□	♂		**10:18 pm**	☽ v/c	

Eastern Standard Time in medium type
Pacific Standard Time in bold type

2001 MAY 2001

18 FRIDAY

☽ □ ♂	1:18 am			☽ v/c	
☽ ⋁ ⚷	4:52 am	**1:52 am**			
☉ ⊼ ⚷	10:08 am	**7:08 am**			
☽ ⚹ ♄	10:25 am	**7:25 am**			
☽ ∟ ⚸	3:04 pm	**12:04 pm**			
☽ ⚹ ♆	8:37 pm	**5:37 pm**			
☽ △ ♀	9:12 pm	**6:12 pm**			
☽ ∟ ♅	10:35 pm	**7:35 pm**			
♀ △ ♇		**10:56 pm**			

4th ♓
☽ enters ♈ 3:41 am **12:41 am**

19 SATURDAY

♀ △ ♇	1:56 am		
☽ ∟ ☉	5:41 am	**2:41 am**	
☽ △ ♇	7:15 am	**4:15 am**	
☽ ☌ ♀	7:36 am	**4:36 am**	
☉ ⊼ ♂	9:10 am	**6:10 am**	
☽ ⚹ ♃	1:26 pm	**10:26 am**	
☽ ∟ ♄	3:20 pm	**12:20 pm**	
☽ ⚹ ☿	8:19 pm	**5:19 pm**	
☽ ⋁ ⚸	8:57 pm	**5:57 pm**	
☽ □ ?	11:07 pm	**8:07 pm**	
♆ ⚹ ♀	11:22 pm	**8:22 pm**	
☽ ⚻ ♀		**9:54 pm**	
☽ ⚹ ♅		**11:53 pm**	

4th ♈

20 SUNDAY

☽ ⚻ ♀	12:54 am		
☽ ⚹ ♅	2:53 am		
☽ △ ⚷	8:06 am	**5:06 am**	
☽ △ ♂	9:48 am	**6:48 am**	☽ v/c
☽ ⚻ ♇	11:14 am	**8:14 am**	
☿ ⋁ ⚸	11:51 am	**8:51 am**	
☽ ⋁ ☉	11:59 am	**8:59 am**	
☽ ☌ ⚷	3:35 pm	**12:35 pm**	
☽ ∟ ♃	5:46 pm	**2:46 pm**	
☽ ⋁ ♄	7:25 pm	**4:25 pm**	
☽ ∟ ☿		**11:24 pm**	

4th ♈
☽ enters ♉ 12:29 pm **9:29 am**
☉ enters ♊   6:44 pm **3:44 pm**

SUN ENTERS GEMINI

MAY

S	M	T	W	T	F	S
		1	2	3	4	5
6	7	8	9	10	11	12
13	14	15	16	17	18	19
20	21	22	23	24	25	26
27	28	29	30	31		

Eastern Standard Time in medium type
Pacific Standard Time in bold type

2001   **MAY**   **2001**

21 MONDAY

4th ♉

☽	⊥	☿	2:24 am	
☽	⊼	♀	3:50 am	**12:50 am**
☽	□	♆	4:27 am	**1:27 am**
☿	⊼	♃	5:29 am	**2:29 am**
☽	⚲	♅	11:19 am	**8:19 am**
☽	⚲	♂	12:50 pm	**9:50 am**
☽	⊼	♇	2:25 pm	**11:25 am**
☽	⊻	♀	6:15 pm	**3:15 pm**
♀	△	❋	6:20 pm	**3:20 pm**
☽	⊻	♃	9:17 pm	**6:17 pm**

22 TUESDAY

4th ♉

☽	△	♃	5:25 am	**2:25 am**	
☿	⚲	♆	5:30 am	**2:30 am**	
☽	☌	❋	5:57 am	**2:57 am**	
☽	⊻	☿	7:21 am	**4:21 am**	
☽	□	♅	9:06 am	**6:06 am**	☽ v/c
☽	⊼	♅	1:49 pm	**10:49 am**	
☽	⊼	♂	3:09 pm	**12:09 pm**	
☽	☌	☉	9:46 pm	**6:46 pm**	
☽	⊥	♀	10:20 pm	**7:20 pm**	
☽	⊻	♆	10:54 pm	**7:54 pm**	
☽	☌	♄		**10:17 pm**	

☽ enters ♊   6:12 pm   **3:12 pm**
New Moon   9:46 pm   **6:46 pm**

23 WEDNESDAY

1st ♊

☽	☌	♄	1:17 am	
☽	⚲	♃	7:33 am	**4:33 am**
☽	☍	♀	7:42 am	**4:42 am**
☽	△	♆	9:22 am	**6:22 am**
☿	△	♅	9:56 am	**6:56 am**
♀	⊥	♀	3:26 pm	**12:26 pm**
☽	☍	♇	6:50 pm	**3:50 pm**
☽	⊥	♆		**10:36 pm**
☽	✶	♀		**10:49 pm**
☽	☌	♃		**11:23 pm**
☉	⊻	♆		**11:31 pm**

24 THURSDAY

1st ♊

☽	⊥	♆	1:36 am		
☽	✶	♀	1:49 am		
☽	☌	♃	2:23 am		
☉	⊻	♆	2:31 am		
☽	⊼	♃	9:12 am	**6:12 am**	
☽	⚲	♆	11:03 am	**8:03 am**	
☽	⊻	❋	12:09 pm	**9:09 am**	
☽	△	♅	12:56 pm	**9:56 am**	
☽	☌	☿	2:36 pm	**11:36 am**	
♀	✶	♃	2:53 pm	**11:53 am**	
☽	☍	♅	5:15 pm	**2:15 pm**	
☽	☍	♂	6:12 pm	**3:12 pm**	☽ v/c

☽ enters ♋   9:42 pm   **6:42 pm**

Eastern Standard Time in medium type
Pacific Standard Time in bold type

2001   **MAY**   **2001**

25 FRIDAY   1st ♋

☉ ∟ ♀	3:12 am	**12:12 am**		
☽ ⚹ ⚷	3:54 am	**12:54 am**		
☽ ⊻ ☉	4:54 am	**1:54 am**		
☽ ⊻ ♄	5:04 am	**2:04 am**		
♅ □ ⚳	6:56 am	**3:56 am**		
☉ ☌ ♄	7:33 am	**4:33 am**		
♀ ∟ ♄	8:19 am	**5:19 am**		
☽ ⚻ ♀	9:47 am	**6:47 am**		
☽ ⚻ ♆	12:26 pm	**9:26 am**		
☽ ⊡ ♅	2:19 pm	**11:19 am**		
☽ ∟ ⚳	2:38 pm	**11:38 am**		
☽ ⚻ ♇	9:37 pm	**6:37 pm**		

26 SATURDAY   1st ♋

♃ ∟ ⚷	5:43 am	**2:43 am**		
☽ ⊻ ♃	5:57 am	**2:57 am**		
☽ ∟ ♄	6:33 am	**3:33 am**		
☽ □ ♀	7:44 am	**4:44 am**	☽ v/c	
☽ ∟ ☉	7:59 am	**4:59 am**		
☽ ⊡ ♀	10:30 am	**7:30 am**		
☽ ☍ ⚴	11:39 am	**8:39 am**		
☿ ☍ ⚶	3:00 pm	**12:00 pm**		
☽ ⚻ ♅	3:32 pm	**12:32 pm**		
☽ ⚹ ⚳	4:56 pm	**1:56 pm**		
☽ ⚻ ⚶	7:34 pm	**4:34 pm**		
☽ ⊻ ☿	7:48 pm	**4:48 pm**		
☽ ⚻ ♂	8:06 pm	**5:06 pm**		
☽ ⊡ ♇	10:46 pm	**7:46 pm**		
☿ ☍ ♂		**10:03 pm**		

☽ enters ♌   **9:12 pm**

27 SUNDAY   1st ♋

☿ ☍ ♂	1:03 am		
☽ ∟ ♃	7:32 am	**4:32 am**	
☽ □ ⚷	7:55 am	**4:55 am**	
☽ ⚹ ♄	7:57 am	**4:57 am**	
♄ ⊻ ⚷	9:30 am	**6:30 am**	
☽ ⚹ ☉	10:58 am	**7:58 am**	
☽ △ ♀	11:09 am	**8:09 am**	
☉ ☍ ♀	1:05 pm	**10:05 am**	
☽ ☍ ♆	2:48 pm	**11:48 am**	
♀ ⊡ ♀	6:38 pm	**3:38 pm**	
☽ ⊡ ⚶	8:38 pm	**5:38 pm**	
☽ ⊡ ♂	8:56 pm	**5:56 pm**	
☽ ∟ ☿	10:03 pm	**7:03 pm**	
☽ △ ♇	11:53 pm	**8:53 pm**	

☽ enters ♌   12:12 am

MAY

S	M	T	W	T	F	S
		1	2	3	4	5
6	7	8	9	10	11	12
13	14	15	16	17	18	19
20	21	22	23	24	25	26
27	28	29	30	31		

Eastern Standard Time in medium type
Pacific Standard Time in bold type

2001 **MAY** **2001**

28 MONDAY

☽	✶	♃	9:08 am	6:08 am	
☉	⚲	♄	11:26 am	8:26 am	
☽	△	♀	1:20 pm	10:20 am	
☽	⚻	♄	1:48 pm	10:48 am	
☽	☍	♅	5:55 pm	2:55 pm	
♀	□	♄	8:29 pm	5:29 pm	
☽	□	♆	9:31 pm	6:31 pm	
☽	△	⚷	9:46 pm	6:46 pm	
☽	△	♂	9:48 pm	6:48 pm	
☽	✶	☿		9:13 pm	☽ v/c
♂	☌	⚷		10:10 pm	
♂	⚻	♅		11:30 pm	
⚷	⚻	♅		11:49 pm	

☽ enters ♍   1st ♌
               11:38 pm

MEMORIAL DAY (OBSERVED) • SHAVUOT

29 TUESDAY

☽	✶	☿	12:13 am		☽ v/c
♂	☌	⚷	1:10 am		
♂	⚻	♅	2:30 am		
⚷	⚻	♅	2:49 am		
☽	□	♄	10:54 am	7:54 am	
☽	△	♆	12:00 pm	9:00 am	
☽	□	♀	12:37 pm	9:37 am	
☽	⚲	♃	3:00 pm	12:00 pm	
☽	⚲	♀	4:19 pm	1:19 pm	
☽	□	☉	5:09 pm	2:09 pm	
☽	⚻	♆	5:19 pm	2:19 pm	
☉	△	♆	7:34 pm	4:34 pm	
♀	⚻	♃		9:24 pm	
☽	□	♇		11:27 pm	

☽ enters ♍ 2:38 am **7:02 am**   1st ♌
       ♅ ℞ 10:11 am **7:11 am**
2nd Quarter 5:09 pm **2:09 pm**

30 WEDNESDAY

♀	⚻	♃	12:24 am		
☽	□	♇	2:27 am		
☽	□	♃	12:45 pm	9:45 am	
☽	⚲	♃	2:18 pm	11:18 am	
☽	△	♄	4:22 pm	1:22 pm	
☽	⚲	♆	6:50 pm	3:50 pm	
☽	⚻	♀	7:35 pm	4:35 pm	
☽	⚻	♅	8:50 pm	5:50 pm	
☽	□	♂	11:58 pm	8:58 pm	
☽	□	⚷		9:31 pm	
☽	△	☿		11:45 pm	

2nd ♍

31 THURSDAY

☽	□	⚷	12:31 am		
☽	△	☿	2:45 am		
☽	□	☿	4:40 am	1:40 am	☽ v/c
☽	△	♄	2:36 pm	11:36 am	
☽	✶	♀	2:48 pm	11:48 am	
♀	✶	♅	3:12 pm	12:12 pm	
☽	⚻	♆	4:52 pm	1:52 pm	
☽	△	♆	8:37 pm	5:37 pm	
♄	☍	♀	9:08 pm	6:08 pm	
☽	⚲	♅	10:39 pm	7:39 pm	
☽	△	☉		9:18 pm	

☽ enters ♎ 5:41 am **2:41 am**   2nd ♍

Eastern Standard Time in medium type
Pacific Standard Time in bold type

JUNE 2001

GEMINI ♊
Duality: Masculine
Quality: Mutable
Element: Air
House: 3rd
Planetary Ruler: Mercury
Rules: Hands, Arms, Shoulders
Keyword: Diversity
Keynote: I think.

---

1 FRIDAY

2nd ♎

☽	△	☉	12:18 am	
☽	⚻	⚹	5:49 am	**2:49 am**
☽	✶	♇	5:53 am	**2:53 am**
☽	⊥	♀	4:18 pm	**1:18 pm**
☽	⚻	♄	4:54 pm	**1:54 pm**
☽	△	♃	5:25 pm	**2:25 pm**
☽	□	?	7:54 pm	**4:54 pm**
☽	△	♅		**9:49 pm**
♀	△	♂		**11:03 pm**

2 SATURDAY

2nd ♎
☽ enters ♏ 9:56 am **6:56 am**
⚹ enters ♊ 12:00 pm **9:00 pm**

☽	△	♅	12:49 am	
♀	△	♂	2:03 am	
☽	✶	♂	3:07 am	**12:07 am**
☽	☍	♀	3:13 am	**12:13 am**
☽	✶	♃	4:22 am	**1:22 am**
☽	⚻	☉	4:29 am	**1:29 am**
☽	⊥	♇	8:07 am	**5:07 am**
☽	⊼	⚹	9:17 am	**6:17 am**
☽	△	☿	9:41 am	**6:41 am** ☽ v/c
☽	⚼	♀	6:11 pm	**3:11 pm**
♀	△	♃	7:10 pm	**4:10 pm**
☽	⊼	♄	7:37 pm	**4:37 pm**
☽	⚻	♃	8:20 pm	**5:20 pm**
☿	⚼	⚹	8:28 pm	**5:28 pm**
☽	☍	♆	11:10 pm	**8:10 pm**
☽	□	♆		**10:16 pm**

3 SUNDAY

2nd ♏
☿ ℞ **9:21 pm**

☽	□	♆	1:16 am	
☽	⊥	♂	5:15 am	**2:15 am**
☽	⊥	♃	6:53 am	**3:53 am**
☽	⊼	☉	9:11 am	**6:11 am**
☽	⚼	♇	10:47 am	**7:47 am**
☽	⚻	☿	12:36 pm	**9:36 am**
☽	⊼	♃	11:46 pm	**8:46 pm**
☽	✶	?		**9:59 pm**

PENTECOST

Eastern Standard Time in medium type
Pacific Standard Time in bold type

2001 JUNE 2001

4 MONDAY
2nd ♏

☽	✶	♃	12:59 am		
☽	□	♅	6:29 am	3:29 am	☽ v/c
☉	☍	♇	6:50 am	3:50 am	
☽	⩖	♂	7:49 am	4:49 am	
☽	⩖	⚷	9:55 am	6:55 am	
☽	⊼	♀	1:04 pm	10:04 am	
☽	⊼	☿	3:52 pm	12:52 pm	
☽	☍	⚵	5:52 pm	2:52 pm	
☽	☌	♀	11:23 pm	8:23 pm	
♀	⚼	♇		10:21 pm	
☽	☍	♄		11:35 pm	

☿ ℞ 12:21 am
☽ enters ♐ 3:58 pm **12:58 pm**

5 TUESDAY
2nd ♐

♀	⚼	♇	1:21 am		
☽	☍	♄	2:35 am		
☽	⊥	♃	4:17 am	1:17 am	
☽	⊼	⚸	7:37 am	4:37 am	
☽	✶	♆	7:53 am	4:53 am	
♆	□	⚸	3:43 pm	12:43 pm	
☽	☌	♇	5:45 pm	2:45 pm	
☽	⚼	♀	7:05 pm	4:05 pm	
☽	☍	☉	8:39 pm	5:39 pm	
♃	⊼	⚵	10:31 pm	7:31 pm	
☿	✶	♀		9:40 pm	

Full Moon 8:39 pm **5:39 pm**

6 WEDNESDAY
3rd ♐

☿	✶	♀	12:40 am		
☽	⩖	♃	8:12 am	5:12 am	
☽	☍	♃	8:28 am	5:28 am	
☽	⊥	♆	12:06 pm	9:06 am	
☽	⚼	⚸	12:50 pm	9:50 am	
☽	✶	♅	2:26 pm	11:26 am	
☽	☌	♂	2:37 pm	11:37 am	
☽	☌	⚷	5:45 pm	2:45 pm	
♂	✶	♅	10:54 pm	7:54 pm	
☽	☍	☿	11:41 pm	8:41 pm	☽ v/c
☽	△	♀		10:57 pm	☽ v/c

♀ enters ♉ 5:25 am **2:25 am**
☽ enters ♑ **9:23 pm**

7 THURSDAY
3rd ♐

☽	△	♀	1:57 am		☽ v/c
☽	⊼	⚵	5:12 am	2:12 am	
☽	⩖	♀	6:53 am	3:53 am	
☽	⊼	♄	12:06 pm	9:06 am	
☽	⩖	♆	4:59 pm	1:59 pm	
☽	△	⚸	6:48 pm	3:48 pm	
☽	⊥	♅	7:23 pm	4:23 pm	
♂	⚼	⚸	8:50 pm	5:50 pm	

☽ enters ♑ 12:23 am

Eastern Standard Time in medium type
Pacific Standard Time in bold type

2001   **JUNE**   **2001**

8 FRIDAY

3rd ♑

☽	⊻	♇	3:14 am	**12:14**	**am**
♀	☍	⚹	5:46 am	**2:46**	**am**
☽	⊼	☉	11:20 am	**8:20**	**am**
☽	∟	♀	11:33 am	**8:33**	**am**
☽	⚁	⚹	11:59 am	**8:59**	**am**
☽	⚃	♄	5:51 pm	**2:51**	**pm**
☽	☌	⚴	5:51 pm	**2:51**	**pm**
♄	⚃	⚴	5:54 pm	**2:54**	**pm**
☽	⊼	♃	7:53 pm	**4:53**	**pm**
☽	⊻	♂	11:45 pm	**8:45**	**pm**
☽	⊻	♅		**9:56**	**pm**

9 SATURDAY

☽ enters ♒   11:20 am   **8:20 am**

3rd ♑

☽	⊻	♅	12:56 am		
☽	⊻	⚷	4:06 am	**1:06**	**am**
♀	⊼	♀	4:52 am	**1:52**	**am**
☽	∟	♇	8:54 am	**5:54**	**am**
☽	⊼	☿	9:12 am	**6:12**	**am**
☽	⚹	♀	4:46 pm	**1:46**	**pm**
☽	□	♀	6:06 pm	**3:06**	**pm**
☽	△	⚹	7:25 pm	**4:25**	**pm**
☽	⚃	☉	7:47 pm	**4:47**	**pm**
☽	△	♄		**9:08**	**pm**
☽	⚃	♃		**11:28**	**pm**

10 SUNDAY

3rd ♒

☽	△	♄	12:08 am		
☽	⚃	♃	2:28 am		
☽	☌	♆	4:28 am	**1:28**	**am**
☽	∟	♂	5:02 am	**2:02**	**am**
☽	□	⚷	8:36 am	**5:36**	**am**
☽	∟	⚷	10:02 am	**7:02**	**am**
☽	⚃	☿	2:24 pm	**11:24**	**am**
☽	⚹	♇	2:59 pm	**11:59**	**am**

			JUNE			
S	M	T	W	T	F	S
					1	2
3	4	5	6	7	8	9
10	11	12	13	14	15	16
17	18	19	20	21	22	23
24	25	26	27	28	29	30

Eastern Standard Time in medium type
Pacific Standard Time in bold type

2001   **JUNE**   **2001**

11 MONDAY

3rd ≈

♂ ⊥ ♆	3:50 am	**12:50 am**			
☽ △ ☉	4:42 am	**1:42 am**			
☽ ⊻ ⚷	5:23 am	**2:23 am**			
♀ ⊻ ⚹	9:18 am	**6:18 am**			
☽ △ ♃	9:23 am	**6:23 am**			
☽ ⚹ ♂	10:35 am	**7:35 am**			
☉ ⊼ ⚷	12:08 pm	**9:08 am**			
☽ ☌ ♅	1:17 pm	**10:17 am**			
☽ ⚹ ⚳	4:13 pm	**1:13 pm**			
☽ △ ☿	7:38 pm	**4:38 pm**	☽ v/c		
⚳ ⊡ ⚕	8:16 pm	**5:16 pm**			

☽ enters ♓   11:53 pm   **8:53 pm**

12 TUESDAY

3rd ♓

☽ ⊡ ♀	4:05 am	**1:05 am**	
☽ ⊡ ⚹	11:15 am	**8:15 am**	
☽ ⊥ ⚷	11:23 am	**8:23 am**	
♂ ☍ ♃	12:01 pm	**9:01 am**	
☽ ⚹ ♀	12:11 pm	**9:11 am**	
⚷ ⊡ ⚹	1:23 pm	**10:23 am**	
☽ ⊡ ♄	1:28 pm	**10:28 am**	
☽ ⊻ ♆	5:04 pm	**2:04 pm**	
☽ ⚹ ⚕	11:29 pm	**8:29 pm**	

13 WEDNESDAY

3rd ♓
4th Quarter   10:28 pm   **7:28 pm**

☽ ⊡ ♇	3:31 am	**12:31 am**	
♀ ⊻ ♄	5:34 am	**2:34 am**	
☉ ☍ ♂	12:46 pm	**9:46 am**	
☿ ⊥ ⚕	3:50 pm	**12:50 pm**	
☽ ⚹ ⚷	5:09 pm	**2:09 pm**	
☽ ⊥ ♀	9:02 pm	**6:02 pm**	
☽ ⊡ ♂	9:28 pm	**6:28 pm**	
☽ ⊡ ☉	10:28 pm	**7:28 pm**	
☽ ⊡ ♃	11:02 pm	**8:02 pm**	
☽ ⊥ ♆	11:07 pm	**8:07 pm**	
♀ ⊡ ♂		**10:02 pm**	
☽ ⊻ ♅		**10:38 pm**	

14 THURSDAY

4th ♓

☽ enters ♈   12:03 pm   **9:03 am**

♀ ⊡ ♂	1:02 am		
☽ ⊻ ♅	1:38 am		
♃ ⊡ ♆	3:22 am	**12:22 am**	
☽ ⊡ ⚷	4:14 am	**1:14 am**	
☽ ⊡ ☿	5:26 am	**2:26 am**	☽ v/c
☉ ⊡ ♆	6:33 am	**3:33 am**	
☽ ⊥ ⚕	6:33 am	**3:33 am**	
☉ ☌ ♃	7:38 am	**4:38 am**	
☽ △ ♀	2:55 pm	**11:55 am**	
♄ ☌ ⚹	6:59 pm	**3:59 pm**	
♀ ⊡ ♆	9:46 pm	**6:46 pm**	
☽ ⚹ ♄		**10:50 pm**	
☽ ⚹ ⚹		**11:06 pm**	

FLAG DAY

Eastern Standard Time in medium type
Pacific Standard Time in bold type

2001   **JUNE**   **2001**

15 FRIDAY

4th ♈

☽ ✶ ♄	1:50 am		
☽ ✶ ⚷	2:06 am		
♀ ⊥ ♃	3:40 am	**12:40 am**	
☽ ✶ ♆	4:37 am	**1:37 am**	
☽ ⚹ ♀	5:14 am	**2:14 am**	
☽ ⊥ ♅	7:05 am	**4:05 am**	
☿ ☍ ⚴	11:07 am	**8:07 am**	
☽ ⚹ ⚸	12:55 pm	**9:55 am**	
☉ △ ♅	1:57 pm	**10:57 am**	
☽ △ ♇	2:36 pm	**11:36 am**	
☽ ⚼ ♀	7:31 pm	**4:31 pm**	
☽ □ ⚵		**11:59 pm**	

16 SATURDAY

☽ enters ♉   9:39 pm   **6:39 pm**

4th ♈

☽ □ ⚵	2:59 am		
☽ △ ♂	6:23 am	**3:23 am**	
☽ ⊥ ♄	6:57 am	**3:57 am**	
☽ ⊥ ⚷	8:21 am	**5:21 am**	
☉ ☌ ☿	8:26 am	**5:26 am**	
☽ ✶ ♃	10:24 am	**7:24 am**	
☽ ✶ ♅	11:44 am	**8:44 am**	
☽ ✶ ☿	12:57 pm	**9:57 am**	
☽ ✶ ☉	1:32 pm	**10:32 am**	☽ v/c
☽ △ ⚴	1:57 pm	**10:57 am**	
☿ ⊥ ♀	4:44 pm	**1:44 pm**	
☉ ☍ ⚴	6:50 pm	**3:50 pm**	
☽ ⚼ ♇	7:01 pm	**4:01 pm**	
☽ ⚻ ♀	11:19 pm	**8:19 pm**	

17 SUNDAY

4th ♉

♆ △ ⚷	5:02 am	**2:02 am**	
♀ ⚼ ⚴	6:25 am	**3:25 am**	
☽ ⚼ ♂	9:40 am	**6:40 am**	
☽ ⚹ ♄	11:10 am	**8:10 am**	
☽ □ ♆	1:10 pm	**10:10 am**	
♇ ⚻ ⚷	1:20 pm	**10:20 am**	
☽ ⚹ ⚷	1:34 pm	**10:34 am**	
☽ ⊥ ♃	2:44 pm	**11:44 am**	
☽ ⊥ ☿	3:34 pm	**12:34 pm**	
☿ △ ♅	5:08 pm	**2:08 pm**	
☽ ⚼ ⚴	5:32 pm	**2:32 pm**	
☽ ☌ ♀	6:31 pm	**3:31 pm**	
☽ ⊥ ☉	7:25 pm	**4:25 pm**	
☽ ⚻ ♇	10:31 pm	**7:31 pm**	
☽ ☌ ⚷	10:50 pm	**7:50 pm**	

FATHER'S DAY

JUNE

S	M	T	W	T	F	S
					1	2
3	4	5	6	7	8	9
10	11	12	13	14	15	16
17	18	19	20	21	22	23
24	25	26	27	28	29	30

Eastern Standard Time in medium type
Pacific Standard Time in bold type

2001   **JUNE**   **2001**

18 MONDAY
4th ♉

☿ ♂ ♃	5:12 am	**2:12 am**		
☽ △ ♀	9:30 am	**6:30 am**		
☽ ⊼ ♂	12:07 pm	**9:07 am**		
☽ ⚺ ☿	5:25 pm	**2:25 pm**		
☽ ⚺ ♃	6:07 pm	**3:07 pm**		
☽ □ ♅	6:21 pm	**3:21 pm**	☽ v/c	
☽ ⊼ ⚷	8:13 pm	**5:13 pm**		
☽ ⚺ ☉		**9:12 pm**		

19 TUESDAY
4th ♉

☽ enters ♊   3:42 am   **12:42 am**

☽ ⚺ ☉	12:12 am		
☽ ☍ ♀	4:25 am	**1:25 am**	
♃ △ ♅	7:25 am	**4:25 am**	
☽ ⚻ ♀	11:29 am	**8:29 am**	
☽ ♂ ♄	4:52 pm	**1:52 pm**	
☽ △ ♆	6:11 pm	**3:11 pm**	
☽ ♂ ✦	8:58 pm	**5:58 pm**	
♀ ⊼ ♇	9:14 pm	**6:14 pm**	
☽ ☍ ♇		**11:57 pm**	

20 WEDNESDAY
4th ♊

☉ enters ♋   **11:38 pm**

☽ ☍ ♇	2:57 am			
☽ ⚺ ♀	3:25 am	**12:25 am**		
☽ ⚺ ⚹	4:54 am	**1:54 am**		
☿ ⚻ ♆	5:48 am	**2:48 am**		
☽ ⊼ ♀	12:45 pm	**9:45 am**		
☽ ☍ ♂	2:44 pm	**11:44 am**		
☽ ♂ ☿	7:09 pm	**4:09 pm**		
☽ ⚻ ♆	7:35 pm	**4:35 pm**		
☽ △ ♅	9:44 pm	**6:44 pm**		
☽ ♂ ♃	10:24 pm	**7:24 pm**	☽ v/c	
☽ ☍ ⚷	11:19 pm	**8:19 pm**		
☉ ⊼ ♀		**11:48 pm**		

SUN ENTERS CANCER PST
LITHA (SUMMER SOLSTICE) 11:38 PM EST

21 THURSDAY
4th ♊

☉ enters ♋	2:38 am	
☿ enters ♏	3:39 am	**12:39 am**
☽ enters ♋	6:40 am	**3:40 am**
New Moon	6:58 am	**3:58 am**

☉ ⊼ ♀	2:48 am		
☉ ⚻ ⚹	3:19 am	**12:19 am**	
☽ ⚻ ♀	6:34 am	**3:34 am**	
☽ ⊼ ♀	6:38 am	**3:38 am**	
☽ ⚻ ⚹	6:49 am	**3:49 am**	
☽ ♂ ☉	6:58 am	**3:58 am**	
♀ ♂ ⚹	12:10 pm	**9:10 am**	
☽ ⚺ ♄	7:41 pm	**4:41 pm**	
☽ ⊼ ♆	8:27 pm	**5:27 pm**	
☽ ⚻ ♅	10:35 pm	**7:35 pm**	
☽ ⚺ ✦		**10:18 pm**	

SUN ENTERS CANCER EST
LITHA (SUMMER SOLSTICE) 2:38 AM EST
SOLAR ECLIPSE ☌ (0° ♋ 10') 7:05 AM EST/4:05 AM PST

Eastern Standard Time in medium type
Pacific Standard Time in bold type

2001 — JUNE — 2001

22 FRIDAY
1st ♋

☽	⚹	⚷	1:18 am		
☽	⊼	♇	4:52 am	**1:52 am**	
☽	⬒	♀	7:02 am	**4:02 am**	
☽	⚼	⚴	8:15 am	**5:15 am**	
☽	✶	♀	9:11 am	**6:11 am**	☽ v/c
☽	☍	♃	1:47 pm	**10:47 am**	
☽	⊼	♂	3:19 pm	**12:19 pm**	
♃	☍	⚸	6:46 pm	**3:46 pm**	
☽	⚺	☿	7:18 pm	**4:18 pm**	
☽	⦦	♄	8:29 pm	**5:29 pm**	
☽	⊼	♅	11:06 pm	**8:06 pm**	
☽	⊼	⚸		**9:29 pm**	
☽	⚺	♃		**9:36 pm**	
☽	⦦	⚷		**11:52 pm**	

23 SATURDAY
1st ♋
☽ enters ♌ 7:55 am **4:55 am**

☽	⊼	⚸	12:29 am		
☽	⚺	♃	12:36 am		
☽	⦦	⚷	2:52 am		
☽	⬒	♇	5:20 am	**2:20 am**	
☽	△	♀	7:14 am	**4:14 am**	
☽	⚺	☉	11:36 am	**8:36 am**	
☽	⬒	♂	3:17 pm	**12:17 pm**	
☽	⦦	☿	7:12 pm	**4:12 pm**	
☽	✶	♄	9:08 pm	**6:08 pm**	
☽	☍	♆	9:25 pm	**6:25 pm**	
☉	⦦	♀	10:03 pm	**7:03 pm**	
☽	⬒	⚸		**9:50 pm**	
☽	⦦	♃		**10:27 pm**	

24 SUNDAY
1st ♌

☽	⬒	⚸	12:50 am		
☽	⦦	♃	1:27 am		
☽	✶	⚷	4:20 am	**1:20 am**	
☽	△	♇	5:45 am	**2:45 am**	
☽	□	⚴	10:35 am	**7:35 am**	
☽	⦦	☉	1:46 pm	**10:46 am**	
☽	□	♀	1:52 pm	**10:52 am**	
☽	⊼	♀	2:04 pm	**11:04 am**	
☽	△	♂	3:16 pm	**12:16 pm**	
♀	△	♃	4:10 pm	**1:10 pm**	
☽	✶	☿	7:15 pm	**4:15 pm**	
☽	☍	♅		**9:01 pm**	
☽	△	⚸		**10:15 pm**	
♄	△	♆		**11:17 pm**	
☽	✶	♃		**11:22 pm**	☽ v/c

	JUNE					
S	M	T	W	T	F	S
					1	2
3	4	5	6	7	8	9
10	11	12	13	14	15	16
17	18	19	20	21	22	23
24	25	26	27	28	29	30

Eastern Standard Time in medium type
Pacific Standard Time in bold type

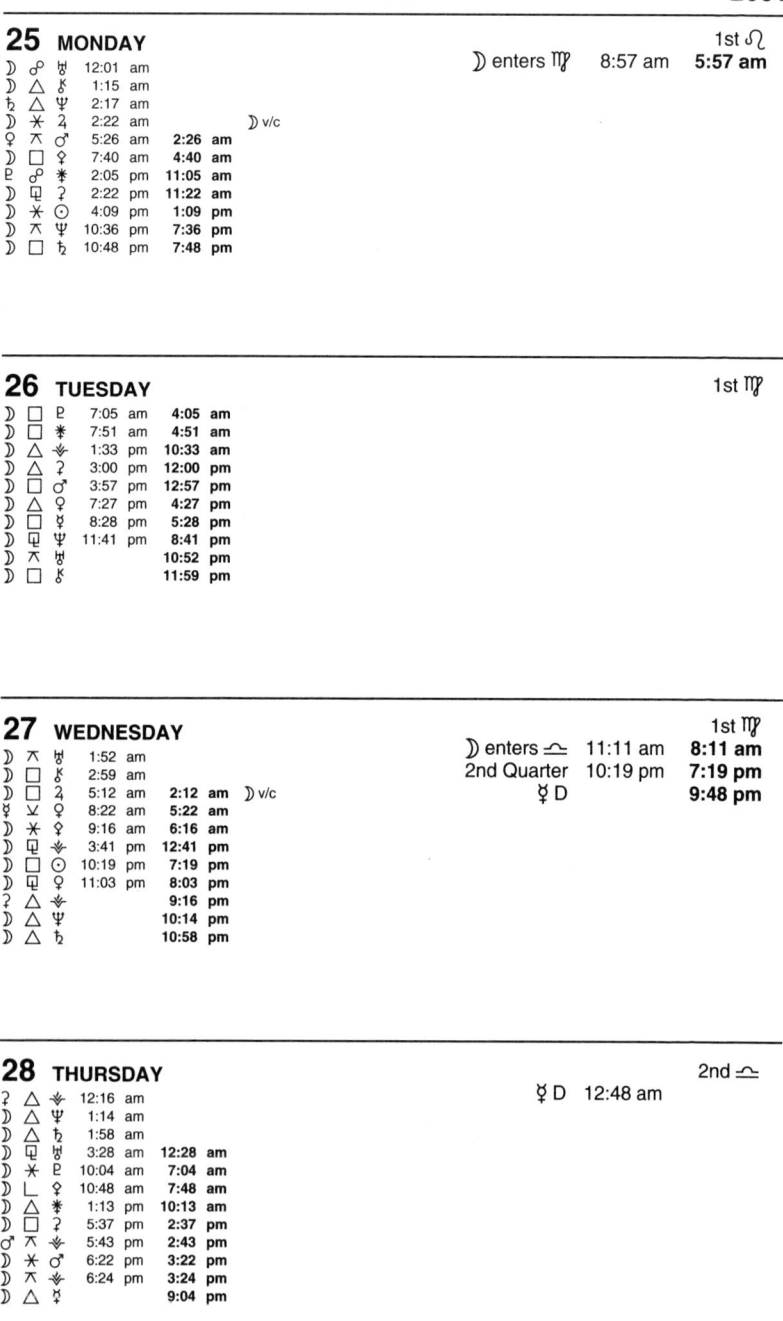

2001 JUNE/JULY 2001

29 FRIDAY

☽	△	☿	12:04 am		
☽	⊼	♀	3:23 am	**12:23 am**	
☽	⚏	♄	4:23 am	**1:23 am**	
☽	△	♅	5:39 am	**2:39 am**	
☽	✶	⚷	6:39 am	**3:39 am**	
☽	△	♃	10:07 am	**7:07 am**	☽ v/c
☽	⊥	♇	12:23 pm	**9:23 am**	
☽	⊻	♀	12:54 pm	**9:54 am**	
☉	⊼	♆	4:00 pm	**1:00 pm**	
☽	⚏	⚳	4:52 pm	**1:52 pm**	
☽	⊥	♂	8:26 pm	**5:26 pm**	

☽ enters ♏ 3:28 pm **12:28 pm**

2nd ♎

30 SATURDAY

☽	⚏	☿	3:01 am	**12:01 am**
☽	□	♆	6:06 am	**3:06 am**
☽	△	☉	7:13 am	**4:13 am**
☽	⊼	♄	7:26 am	**4:26 am**
♀	□	♅	7:46 am	**4:46 am**
☽	⊥	⚷	9:23 am	**6:23 am**
☉	⊻	♄	10:38 am	**7:38 am**
☽	⚏	♃	1:31 pm	**10:31 am**
☽	⊻	♇	3:20 pm	**12:20 pm**
♀	⊼	⚷	6:53 pm	**3:53 pm**
☽	⊼	⚳	9:14 pm	**6:14 pm**
☽	✶	⚴	10:28 pm	**7:28 pm**
☽	⊻	♂	11:06 pm	**8:06 pm**
☉	⚏	♅	11:47 pm	**8:47 pm**
☽	☍	⚵		**10:50 pm**

2nd ♏

CANCER ♋
Duality: Feminine
Quality: Cardinal
Element: Water
House: 4th
Planetary Ruler: Moon
Rules: Breasts and Stomach
Keyword: Sympathy
Keynote: I feel.

1 SUNDAY

☽	☍	⚵	1:50 am	
☽	⊼	☿	6:48 am	**3:48 am**
☽	□	♅	11:50 am	**8:50 am**
☽	⊻	⚷	12:43 pm	**9:43 am**
☽	⚏	☉	12:49 pm	**9:49 am**
☽	☍	♀	2:25 pm	**11:25 am**	☽ v/c
☽	⊼	♃	5:35 pm	**2:35 pm**
⚴	⊼	⚴	5:52 pm	**2:52 pm**
☽	☌	♀	6:59 pm	**3:59 pm**
☽	⊥	⚴		**10:47 pm**

☽ enters ♐ 10:13 pm **7:13 pm**

2nd ♏

Eastern Standard Time in medium type
Pacific Standard Time in bold type

2001   **JULY**   **2001**

2 MONDAY
2nd ♐

☽	∟	♄	1:47 am	
♂	☍	⚹	3:41 am	**12:41 am**
☽	⚹	♆	1:25 pm	**10:25 am**
☽	☍	♄	3:26 pm	**12:26 pm**
☽	⚻	☉	7:11 pm	**4:11 pm**
☽	☌	♇	11:03 pm	**8:03 pm**

3 TUESDAY
2nd ♐

☽	⚺	♄	5:39 am	**2:39 am**
☽	☌	♂	6:16 am	**3:16 am**
☽	☍	⚹	8:04 am	**5:04 am**
☽	⚻	⚸	11:55 am	**8:55 am**
♀	⚺	♃	1:47 pm	**10:47 am**
♀	☍	♀	4:15 pm	**1:15 pm**
☽	☍	☿	4:59 pm	**1:59 pm**
☽	∟	♆	5:58 pm	**2:58 pm**
☽	⚹	♅	8:26 pm	**5:26 pm**
☽	☌	⚸	9:11 pm	**6:11 pm**
♃	⚻	♀	10:33 pm	**7:33 pm**

4 WEDNESDAY
2nd ♐

☽	⚺	♀	3:28 am	**12:28 am**	
☽	☍	♃	3:36 am	**12:36 am**	☽ v/c
☽	⚻	♀	4:38 am	**1:38 am**	
☿	⚼	♆	4:07 pm	**1:07 pm**	
☉	⚼	♀	4:08 pm	**1:08 pm**	
☽	⚼	⚸	5:53 pm	**2:53 pm**	
☉	⚻	♇	9:22 pm	**6:22 pm**	
☽	⚺	♆	11:03 pm	**8:03 pm**	
☽	∟	♅		**10:33 pm**	
☽	⚻	♄		**10:48 pm**	

☽ enters ♑   7:21 am   **4:21 am**

INDEPENDENCE DAY

5 THURSDAY
2nd ♑

☽	∟	♅	1:33 am		
☽	⚻	♄	1:48 am		
☽	∟	♀	8:32 am	**5:32 am**	
☽	⚺	♇	9:03 am	**6:03 am**	
☽	☍	☉	10:04 am	**7:04 am**	☽ v/c
☽	⚼	♀	12:50 pm	**9:50 am**	
☽	☌	♄	2:58 pm	**11:58 am**	
☽	⚺	♂	3:39 pm	**12:39 pm**	
☽	⚻	⚹	9:27 pm	**6:27 pm**	
☽	△	⚸		**9:24 pm**	

Full Moon   10:04 am   **7:04 am**
♀ enters ♊   11:44 am   **8:44 am**

LUNAR ECLIPSE ☍ **(13º ♑ 39') 9:56 AM EST/6:56 AM PST**

Eastern Standard Time in medium type
Pacific Standard Time in bold type

2001   **JULY**   **2001**

6 FRIDAY

☽	△	♇	12:24 am		
☽	⊼	☿	6:37 am	**3:37**	**am**
☽	⋎	♅	7:09 am	**4:09**	**am**
☽	⊡	♄	7:45 am	**4:45**	**am**
☽	⋎	⚷	7:45 am	**4:45**	**am**
♀	⊡	♆	9:02 am	**6:02**	**am**
☽	⚹	♀	2:04 pm	**11:04**	**am**
☽	∟	♇	2:46 pm	**11:46**	**am**
☿	△	♅	3:42 pm	**12:42**	**pm**
☽	⊼	♃	3:48 pm	**12:48**	**pm**
☽	∟	♂	9:04 pm	**6:04**	**pm**
☽	△	♀	9:37 pm	**6:37**	**pm**
☿	☍	⚷		**9:42**	**pm**

☽ enters ♒   6:33 pm   **3:33 pm**

3rd ♑

7 SATURDAY

☿	☍	⚷	12:42 am		
☽	⊡	⚳	4:55 am	**1:55**	**am**
☽	☌	♆	10:34 am	**7:34**	**am**
☽	∟	⚷	1:39 pm	**10:39**	**am**
☉	☍	♃	1:44 pm	**10:44**	**am**
☽	△	♄	2:05 pm	**11:05**	**am**
☽	⊡	☿	2:36 pm	**11:36**	**am**
☽	⚹	♇	8:50 pm	**5:50**	**pm**
☽	⊡	♃	10:32 pm	**7:32**	**pm**
☉	⊼	♂	11:10 pm	**8:10**	**pm**
☽	⋎	♃		**10:54**	**pm**
☽	⚹	♂		**11:50**	**pm**

3rd ♒

8 SUNDAY

☽	⋎	♃	1:54 am		
☽	⚹	♂	2:50 am		
☽	⊼	☉	3:13 am	**12:13**	**am**
☽	△	⚳	12:44 pm	**9:44**	**am**
☽	□	♇	2:38 pm	**11:38**	**am**
☽	☌	♅	7:22 pm	**4:22**	**pm**
☽	⚹	⚷	7:49 pm	**4:49**	**pm**
☽	△	☿	11:12 pm	**8:12**	**pm**
☽	□	♀		**11:08**	**pm**

3rd ♒

JULY

S	M	T	W	T	F	S
1	2	3	4	5	6	7
8	9	10	11	12	13	14
15	16	17	18	19	20	21
22	23	24	25	26	27	28
29	30	31				

Eastern Standard Time in medium type
Pacific Standard Time in bold type

2001 JULY 2001

9 MONDAY
3rd ♒

☽ □ ♀	2:08 am				
☽ △ ♃	5:28 am	**2:28 am**	☽ v/c		
☽ ⊥ ♄	7:43 am	**4:43 am**			
☽ ⊡ ☉	12:15 pm	**9:15 am**			
☽ □ ♀	4:21 pm	**1:21 pm**			
☽ ⊻ ♆	11:08 pm	**8:08 pm**			

☽ enters ♓ 7:05 am **4:05 am**

10 TUESDAY
3rd ♓

☽ □ ♄	3:23 am	**12:23 am**	
☽ □ ♇	9:28 am	**6:28 am**	
☿ ⊼ ♀	9:59 am	**6:59 am**	
☽ ✶ ♄	1:32 pm	**10:32 am**	
☽ □ ♂	2:51 pm	**11:51 am**	
☽ △ ☉	9:14 pm	**6:14 pm**	

11 WEDNESDAY
3rd ♓

☽ □ ⚸	4:33 am	**1:33 am**	
☽ ✶ ⚴	5:17 am	**2:17 am**	
☽ ⊥ ♆	5:21 am	**2:21 am**	
☽ ⊻ ♅	7:52 am	**4:52 am**	
☽ □ ⚸	8:10 am	**5:10 am**	
☽ △ ♀	2:25 pm	**11:25 am**	
☽ □ ☿	5:17 pm	**2:17 pm**	
☽ □ ♃	7:09 pm	**4:09 pm**	☽ v/c
♆ ⊡ ⚸	8:18 pm	**5:18 pm**	

☽ enters ♈ 7:36 pm **4:36 pm**

12 THURSDAY
3rd ♈

☽ ✶ ♀	10:44 am	**7:44 am**	
☽ ✶ ♆	11:12 am	**8:12 am**	
☽ ⊥ ⚴	12:10 pm	**9:10 am**	
☽ ⊥ ♅	1:41 pm	**10:41 am**	
♀ △ ♆	3:49 pm	**12:49 pm**	
☽ ✶ ♄	4:02 pm	**1:02 pm**	
☿ ☌ ♃	5:29 pm	**2:29 pm**	
☽ ⊡ ♀	8:05 pm	**5:05 pm**	
☽ △ ♇	9:17 pm	**6:17 pm**	
⚸ ⊻ ⚴	9:40 pm	**6:40 pm**	
☽ □ ♄		**9:18 pm**	
☽ △ ♂		**11:05 pm**	

☿ enters ♋ 5:47 pm **2:47 pm**
♃ enters ♋ 7:02 pm **4:02 pm**

Eastern Standard Time in medium type
Pacific Standard Time in bold type

2001   JULY   **2001**

13 FRIDAY

☽	□	⚷	12:18 am		
☽	△	♂	2:05 am		
☽	□	☉	1:45 pm	**10:45 am**	
☽	⊻	⚳	6:21 pm	**3:21 pm**	
☽	⚹	♆	6:43 pm	**3:43 pm**	
☽	⚹	♅	6:52 pm	**3:52 pm**	☽ v/c
☽	⊥	♀	6:55 pm	**3:55 pm**	
☽	△	⚴	7:02 pm	**4:02 pm**	
☽	⊥	♄	9:29 pm	**6:29 pm**	
♅	△	♆	9:40 pm	**6:40 pm**	
⚴	☍	♆		**9:53 pm**	
☽	⚻	♀		**10:06 pm**	
☽	⚟	♇		**11:19 pm**	

4th Quarter   1:45 pm   **10:45 am**   3rd ♈

14 SATURDAY

⚴	☍	♆	12:53 am		
☽	⚻	♀	1:06 am		
☽	⚟	♇	2:19 am		
☽	⚟	♂	6:49 am	**3:49 am**	
☽	⚹	♃	6:51 am	**3:51 am**	
☽	⚹	☿	10:10 am	**7:10 am**	
♅	□	♆	10:18 am	**7:18 am**	
⚴	⚻	♆	2:27 pm	**11:27 am**	
☽	□	♆	8:55 pm	**5:55 pm**	
☽	⚟	⚴	11:21 pm	**8:21 pm**	
☽	⊥	♅		**9:30 pm**	
☽	⊻	♀		**11:03 pm**	
☽	⊻	♄		**11:05 pm**	
♀	☌	♄		**11:32 pm**	

☽ enters ♉   6:13 am   **3:13 am**   4th ♈

15 SUNDAY

☽	⊥	♅	12:30 am		
☽	⊻	♀	2:03 am		
☽	⊻	♄	2:05 am		
♀	☌	♄	2:32 am		
☽	⚟	♇	6:29 am	**3:29 am**	
☽	△	⚷	8:28 am	**5:28 am**	
☽	⚟	♂	10:44 am	**7:44 am**	
☽	⊥	♃	11:23 am	**8:23 am**	
☽	⊥	☿	5:18 pm	**2:18 pm**	
☽	⚹	☉		**11:23 pm**	
☽	□	♅		**11:41 pm**	☽ v/c
☽	⚟	⚴		**11:45 pm**	

4th ♉

JULY						
S	M	T	W	T	F	S
1	2	3	4	5	6	7
8	9	10	11	12	13	14
15	16	17	18	19	20	21
22	23	24	25	26	27	28
29	30	31				

Eastern Standard Time in medium type
Pacific Standard Time in bold type

2001 JULY 2001

16 MONDAY

☽	⚹	☉	2:23 am		
☽	□	♅	2:41 am		
☽	⊼	⚷	2:45 am		
☽	☌	⚷	3:55 am	**12:55 am**
☽	⚺	⚴	5:13 am	**2:13 am**
☉	⊼	♅	6:20 am	**3:20 am**
☉	⊼	⚷	7:08 am	**4:08 am**
☽	☍	♀	8:33 am	**5:33 am**
☽	⚼	♃	11:14 am	**8:14 am**
☽	⚺	♃	2:56 pm	**11:56 am**
☽	⚺	☿	11:20 pm	**8:20 pm**

☽ v/c

4th ♉
☽ enters ♊   1:26 pm   **10:26 am**

17 TUESDAY

☽	△	♆	3:02 am	**12:02 am**
♀	☍	♇	4:46 am	**1:46 am**
☽	⚼	☉	6:55 am	**3:55 am**
☽	☌	♄	8:22 am	**5:22 am**
☉	⚹	⚷	11:56 am	**8:56 am**
☽	☍	♇	11:58 am	**8:58 am**
☽	☌	♀	12:37 pm	**9:37 am**
☽	⊼	♃	1:06 pm	**10:06 am**
☽	☍	♂	3:51 pm	**12:51 pm**
♀	⊼	♃	5:52 pm	**2:52 pm**
♅	⚹	⚷	11:58 pm	**8:58 pm**

4th ♊

18 WEDNESDAY

☽	⚼	♆	4:43 am	**1:43 am**
☉	⚼	♄	6:17 am	**3:17 am**
☽	☍	⚷	6:45 am	**3:45 am**
☽	△	♅	6:46 am	**3:46 am**
☿	⊼	♆	8:17 am	**5:17 am**
☽	⚺	⚴	9:24 am	**6:24 am**
☽	⚺	☉	10:21 am	**7:21 am**
☽	☌	⚴	11:26 am	**8:26 am**
☽	⊼	♀	12:21 pm	**9:21 am**
☽	☌	♃	7:08 pm	**4:08 pm**
☿	⚼	♅		**11:14 pm**

☽ v/c

4th ♊
♀ D   7:45 am   **4:45 am**
☽ enters ♋   4:56 pm   **1:56 pm**

19 THURSDAY

☿	⚼	♅	2:14 am	
♀	☍	♂	4:19 am	**1:19 am**
☽	⊼	♆	5:37 am	**2:37 am**
☽	⚼	♅	7:36 am	**4:36 am**
☽	☌	☿	8:17 am	**5:17 am**
♀	⊼	⚴	10:10 am	**7:10 am**
☽	⚼	⚴	10:50 am	**7:50 am**
☽	⚺	♄	11:05 am	**8:05 am**
☽	⚼	♀	1:06 pm	**10:06 am**
☽	⊼	♇	2:04 pm	**11:04 am**
☽	☍	♃	2:31 pm	**11:31 am**
☉	△	♀	4:28 pm	**1:28 pm**
☽	⊼	♂	5:45 pm	**2:45 pm**
☽	⚺	♀	6:51 pm	**3:51 pm**
☉	⚺	⚴		**10:52 pm**

4th ♋
♂ D   5:45 pm   **2:45 pm**

Eastern Standard Time in medium type
Pacific Standard Time in bold type

2001 JULY 2001

20 FRIDAY
4th ♋

☉	⋁	⚹	1:52 am			
☉	⊡	♇	7:09 am	4:09 am		
☽	⊼	⚷	7:48 am	4:48 am		
☽	⊼	♅	7:52 am	4:52 am		
☿	⋁	♄	10:26 am	7:26 am		
☽	⌐	♄	11:30 am	8:30 am		
☽	⚹	⚹	11:41 am	8:41 am		
☿	⌐	⚹	12:10 pm	9:10 am		
☽	△	♀	1:20 pm	10:20 am		
☽	⊡	♇	2:15 pm	11:15 am		
☽	⋁	⚹	2:24 pm	11:24 am		
☽	☌	☉	2:44 pm	11:44 am	☽ v/c	
☽	⊡	♂	5:54 pm	2:54 pm		
☽	⋁	♃	8:33 pm	5:33 pm		
☽	⌐	♀	8:55 pm	5:55 pm		

New Moon 2:44 pm **11:44 am**
☽ enters ♌ 5:43 pm **2:43 pm**

♇ ⋁ ♃ 10:48 pm
☿ ⊡ ♀ 11:34 pm

21 SATURDAY
1st ♌

♇	⋁	♃	1:48 am		
☿	⊡	♀	2:34 am		
☽	☍	♆	5:52 am	2:52 am	
☽	⊡	⚷	7:41 am	4:41 am	
☿	☍	♃	9:16 am	6:16 am	
☿	⊼	♇	10:02 am	7:02 am	
☽	⚹	♄	11:36 am	8:36 am	
☽	⊼	♃	1:59 pm	10:59 am	
☽	△	♇	2:08 pm	11:08 am	
☽	⋁	☿	2:41 pm	11:41 am	
☽	⌐	⚹	3:15 pm	12:15 pm	
☽	△	♂	5:49 pm	2:49 pm	
☽	⌐	♃	8:46 pm	5:46 pm	
☽	⚹	♀	10:43 pm	7:43 pm	

22 SUNDAY
1st ♌

☽	△	⚷	7:28 am	4:28 am		
☽	☍	♅	7:34 am	4:34 am	☽ v/c	
☽	☐	⚹	12:37 pm	9:37 am		
☽	☐	♀	1:11 pm	10:11 am		
☽	⊡	♃	1:33 pm	10:33 am		
☽	⚹	⚹	4:04 pm	1:04 pm		
☿	⊼	♂	5:28 pm	2:28 pm		
☽	⋁	☉	5:45 pm	2:45 pm		
☉	⊡	♂	5:45 pm	2:45 pm		
☽	⌐	☿	5:47 pm	2:47 pm		
☽	⚹	♃	9:00 pm	6:00 pm		

☉ enters ♌ 1:26 pm **10:26 am**
☽ enters ♍ 5:29 pm **2:29 pm**

SUN ENTERS LEO

JULY

S	M	T	W	T	F	S
1	2	3	4	5	6	7
8	9	10	11	12	13	14
15	16	17	18	19	20	21
22	23	24	25	26	27	28
29	30	31				

Eastern Standard Time in medium type
Pacific Standard Time in bold type

JULY 2001

23 MONDAY
1st ♍

☽	⊼	♆	5:36 am	**2:36 am**	
☽	□	♄	11:48 am	**8:48 am**	
☽	∟	♀	1:15 pm	**10:15 am**	
☽	△	♃	1:17 pm	**10:17 am**	
☽	□	♇	2:00 pm	**11:00 am**	
☽	⚼	⚷	2:38 pm	**11:38 am**	
♀	☍	⚷	3:39 pm	**12:39 pm**	
☽	□	♂	5:56 pm	**2:56 pm**	
☽	∟	☉	7:31 pm	**4:31 pm**	
☽	⚹	☿	9:22 pm	**6:22 pm**	
☽	□	♀		**11:48 pm**	☽ v/c

24 TUESDAY
1st ♍

☀ enters ♋ 5:05 am **2:05 am**
☽ enters ♎ 6:08 pm **3:08 pm**

☽	□	♀	2:48 am		☽ v/c
☽	⚼	♆	5:52 am	**2:52 am**	
☽	□	⚷	7:38 am	**4:38 am**	
☽	⊼	♅	7:46 am	**4:46 am**	
☽	⚹	♀	1:49 pm	**10:49 am**	
☽	△	⚷	2:17 pm	**11:17 am**	
☽	□	☀	6:40 pm	**3:40 pm**	
☽	⚹	☉	9:51 pm	**6:51 pm**	
☽	□	♃	10:32 pm	**7:32 pm**	

25 WEDNESDAY
1st ♎

☽	△	♆	6:40 am	**3:40 am**
☽	⚼	♅	8:36 am	**5:36 am**
☉	⚺	♃	10:47 am	**7:47 am**
☽	△	♄	1:36 pm	**10:36 am**
☽	□	♃	2:10 pm	**11:10 am**
☽	∟	♀	2:58 pm	**11:58 am**
☽	⚹	♇	3:30 pm	**12:30 pm**
☽	⚼	⚷	4:00 pm	**1:00 pm**
♀	⚼	♆	5:39 pm	**2:39 pm**
☽	⚹	♂	7:57 pm	**4:57 pm**

26 THURSDAY
1st ♎

☽ enters ♏ 9:17 pm **6:17 pm**

☽	□	☿	7:22 am	**4:22 am**	
☽	△	♀	9:30 am	**6:30 am**	
☽	⚹	⚷	9:59 am	**6:59 am**	
☽	△	♅	10:10 am	**7:10 am**	☽ v/c
♀	☍	⚷	3:15 pm	**12:15 pm**	
☽	⚼	♄	3:33 pm	**12:33 pm**	
☽	⚺	♀	4:53 pm	**1:53 pm**	
♀	△	♅	5:18 pm	**2:18 pm**	
☽	∟	♇	5:19 pm	**2:19 pm**	
☽	⊼	⚷	6:31 pm	**3:31 pm**	
♄	⊼	♃	7:00 pm	**4:00 pm**	
☽	∟	♂	10:06 pm	**7:06 pm**	
☽	△	☀		**9:05 pm**	
☿	⊼	⚷		**10:17 pm**	
☿	⊼	♅		**11:29 pm**	
☽	△	♃		**11:46 pm**	

Eastern Standard Time in medium type
Pacific Standard Time in bold type

2001   **JULY**   **2001**

27 FRIDAY

1st ♏

☽	△	⚵	12:05 am		
☿	⊼	⚷	1:17 am		
☿	⊼	♅	2:29 am		
☽	△	♃	2:46 am		
☽	□	☉	5:08 am	2:08 am
☽	□	♆	10:30 am	7:30 am
☽	⊥	⚷	12:21 pm	9:21 am
☽	⚼	♀	2:23 pm	11:23 am
☿	⊻	♀	2:42 pm	11:42 am
☽	✶	⚴	5:54 pm	2:54 pm
☽	⊼	♄	6:22 pm	3:22 pm
☽	⊻	♇	7:58 pm	4:58 pm
☽	⊻	♂		10:10 pm

2nd Quarter   5:08 am   **2:08 am**

28 SATURDAY

2nd ♏

☽	⊻	♂	1:10 am			
☽	⚼	⚵	4:12 am	1:12 am		
☽	⚼	♃	6:12 am	3:12 am		
☽	⊻	⚷	3:33 pm	12:33 pm		
☽	□	♅	3:45 pm	12:45 pm		
☿	⊥	♄	5:42 pm	2:42 pm		
☽	⊼	♀	8:22 pm	5:22 pm		
☽	⊥	⚴	9:00 pm	6:00 pm		
☽	△	☿	10:50 pm	7:50 pm	☽ v/c	
☽	☌	♀	11:20 pm	8:20 pm		
☿	△	♀		11:02 pm		
☽	☍	⚵		11:15 pm		
☿	⚼	♇		11:43 pm		

29 SUNDAY

2nd ♏

☿	△	♀	2:02 am		
☽	☍	⚵	2:15 am		
☿	⚼	♇	2:43 am		
☽	⊼	⚵	9:16 am	6:16 am
☽	⊼	♃	10:30 am	7:30 am
☽	△	☉	4:34 pm	1:34 pm
☽	✶	♆	5:40 pm	2:40 pm
☿	✶	⚵	11:34 pm	8:34 pm
☽	⊻	⚴		9:54 pm
☽	☍	♄		11:32 pm

☽ enters ♐   3:44 am   **12:44 am**

	JULY					
S	M	T	W	T	F	S
1	2	3	4	5	6	7
8	9	10	11	12	13	14
15	16	17	18	19	20	21
22	23	24	25	26	27	28
29	30	31				

Eastern Standard Time in medium type
Pacific Standard Time in bold type

2001   **JULY/AUGUST**   **2001**

30 MONDAY

☽	⚹	♄	12:54 am	
☽	☍	♄	2:32 am	
☽	☌	♇	3:45 am	**12:45 am**
☉	☍	♆	6:48 am	**3:48 am**
♀	⚻	♀	8:03 am	**5:03 am**
☽	⊡	☿	8:45 am	**5:45 am**
☽	☌	♂	9:54 am	**6:54 am**
☿	⊡	♂	4:07 pm	**1:07 pm**
☽	∟	♆	10:23 pm	**7:23 pm**
☽	⊡	☉	11:43 pm	**8:43 pm**
☽	☌	⚴		**9:18 pm**
☽	⚹	♅		**9:31 pm**

2nd ♐
☿ enters ♌   5:18 am   **2:18 am**

31 TUESDAY

☽	☌	⚴	12:18 am		
☽	⚹	♅	12:31 am		
♃	☌	⚸	4:45 am	**1:45 am**	
☉	⊡	⚴	6:58 am	**3:58 am**	
☽	⚻	♀	9:01 am	**6:01 am**	
☽	☍	♀	11:24 am	**8:24 am**	☽ v/c
☽	⚻	⚸	1:19 pm	**10:19 am**	
☽	⚻	☿	7:51 pm	**4:51 pm**	
☽	☍	♃	9:21 pm	**6:21 pm**	☽ v/c
☽	☍	⚸	9:51 pm	**6:51 pm**	

2nd ♐
⚸ enters ♊   11:31 am   **8:31 am**
☽ enters ♑   1:16 pm   **10:16 am**

LEO ♌
Duality: Masculine
Quality: Fixed
Element: Fire
House: 5th
Planetary Ruler: Sun
Rules: Back, Spine, and Heart
Keyword: Faith
Keynote: I will.

1 WEDNESDAY

☽	⚻	♆	3:41 am	**12:41 am**
☿	⚻	♃	5:24 am	**2:24 am**
☽	∟	♅	5:50 am	**2:50 am**
☽	⚻	☉	7:38 am	**4:38 am**
☽	☌	⚸	10:35 am	**7:35 am**
☿	⚻	⚴	11:09 am	**8:09 am**
☽	⚻	♄	1:29 pm	**10:29 am**
☽	⚻	♇	2:15 pm	**11:15 am**
☽	∟	♀	2:48 pm	**11:48 am**
♀	⚻	♆	3:12 pm	**12:12 pm**
☽	⊡	⚸	7:46 pm	**4:46 pm**
☽	⚻	♂	9:29 pm	**6:29 pm**

2nd ♑
♀ enters ♋   7:18 am   **4:18 am**

LAMMAS

Eastern Standard Time in medium type
Pacific Standard Time in bold type

2001 AUGUST 2001

2 THURSDAY
☽ ⌑ ⚷ 11:23 am **8:23 am**
☽ ⌑ ♅ 11:35 am **8:35 am**
☉ ⊼ ♃ 4:25 pm **1:25 pm**
☿ ☍ ♆ 4:58 pm **1:58 pm**
☽ ⊡ ♄ 7:39 pm **4:39 pm**
☽ ∟ ♇ 8:10 pm **5:10 pm**
☽ ⚹ ♀ 9:00 pm **6:00 pm**
☽ △ ⚵ **11:36 pm**

☽ enters ♒   2nd ♑
             9:53 pm

3 FRIDAY
☽ △ ⚵ 2:36 am
☿ ⊡ ⚷ 3:56 am **12:56 am**
☽ ∟ ♂ 3:58 am **12:58 am**
☽ ⊼ ♀ 5:19 am **2:19 am**
☽ ⊼ ♃ 10:13 am **7:13 am**
☽ ⊼ ⚹ 12:39 pm **9:39 am**
☽ ☌ ♆ 3:30 pm **12:30 pm**
☽ ∟ ⚷ 5:27 pm **2:27 pm**
☽ ☍ ☿ 8:23 pm **5:23 pm**
☽ ⌑ ♃ 9:57 pm **6:57 pm**
☽ ☍ ☉ **9:56 pm**
☽ △ ♄ **11:05 pm**
☽ ⚹ ♇ **11:22 pm**

☽ enters ♒ 12:53 am   2nd ♑
Full Moon   **9:56 pm**

4 SATURDAY
☽ ☍ ☉ 12:56 am
☽ △ ♄ 2:05 am
☽ ⚹ ♇ 2:22 am
☿ ⊼ ♃ 4:56 am **1:56 am**
☽ ⚹ ♂ 10:45 am **7:45 am**
☽ ⊡ ♀ 2:51 pm **11:51 am**
☉ ⚹ ♄ 4:37 pm **1:37 pm**
☽ ⊡ ♃ 5:03 pm **2:03 pm**
☉ △ ♇ 6:31 pm **3:31 pm**
☽ ⊡ ⚹ 8:28 pm **5:28 pm**
☽ ⚹ ⚷ 11:42 pm **8:42 pm**
☽ ☌ ♅ 11:52 pm **8:52 pm** ☽ v/c

Full Moon 12:56 am   2nd ♒

5 SUNDAY
☽ ∟ ♃ 3:57 am **12:57 am**
☿ ⚹ ♄ 6:11 am **3:11 am**
☿ △ ♇ 6:27 am **3:27 am**
☽ ⊡ ♀ 10:09 am **7:09 am**
♄ ☍ ♇ 12:03 pm **9:03 am**
☉ ☌ ☿ 4:51 pm **1:51 pm**
☽ ⊡ ⚵ 4:55 pm **1:55 pm**
♀ ☌ ♃ 5:50 pm **2:50 pm**
♆ ⊼ ⚹ 10:30 pm **7:30 pm**
☽ △ ♃ 11:58 pm **8:58 pm**
☽ △ ♀   **9:30 pm**

☽ enters ♓ 1:30 pm **10:30 am**   3rd ♒

Eastern Standard Time in medium type
Pacific Standard Time in bold type

2001 AUGUST 2001

6 MONDAY
3rd ♓

☽ △ ♀	12:30 am	
☽ ⊻ ♆	4:04 am	**1:04 am**
☽ △ ⚹	4:22 am	**1:22 am**
☽ ⚹ ♄	10:01 am	**7:01 am**
☽ □ ♇	3:02 pm	**12:02 pm**
☽ □ ♄	3:15 pm	**12:15 pm**
☽ ⊼ ☉	6:59 pm	**3:59 pm**
☽ ⊼ ☿	9:54 pm	**6:54 pm**
☽ □ ♂		**9:39 pm** ☽ v/c

7 TUESDAY
3rd ♓
☽ enters ♈ **11:05 pm**

☽ □ ♂	12:39 am		☽ v/c
☽ ∟ ♆	10:19 am	**7:19 am**	
☽ □ ⚷	12:14 pm	**9:14 am**	
♀ ⊼ ♆	12:19 pm	**9:19 am**	
☽ ⊻ ♅	12:21 pm	**9:21 am**	
☿ △ ♂	3:38 pm	**12:38 pm**	
♅ ⊡ ⚹	4:00 pm	**1:00 pm**	
☽ △ ♀	11:24 pm	**8:24 pm**	

8 WEDNESDAY
3rd ♓
☽ enters ♈ 2:05 am

☽ ⊡ ☉	3:50 am	**12:50 am**
☽ ⚹ ⚷	7:04 am	**4:04 am**
♀ ⊡ ♅	8:38 am	**5:38 am**
☽ ⊡ ☿	10:16 am	**7:16 am**
☽ □ ♃	1:27 pm	**10:27 am**
☽ ⚹ ♆	4:20 pm	**1:20 pm**
☽ ∟ ♅	6:20 pm	**3:20 pm**
☽ □ ♀	7:24 pm	**4:24 pm**
☽ □ ⚹	7:42 pm	**4:42 pm**
☽ □ ⚷	9:43 pm	**6:43 pm**
♀ ☌ ⚹		**10:03 pm**

9 THURSDAY
3rd ♈

♀ ☌ ⚹	1:03 am	
☽ △ ♇	3:13 am	**12:13 am**
☽ ⚹ ♄	3:52 am	**12:52 am**
☽ ⊡ ♀	5:40 am	**2:40 am**
☿ ∟ ♃	6:58 am	**3:58 am**
☽ △ ☉	12:17 pm	**9:17 am**
☽ ∟ ⚷	1:41 pm	**10:41 am**
☽ △ ♂	1:56 pm	**10:56 am**
♀ ☍ ♃	5:41 pm	**2:41 pm**
☽ △ ☿	9:54 pm	**6:54 pm**
☽ △ ⚷	11:50 pm	**8:50 pm**
☽ ⚹ ♅	11:53 pm	**8:53 pm** ☽ v/c

Eastern Standard Time in medium type
Pacific Standard Time in bold type

2001 AUGUST 2001

10 FRIDAY

☽	🖳	♇	8:42 am	**5:42**	**am**
♀	☍	⚸	8:55 am	**5:55**	**am**
☽	⊥	♄	9:33 am	**6:33**	**am**
☿	△	⚷	9:46 am	**6:46**	**am**
☿	☍	♅	9:57 am	**6:57**	**am**
☽	⚼	♀	11:27 am	**8:27**	**am**
☉	△	♂	4:47 pm	**1:47**	**pm**
☽	⚺	⚹	7:41 pm	**4:41**	**pm**
☽	🖳	♂	7:52 pm	**4:52**	**pm**
☽	✶	♃		**10:17**	**pm**

☽ enters ♉ 1:23 pm **10:23 am**

3rd ♈

11 SATURDAY

☽	✶	♃	1:17 am		
☽	□	♆	3:00 am	**12:00**	**am**
☿	🖳	♃	4:37 am	**1:37**	**am**
☽	🖳	⚷	4:51 am	**1:51**	**am**
☽	△	♃	7:48 am	**4:48**	**am**
♅	✶	⚷	8:22 am	**5:22**	**am**
☽	✶	⚸	9:03 am	**6:03**	**am**
☽	✶	♀	12:02 pm	**9:02**	**am**
☽	⚼	♇	1:31 pm	**10:31**	**am**
☿	⊥	⚸	1:51 pm	**10:51**	**am**
☽	⚺	♄	2:32 pm	**11:32**	**am**
☽	⚼	♂		**10:03**	**pm**
☽	□	☉		**11:53**	**pm**

4th Quarter **11:53 pm**

3rd ♉

12 SUNDAY

☽	⚼	♂	1:03 am			
☽	□	☉	2:53 am			
♀	⚼	♇	4:05 am	**1:05**	**am**	
☽	⊥	♃	6:07 am	**3:07**	**am**	
☽	□	♅	9:03 am	**6:03**	**am**	
☽	⚼	⚷	9:05 am	**6:05**	**am**	
☽	🖳	♃	11:48 am	**8:48**	**am**	
☽	⊥	⚸	2:28 pm	**11:28**	**am**	
♀	⚺	♄	4:58 pm	**1:58**	**pm**	
☽	□	☿	5:32 pm	**2:32**	**pm**	☽ v/c
☽	⊥	♀	6:51 pm	**3:51**	**pm**	
☽	☍	♀	8:48 pm	**5:48**	**pm**	

4th Quarter 2:53 am
☽ enters ♊ 9:59 pm **6:59 pm**

3rd ♉

AUGUST

S	M	T	W	T	F	S
			1	2	3	4
5	6	7	8	9	10	11
12	13	14	15	16	17	18
19	20	21	22	23	24	25
26	27	28	29	30	31	

Eastern Standard Time in medium type
Pacific Standard Time in bold type

AUGUST 2001

13 MONDAY
☽	☌	♆	5:12 am	**2:12 am**	
☽	⚺	♃	10:00 am	**7:00 am**	
☽	△	♆	10:40 am	**7:40 am**	
☿	⚻	♀	2:36 pm	**11:36 am**	
☽	⚻	♄	2:54 pm	**11:54 am**	
☿	□	♀	5:43 pm	**2:43 pm**	
☽	⚺	⚹	6:49 pm	**3:49 pm**	
♀	⚼	♀	7:58 pm	**4:58 pm**	
☽	☍	♇	8:36 pm	**5:36 pm**	
☽	☌	♄	9:53 pm	**6:53 pm**	
☽	⚺	♀		**9:27 pm**	

☿ enters ♍

4th ♊
9:04 pm

14 TUESDAY
☽	⚺	♀	12:27 am		
☉	⚻	♃	8:14 am	**5:14 am**	
☽	☍	♂	8:38 am	**5:38 am**	
☽	⚼	♆	1:07 pm	**10:07 am**	
☽	⚹	☉	1:11 pm	**10:11 am**	
☽	△	♅	2:42 pm	**11:42 am**	☽ v/c
☽	☍	⚷	2:49 pm	**11:49 am**	
☽	⚻	♀		**11:26 pm**	
♃	⚻	♆		**11:43 pm**	

☿ enters ♍ 12:04 am
☽ enters ♋

4th ♊
11:55 pm

15 WEDNESDAY
☽	⚻	♀	2:26 am		
♃	⚻	♆	2:43 am		
☽	⚹	☿	7:01 am	**4:01 am**	
☉	☍	♅	10:25 am	**7:25 am**	
☽	⚺	♆	10:44 am	**7:44 am**	
☉	△	⚷	12:32 pm	**9:32 am**	
♇	⚻	⚹	2:18 pm	**11:18 am**	
☽	⚻	♆	2:39 pm	**11:39 am**	
☽	☌	♃	2:50 pm	**11:50 am**	
☽	⚼	♅	4:09 pm	**1:09 pm**	
☽	⚻	☉	4:35 pm	**1:35 pm**	
☽	☍	⚷	6:24 pm	**3:24 pm**	
☽	⚻	♇	11:59 pm	**8:59 pm**	
☽	☌	⚹		**9:22 pm**	
☽	⚺	♄		**10:27 pm**	

☽ enters ♋ 2:55 am

4th ♊

16 THURSDAY
☽	☌	⚹	12:22 am		
☽	⚺	♄	1:27 am		
☽	⚼	♀	3:52 am	**12:52 am**	
☽	☌	♀	8:03 am	**5:03 am**	☽ v/c
☽	⚻	☿	11:37 am	**8:37 am**	
☽	⚻	♆	12:06 pm	**9:06 am**	
☽	⚻	♂	12:23 pm	**9:23 am**	
☿	□	♆	4:06 pm	**1:06 pm**	
☽	⚻	♅	4:48 pm	**1:48 pm**	
☽	⚻	⚷	5:00 pm	**2:00 pm**	
☉	⚼	⚷	6:03 pm	**3:03 pm**	
☽	⚺	☉	7:00 pm	**4:00 pm**	
☽	⚼	♇		**9:29 pm**	
☽	⚻	♄		**11:02 pm**	

♀ enters ♐ 5:39 pm **2:39 pm**

4th ♋

Eastern Standard Time in medium type
Pacific Standard Time in bold type

2001 AUGUST 2001

17 FRIDAY

☽ ⚲ ♇	12:29 am			
☽ ⊥ ♄	2:02 am			
☽ △ ♀	4:33 am	**1:33 am**		
♄ ⊻ ⚷	9:13 am	**6:13 am**		
☽ ⚹ ⚹	12:45 pm	**9:45 am**		
☽ ⚲ ♂	1:08 pm	**10:08 am**		
☽ ⊻ ☿	3:09 pm	**12:09 pm**		
☽ ☍ ♆	3:26 pm	**12:26 pm**		
☽ ⊻ ♃	4:19 pm	**1:19 pm**		
☽ ⚲ ⚷	5:04 pm	**2:04 pm**		
☿ ⊼ ♆	5:33 pm	**2:33 pm**		
☽ ⊼ ⚴	6:53 pm	**3:53 pm**		
☽ △ ♇		**9:24 pm**		
☿ ⚹ ♃		**10:57 pm**		
☽ ⚹ ♄		**11:03 pm**		
☽ ⊻ ⚷		**11:36 pm**		

☽ enters ♌ 4:25 am **1:25 am**

4th ♋

18 SATURDAY

☽ △ ♇	12:24 am			
☿ ⚹ ♃	1:57 am			
☽ ⚹ ♄	2:03 am			
☽ ⊻ ⚷	2:36 am			
☽ ⊻ ♀	12:10 pm	**9:10 am**		
☽ △ ♂	1:26 pm	**10:26 am**		
☽ ⊥ ♃	4:18 pm	**1:18 pm**		
☽ ☍ ♅	4:28 pm	**1:28 pm**		
☽ △ ⚴	4:44 pm	**1:44 pm**		
☽ ⚲ ⚴	6:28 pm	**3:28 pm**		
☿ △ ⚴	9:48 pm	**6:48 pm**		
☽ ☌ ☉	9:55 pm	**6:55 pm**	☽ v/c	
♀ ⊥ ⚷		**9:55 pm**		
♃ ⚲ ♅		**11:39 pm**		

New Moon 9:55 pm **6:55 pm**

4th ♌

19 SUNDAY

♀ ⊥ ⚷	12:55 am			
♃ ⚲ ♅	2:39 am			
☽ ⊥ ⚹	3:04 am	**12:04 am**		
☽ □ ♀	4:34 am	**1:34 am**		
♀ ⊼ ♂	11:15 am	**8:15 am**		
☽ □ ⚷	12:55 pm	**9:55 am**		
☽ ⊥ ♀	1:41 pm	**10:41 am**		
☽ ⊼ ♆	2:37 pm	**11:37 am**		
☽ ⚹ ♃	4:09 pm	**1:09 pm**		
☽ △ ⚴	5:56 pm	**2:56 pm**		
☽ ☌ ☿	8:39 pm	**5:39 pm**		
☽ □ ♇	11:35 pm	**8:35 pm**		
☽ □ ♄		**10:26 pm**		

☽ enters ♍ 3:53 am **12:53 am**

1st ♌

		AUGUST				
S	M	T	W	T	F	S
			1	2	3	4
5	6	7	8	9	10	11
12	13	14	15	16	17	18
19	20	21	22	23	24	25
26	27	28	29	30	31	

Eastern Standard Time in medium type
Pacific Standard Time in bold type

2001 AUGUST 2001

20 MONDAY
1st ♍

☽	□	♄	1:26 am		
☽	⚹	⚷	3:31 am	**12:31**	**am**
☽	□	♂	1:48 pm	**10:48**	**am**
☽	⚻	♆	2:15 pm	**11:15**	**am**
☽	⚹	♀	3:21 pm	**12:21**	**pm** ☽ v/c
☽	⚼	♅	3:34 pm	**12:34**	**pm**
☽	□	⚸	3:56 pm	**12:56**	**pm**
♀	⚼	♅	6:08 pm	**3:08**	**pm**
☿	□	♇	10:23 pm	**7:23**	**pm**
♀	⚼	⚸	10:52 pm	**7:52**	**pm**
☽	⚺	☉		**9:29**	**pm**

21 TUESDAY
1st ♍

☽ enters ♎ 3:19 am **12:19 am**

☽	⚺	☉	12:29 am		
☽	⚹	♀	4:38 am	**1:38**	**am**
♂	⚻	♆	6:41 am	**3:41**	**am**
☽	△	⚷	1:28 pm	**10:28**	**am**
☽	△	♆	2:16 pm	**11:16**	**am**
☽	⚻	♅	3:36 pm	**12:36**	**pm**
☿	□	♄	4:10 pm	**1:10**	**pm**
☽	□	♃	4:32 pm	**1:32**	**pm**
☽	□	⚴	5:39 pm	**2:39**	**pm**
♀	⚻	⚷	7:47 pm	**4:47**	**pm**
☽	⚹	♇	11:39 pm	**8:39**	**pm**
☽	△	♄		**10:47**	**pm**
☽	⚻	☉		**11:30**	**pm**

22 WEDNESDAY
1st ♎

☉ enters ♍ 8:27 pm **5:27 pm**

☽	△	♄	1:47 am		
☽	⚻	☉	2:30 am		
☽	⚺	☿	3:00 am	**12:00**	**am**
☽	⚻	♀	5:23 am	**2:23**	**am**
☽	□	⚷	5:37 am	**2:37**	**am**
☽	⚻	⚷	2:37 pm	**11:37**	**am**
☽	⚹	♂	3:53 pm	**12:53**	**pm**
☽	△	♅	4:16 pm	**1:16**	**pm**
☽	⚹	⚸	4:46 pm	**1:46**	**pm**
☽	□	♀	8:34 pm	**5:34**	**pm** ☽ v/c
☽	⚻	♇		**9:39**	**pm**
☽	⚻	♄		**11:58**	**pm**

SUN ENTERS VIRGO

23 THURSDAY
1st ♎

☽ enters ♏ 4:50 am **1:50 am**
♇ D 11:06 am **8:06 am**

☽	⚻	♇	12:39 am		
☽	⚻	♄	2:58 am		
♂	⚹	♅	4:59 am	**1:59**	**am**
☽	⚹	☉	5:27 am	**2:27**	**am**
♆	△	⚷	6:51 am	**3:51**	**am**
☽	⚺	♀	6:57 am	**3:57**	**am**
☽	⚻	☿	7:33 am	**4:33**	**am**
☿	⚹	⚷	10:59 am	**7:59**	**am**
☽	□	♆	4:26 pm	**1:26**	**pm**
☽	⚼	⚷	4:38 pm	**1:38**	**pm**
☽	⚻	♂	6:13 pm	**3:13**	**pm**
☽	⚻	⚸	6:22 pm	**3:22**	**pm**
☽	△	♃	7:36 pm	**4:36**	**pm**
☽	⚹	⚴	8:01 pm	**5:01**	**pm**
♂	☌	⚸	11:47 pm	**8:47**	**pm**
☽	⚺	♇		**11:33**	**pm**

Eastern Standard Time in medium type
Pacific Standard Time in bold type

2001 AUGUST 2001

24 FRIDAY
1st ♏

☽	⊻	♇	2:33 am		
☽	⊼	♄	5:04 am	2:04	am
☉	□	♀	8:53 am	5:53	am
☽	△	♅	11:07 am	8:07	am
☽	✶	☿	1:24 pm	10:24	am
☽	□	♆	8:17 pm	5:17	pm
☽	⊻	⚷	8:58 pm	5:58	pm
♀	⚏	♇	9:26 pm	6:26	pm
☽	⊻	♂	9:38 pm	6:38	pm
☽	⚏	♃	10:37 pm	7:37	pm
☽	⊥	⚴	10:38 pm	7:38	pm
♃	☍	⚴	11:54 pm	8:54	pm

25 SATURDAY
1st ♏

☽	△	♀	6:16 am	3:16 am	☽ v/c
☽	☌	♀	1:08 pm	10:08 am	
☽	□	☉	2:55 pm	11:55 am	
☽	⚏	♆	3:32 pm	12:32 pm	
☽	✶	♆	10:23 pm	7:23 pm	
☽	☍	⚷	11:47 pm	8:47 pm	
☽	⊻	⚴		11:17 pm	
☽	⊼	♃		11:41 pm	

☽ enters ♐ 9:59 am **6:59 am**
2nd Quarter 2:55 pm **11:55 am**

26 SUNDAY
2nd ♐

☽	⊻	⚴	2:17 am		
☽	⊼	♃	2:41 am		
♀	⊥	♄	4:34 am	1:34	am
☉	⊥	♅	8:37 am	5:37	am
☽	☌	♇	9:24 am	6:24	am
☿	⚏	♆	10:08 am	7:08	am
☽	☍	♄	12:21 pm	9:21	am
☽	⚏	♀	1:07 pm	10:07	am
☽	⊼	♅	9:03 pm	6:03	pm
☿	⊼	♅	9:05 pm	6:05	pm
☽	⊥	♆		11:50	pm

⚷ D 4:19 am **1:19 am**
♀ enters ♌ 11:12 pm **8:12 pm**

AUGUST

S	M	T	W	T	F	S
			1	2	3	4
5	6	7	8	9	10	11
12	13	14	15	16	17	18
19	20	21	22	23	24	25
26	27	28	29	30	31	

Eastern Standard Time in medium type
Pacific Standard Time in bold type

AUGUST 2001

27 MONDAY
2nd ♐

☽ ⊥ ♆	2:50 am			
☿ □ ⚷	3:56 am	12:56 am		
☽ ⋆ ♅	4:15 am	1:15 am		
☽ ☌ ⚷	5:08 am	2:08 am		
☽ □ ☿	5:19 am	2:19 am		
☽ ☌ ♂	7:50 am	4:50 am	☽ v/c	
☽ ⊼ ♀	9:09 pm	6:09 pm		
☽ ⋁ ♀	11:25 pm	8:25 pm		

☽ enters ♑ 7:02 pm **4:02 pm**
♃ D 7:48 pm **4:48 pm**

28 TUESDAY
2nd ♑

☽ △ ☉	5:12 am	2:12 am	
☿ □ ♂	7:42 am	4:42 am	
☽ ⋁ ♆	8:04 am	5:04 am	
☽ ⊥ ♅	9:29 am	6:29 am	
☽ ⊼ ⚷	10:50 am	7:50 am	
☽ ☌ ♃	12:16 pm	9:16 am	
☽ ☍ ♃	1:33 pm	10:33 am	
☽ ⋁ ♇	7:48 pm	4:48 pm	
☽ ⊼ ♄	11:08 pm	8:08 pm	
♀ △ ♀		10:17 pm	

29 WEDNESDAY
2nd ♑

♀ △ ♀	1:17 am			
☽ ⊥ ♀	5:43 am	2:43 am		
☽ ☍ ⚹	10:44 am	7:44 am		
☽ ⊡ ☉	1:39 pm	10:39 am		
☽ ⋁ ♅	3:17 pm	12:17 pm		
☽ ⋁ ⚷	4:26 pm	1:26 pm		
☉ ⊼ ♆	4:36 pm	1:36 pm		
☽ ⊡ ⚷	5:22 pm	2:22 pm		
☽ ⋁ ♂	9:28 pm	6:28 pm		
☽ △ ☿		10:28 pm	☽ v/c	
☽ ⊥ ♇		10:51 pm		

30 THURSDAY
2nd ♑

☽ △ ☿	1:28 am		☽ v/c	
☽ ⊥ ♇	1:51 am			
☽ ⊡ ♄	5:21 am	2:21 am		
☽ ⋆ ♀	12:29 pm	9:29 am		
☽ ☍ ♀	3:39 pm	12:39 pm		
☽ ☌ ♆	8:05 pm	5:05 pm		
☽ ⊼ ☉	10:34 pm	7:34 pm		
☽ ⊥ ⚷	10:42 pm	7:42 pm		
☽ △ ⚷		9:14 pm		
☽ ⋁ ♃		9:33 pm		
☽ ⊼ ♃		11:40 pm		

☽ enters ♒ 6:47 am **3:47 am**

Eastern Standard Time in medium type
Pacific Standard Time in bold type

2001   **AUGUST/SEPTEMBER**   **2001**

31 FRIDAY

☽ △ ⚷	12:14 am			
☽ ⊻ ♀	12:33 am			
☽ ⊼ ♃	2:40 am			
☽ ∟ ♂	4:58 am	**1:58 am**		
☽ ⚹ ♇	8:11 am	**5:11 am**		
☽ △ ♄	11:49 am	**8:49 am**		
☽ ⚏ ☿	12:12 pm	**9:12 am**		
♀ ⊼ ⚷	6:42 am	**3:42 pm**		
☉ △ ♀	11:21 pm	**8:21 pm**		
☉ □ ⚷		**9:36 pm**		
☽ ⊼ ⚴		**11:08 pm**		

☿ enters ♎   7:37 pm   **4:37 pm**

2nd ♒

VIRGO ♍
Duality: Feminine
Quality: Mutable
Element: Earth
House: 6th
Planetary Ruler: Mercury
Rules: Intestines, Nervous System
Keyword: Service
Keynote: I analyze.

---

1 SATURDAY

☉ □ ⚷	12:36 am			
☽ ⊼ ⚴	2:08 am			
☽ ☌ ♅	3:44 am	**12:44 am**		
☽ ⚹ ⚵	5:07 am	**2:07 am**		
☽ ∟ ♀	7:00 am	**4:00 am**		
☽ ⚏ ♃	9:30 am	**6:30 am**		
♀ ☍ ♆	10:55 am	**7:55 am**		
☽ ⚹ ♂	12:36 pm	**9:36 am**	☽ v/c	
☽ ⊼ ☿	10:55 pm	**7:55 pm**		
☽ □ ♀		**11:28 pm**		

☽ enters ♓   7:32 pm   **4:32 pm**

2nd ♒

---

2 SUNDAY

☽ □ ♀	2:28 am			
☽ ⊻ ♆	8:44 am	**5:44 am**		
☽ ⚏ ⚴	9:55 am	**6:55 am**		
☉ ⚹ ♃	10:16 am	**7:16 am**		
☽ ⊼ ♀	11:13 am	**8:13 am**		
♅ ⊼ ⚴	11:59 am	**8:59 am**		
☽ ⚹ ♀	1:26 pm	**10:26 am**		
☽ □ ⚷	2:09 pm	**11:09 am**		
♀ ⚏ ⚵	2:11 pm	**11:11 am**		
☽ △ ♃	4:16 pm	**1:16 pm**		
☽ ☍ ☉	4:43 pm	**1:43 pm**		
☽ □ ♇	8:56 pm	**5:56 pm**		
☽ □ ♄		**9:45 pm**		

Full Moon   4:43 pm   **1:43 pm**

2nd ♓

Eastern Standard Time in medium type
Pacific Standard Time in bold type

2001 SEPTEMBER 2001

3 MONDAY

3rd ♓

☽	□	♄	12:45 am	
☿	⚹	♀	9:23 am	**6:23 am**
♀	⚻	♃	9:54 am	**6:54 am**
☽	⚼	♆	2:55 pm	**11:55 am**
☽	⚺	♅	4:09 pm	**1:09 pm**
☽	△	⚹	5:32 pm	**2:32 pm**
☽	□	⚷	5:46 pm	**2:46 pm**
☽	⚌	♀	8:48 pm	**5:48 pm**
♀	⚹	⚸	9:54 pm	**6:54 pm**
⚷	⚻	⚹	11:05 pm	**8:05 pm**

LABOR DAY

4 TUESDAY

3rd ♓

☽	□	♂	3:37 am	**12:37 am**	☽ v/c
☽	△	♀	4:04 pm	**1:04 pm**	
☽	☍	☿	7:26 pm	**4:26 pm**	
♀	⚺	♃	8:20 pm	**5:20 pm**	
☽	⚹	♆	8:53 pm	**5:53 pm**	
☉	□	♇	8:54 pm	**5:54 pm**	
☽	⚼	♅	10:04 pm	**7:04 pm**	
☽	□	♃		**10:50 pm**	

☽ enters ♈ 7:58 am **4:58 am**

5 WEDNESDAY

3rd ♈

☽	□	♃	1:50 am	
☽	⚹	⚸	3:23 am	**12:23 am**
☽	□	♃	5:13 am	**2:13 am**
☽	△	♀	6:04 am	**3:04 am**
☿	△	♆	7:51 am	**4:51 am**
☽	△	♇	9:02 am	**6:02 am**
☽	⚻	☉	10:05 am	**7:05 am**
☽	⚹	♄	12:57 pm	**9:57 am**
☿	⚌	♅	5:54 pm	**2:54 pm**
☽	⚌	♀	10:28 pm	**7:28 pm**

6 THURSDAY

3rd ♈

☽	⚹	♅	3:40 am	**12:40 am**	
☽	△	⚷	5:29 am	**2:29 am**	
☽	□	⚹	7:50 am	**4:50 am**	
☽	⚼	⚸	9:30 am	**6:30 am**	
♀	△	♇	12:05 pm	**9:05 am**	
☽	⚌	♇	2:36 pm	**11:36 am**	
☽	△	♂	5:31 pm	**2:31 pm**	☽ v/c
☽	⚌	☉	6:08 pm	**3:08 pm**	
☽	⚼	♄	6:32 pm	**3:32 pm**	
☉	□	♄	11:11 pm	**8:11 pm**	

☽ enters ♉ 7:18 pm **4:18 pm**

Eastern Standard Time in medium type
Pacific Standard Time in bold type

2001 SEPTEMBER 2001

7 FRIDAY

3rd ♉

☽	⊼	♀	4:26 am	**1:26 am**	
☿	□	♃	6:04 am	**3:04 am**	
☽	□	♆	7:46 am	**4:46 am**	
☽	⊡	⚷	10:46 am	**7:46 am**	
☽	△	♃	12:56 pm	**9:56 am**	
☽	⊼	☿	1:43 pm	**10:43 am**	
☽	⚹	⚵	3:08 pm	**12:08 pm**	
☽	✶	♃	4:42 pm	**1:42 pm**	
☽	⊼	♇	7:42 pm	**4:42 pm**	
☽	□	♀	11:02 pm	**8:02 pm**	
☽	⚹	♄	11:37 pm	**8:37 pm**	
☽	⊡	♂	11:46 pm	**8:46 pm**	
☽	△	☉		**10:36 pm**	

8 SATURDAY

3rd ♉

☽	△	☉	1:36 am		
☿	△	⚵	5:10 am	**2:10 am**	
♀	✶	♄	5:14 am	**2:14 am**	
♀	⊡	♂	11:33 am	**8:33 am**	
☽	□	♅	1:30 pm	**10:30 am**	☽ v/c
☽	⊼	⚷	3:30 pm	**12:30 pm**	
☽	⊡	♃	5:43 pm	**2:43 pm**	
☽	✶	⚸	8:06 pm	**5:06 pm**	
☿	□	♃	9:30 pm	**6:30 pm**	
☽	⊡	☿	9:37 pm	**6:37 pm**	
☽	⅃	♃	9:37 pm	**6:37 pm**	
⚸	⅃	⚵	10:25 pm	**7:25 pm**	

♂ enters ♑ 12:51 pm **9:51 am**

9 SUNDAY

3rd ♉

☽	⊼	♂	5:20 am	**2:20 am**	
☽	☍	♀	2:36 pm	**11:36 am**	
☽	△	♆	4:32 pm	**1:32 pm**	
☽	⊼	♃	9:50 pm	**6:50 pm**	
☿	✶	♇	11:40 pm	**8:40 pm**	
☽	☌	⚵		**9:27 pm**	
☽	⅃	⚸		**10:07 pm**	
☽	⚹	♃		**10:47 pm**	

☽ enters ♊ 4:41 am **1:41 am**

SEPTEMBER

S	M	T	W	T	F	S
						1
2	3	4	5	6	7	8
9	10	11	12	13	14	15
16	17	18	19	20	21	22
23	24	25	26	27	28	29
30						

Eastern Standard Time in medium type
Pacific Standard Time in bold type

2001 SEPTEMBER 2001

10 MONDAY

3rd ♊

☽	☌	⚷	12:27 am		
☽	⊥	※	1:07 am		
☽	⊻	♃	1:47 am		
☽	☍	♇	4:00 am	**1:00 am**	
☽	△	☿	4:28 am	**1:28 am**	
☽	☌	♄	7:50 am	**4:50 am**	
☽	✶	♀	12:46 pm	**9:46 am**	
☽	□	☉	1:59 pm	**10:59 am**	
☽	⚻	♆	7:48 pm	**4:48 pm**	
☽	△	♅	8:42 pm	**5:42 pm**	☽ v/c
☽	☍	⚷	10:49 pm	**7:49 pm**	

4th Quarter   1:59 pm **10:59 am**

11 TUESDAY

4th ♊

☽	⊻	※	5:13 am	**2:13 am**
☽	☍	♂	1:56 pm	**10:56 am**
☿	△	♄	5:06 pm	**2:06 pm**
☽	⊥	♀	6:01 pm	**3:01 pm**
☽	⊼	♀	9:33 pm	**6:33 pm**
☽	⊼	♆	10:13 pm	**7:13 pm**
☽	⚻	♅	11:03 pm	**8:03 pm**

☽ enters ♋ 11:09 am **8:09 am**

12 WEDNESDAY

4th ♋

☽	☍	♃	3:35 am	**12:35 am**	
☽	⊻	⚷	6:24 am	**3:24 am**	
☽	☌	♃	7:32 am	**4:32 am**	
☽	⊼	♇	9:06 am	**6:06 am**	
☽	⊻	♄	12:45 pm	**9:45 am**	
☽	□	☿	2:32 pm	**11:32 am**	
☽	⊻	♀	10:09 pm	**7:09 pm**	
☽	✶	☉	10:16 pm	**7:16 pm**	☽ v/c
☽	⚻	♀	11:41 pm	**8:41 pm**	
☽	⊼	♅		**9:35 pm**	
☽	⊼	⚷		**11:47 pm**	

13 THURSDAY

4th ♋

☽	⊼	♅	12:35 am		
☽	⊼	⚷	2:47 am		
☉	⊻	♀	4:57 am	**1:57 am**	
♆	✶	♀	5:23 am	**2:23 am**	
♇	⚻	※	5:27 am	**2:27 am**	
☽	⊥	⚷	8:03 am	**5:03 am**	
☽	⚻	♇	10:23 am	**7:23 am**	
☽	☌	※	10:34 am	**7:34 am**	
☽	⊥	♄	1:57 pm	**10:57 am**	
☽	⊼	♂	6:48 pm	**3:48 pm**	
☉	⚻	♆	8:14 pm	**5:14 pm**	
☽	☍	♆		**9:36 pm**	
☽	⊥	☉		**9:55 pm**	
☽	△	♀		**9:59 pm**	
♀	☍	♅		**11:06 pm**	

☽ enters ♌ 2:16 pm **11:16 pm**

Eastern Standard Time in medium type
Pacific Standard Time in bold type

2001 SEPTEMBER 2001

14 FRIDAY
4th ♌

☽	☍	♆	12:36 am	
☽	☐	☉	12:55 am	
☽	△	♀	12:59 am	
♀	☍	♅	2:06 am	
☽	⚼	⚷	3:35 am	**12:35 am**
☽	⚻	♃	6:01 am	**3:01 am**
☉	⚻	♅	7:05 am	**4:05 am**
☽	⚹	⚵	8:56 am	**5:56 am**
☽	⚺	♃	9:55 am	**6:55 am**
☽	△	♇	10:57 am	**7:57 am**
☽	⚹	♄	2:27 pm	**11:27 am**
☽	⚼	♂	8:03 pm	**5:03 pm**
☽	⚹	☿	8:12 pm	**5:12 pm**
☽	☍	♅		**10:29 pm**
☽	⚺	☉		**11:48 pm**

15 SATURDAY
4th ♌

☽ enters ♍ 2:39 pm **11:39 am**

☽	☍	♅	1:29 am		
☽	⚺	☉	2:48 am		
☽	☌	♀	3:35 am	**12:35 am**	☽ v/c
☽	△	⚷	3:47 am	**12:47 am**	
♀	△	⚷	6:04 am	**3:04 am**	
☽	⚼	♃	6:17 am	**3:17 am**	
☽	☐	♃	10:10 am	**7:10 am**	
☽	⚺	⚵	12:46 pm	**9:46 am**	
☉	☐	⚷	6:24 pm	**3:24 pm**	
☽	△	♂	8:48 pm	**5:48 pm**	
☽	☐	☿	9:55 pm	**6:55 pm**	
☽	⚻	♆		**9:33 pm**	
☽	☐	♀		**10:53 pm**	

16 SUNDAY
4th ♍

☽	⚻	♆	12:33 am	
☽	☐	♀	1:53 am	
☽	△	♃	6:11 am	**3:11 am**
☽	☐	⚵	9:10 am	**6:10 am**
☽	⚹	♃	10:05 am	**7:05 am**
☽	☐	♇	10:42 am	**7:42 am**
☽	☐	⚵	1:15 pm	**10:15 am**
☽	☐	♄	2:08 pm	**11:08 am**
♀	⚼	♃	4:00 pm	**1:00 pm**
☽	⚺	☿	11:19 pm	**8:19 pm**
☽	⚼	♆		**9:10 pm**
☽	⚻	♅		**9:48 pm**

SEPTEMBER

S	M	T	W	T	F	S
						1
2	3	4	5	6	7	8
9	10	11	12	13	14	15
16	17	18	19	20	21	22
23	24	25	26	27	28	29
30						

Eastern Standard Time in medium type
Pacific Standard Time in bold type

2001   **SEPTEMBER**   **2001**

17 MONDAY

4th ♍

☽	⚻	♆	12:10 am			
☽	⚼	♅	12:48 am			
☽	□	⚴	3:16 am	**12:16 am**		
☽	☌	☉	5:27 am	**2:27 am**	☽ v/c	
☽	⚺	♀	7:06 am	**4:06 am**		
☽	✶	⚷	1:43 pm	**10:43 am**		
♄	⊥	⚷	5:11 pm	**2:11 pm**		
☿	△	♅	8:51 pm	**5:51 pm**		
☽	□	♂	9:58 pm	**6:58 pm**		
☽	△	♆	11:54 pm	**8:54 pm**		
☽	⚻	♅		**9:31 pm**		
☽	✶	♀		**11:13 pm**		

New Moon	5:27 am	**2:27 am**
☽ enters ♎	2:00 pm	**11:00 pm**
⚷ enters ♌	10:19 pm	**7:19 pm**

18 TUESDAY

1st ♎

☽	⚻	♅	12:31 am		
☽	✶	♀	2:13 am		
☽	□	⚴	6:00 am	**3:00 am**	
☽	⊥	♀	9:03 am	**6:03 am**	
☽	△	⚷	9:08 am	**6:08 am**	
☽	□	♃	10:02 am	**7:02 am**	
☽	✶	♇	10:17 am	**7:17 am**	
☽	△	♄	1:48 pm	**10:48 am**	
♀	⊥	♃	10:36 pm	**7:36 pm**	
☽	△	♅		**9:38 pm**	
☽	☌	☿		**11:40 pm**	
☽	⊥	♀		**11:54 pm**	

ROSH HASHANAH

19 WEDNESDAY

1st ♎

☽	△	♅	12:38 am		
☽	☌	☿	2:40 am		
☽	⊥	♀	2:54 am		
☽	✶	⚴	3:24 am	**12:24 am**	
☿	⊥	♀	7:58 am	**4:58 am**	
☽	⚺	☉	9:00 am	**6:00 am**	
☽	⚻	⚷	9:44 am	**6:44 am**	
☽	⊥	♇	10:43 am	**7:43 am**	
☽	✶	♀	11:38 am	**8:38 am**	☽ v/c
☽	⚻	♄	2:19 pm	**11:19 am**	
☿	✶	⚴	2:34 pm	**11:34 am**	
☽	□	⚷	3:52 pm	**12:52 pm**	
♃	⚼	♇	6:09 pm	**3:09 pm**	
♂	⚺	♆		**9:12 pm**	
☽	□	♆		**9:48 pm**	
☽	✶	♂		**9:50 pm**	

☽ enters ♍	2:27 pm	**11:27 pm**

20 THURSDAY

1st ♏

♂	⚺	♆	12:12 am		
☽	□	♆	12:48 am		
☽	✶	♂	12:50 am		
☽	⚺	♀	4:20 am	**1:20 am**	
☽	⊥	⚴	4:23 am	**1:23 am**	
☽	✶	⚷	7:44 am	**4:44 am**	
☽	⚼	⚷	11:06 am	**8:06 am**	
☽	⚺	♇	11:54 am	**8:54 am**	
☽	⊥	☉	11:59 am	**8:59 am**	
☽	△	♃	12:03 pm	**9:03 am**	
♂	⊥	♅	2:33 pm	**11:33 am**	
☽	⚼	♄	3:39 pm	**12:39 pm**	

♀ enters ♏	9:09 pm	**6:09 pm**

Eastern Standard Time in medium type
Pacific Standard Time in bold type

2001   **SEPTEMBER**   **2001**

21 FRIDAY

1st ♏

☽ □ ♅	3:04 am	**12:04 am**
☽ ⊥ ♂	3:38 am	**12:38 am**
☽ ⩗ ⚷	6:17 am	**3:17 am**
☽ ⩗ ☿	8:55 am	**5:55 am**
☽ ⊥ ⚴	9:57 am	**6:57 am**
☽ ⊡ ♃	2:26 pm	**11:26 am**
☽ ✶ ☉	4:09 pm	**1:09 pm** ☽ v/c
☽ □ ♀	8:08 pm	**5:08 pm**
☽ △ ✸	9:31 pm	**6:31 pm**

☽ enters ♐   6:02 pm   **3:02 pm**

22 SATURDAY

1st ♐

☽ ✶ ♆	5:10 am	**2:10 am**
☽ ⩗ ♂	7:38 am	**4:38 am**
☽ ☌ ♀	10:15 am	**7:15 am**
☽ ⩗ ⚴	1:16 pm	**10:16 am**
☽ ⊥ ☿	1:40 pm	**10:40 am**
☽ ☍ ✸	4:50 pm	**1:50 pm**
☽ ☌ ♇	5:18 pm	**2:18 pm**
☽ ⊼ ♃	5:54 pm	**2:54 pm**
♀ ⩗ ✸	8:23 pm	**5:23 pm**
☽ ☍ ♄	9:19 pm	**6:19 pm**
☽ ⊡ ✸		**11:05 pm**

☉ enters ♎   6:04 pm   **3:04 pm**

SUN ENTERS LIBRA
MABON (FALL EQUINOX) 6:04 PM EST/3:04 PM PST

23 SUNDAY

1st ♐

☽ ⊡ ✸	2:05 am	
☽ ⊥ ♆	8:56 am	**5:56 am**
☽ ✶ ♅	9:31 am	**6:31 am**
☽ ☌ ⚷	1:17 pm	**10:17 am**
☽ ✶ ☿	7:32 pm	**4:32 pm** ☽ v/c

☽ enters ♑   **10:48 pm**

SEPTEMBER

S	M	T	W	T	F	S
						1
2	3	4	5	6	7	8
9	10	11	12	13	14	15
16	17	18	19	20	21	22
23	24	25	26	27	28	29
30						

Eastern Standard Time in medium type
Pacific Standard Time in bold type

2001 **SEPTEMBER** **2001**

24 MONDAY

☽ □ ☉	4:31 am	**1:31 am**
☽ ⊼ ⚹	7:49 am	**4:49 am**
☽ △ ♀	10:10 am	**7:10 am**
☽ ⊻ ♆	1:42 pm	**10:42 am**
☽ ⊔ ♅	2:16 pm	**11:16 am**
☽ ☌ ♂	7:15 pm	**4:15 pm**
☽ ⊻ ♀	8:40 pm	**5:40 pm**
☽ ☌ ♃	11:08 pm	**8:08 pm**
☽ ⊼ ⚷		**11:45 pm**
☽ ⊻ ♇		**11:49 pm**

1st ♐

☽ enters ♑ 1:48 am
2nd Quarter 4:31 am **1:31 am**

25 TUESDAY

☽ ⊼ ⚷	2:45 am	
☽ ⊻ ♇	2:49 am	
☽ ☍ ♃	3:56 am	**12:56 am**
☽ ⊼ ♄	7:03 am	**4:03 am**
☿ ⊡ ⚷	1:13 pm	**10:13 am**
☿ ⊔ ♇	1:32 pm	**10:32 am**
♇ ☍ ⚷	3:31 pm	**12:31 pm**
☽ ⊡ ♀	7:02 pm	**4:02 pm**
☽ ⊻ ♅	7:49 pm	**4:49 pm**
♀ ⊼ ♆	9:32 pm	**6:32 pm**
☽ ⊻ ⚷		**9:09 pm**

2nd ♑

26 WEDNESDAY

☽ ⊻ ⚷	12:09 am	
☽ ⊔ ♀	3:13 am	**12:13 am**
☽ ⊔ ♇	8:45 am	**5:45 am**
☽ ⊡ ⚷	8:52 am	**5:52 am**
☽ □ ☿	9:38 am	**6:38 am** ☽ v/c
☽ ⊡ ♄	1:01 pm	**10:01 am**
☽ △ ☉	9:14 pm	**6:14 pm**
☽ ☍ ⚹	9:50 pm	**6:50 pm**
☽ ☌ ♆		**10:24 pm**

2nd ♑

☽ enters ♒ 1:05 pm **10:05 am**
♄ ℞ 7:04 pm **4:04 pm**

27 THURSDAY

☽ ☌ ♆	1:24 am	
☽ ⊼ ♀	4:39 am	**1:39 am**
♂ ⊻ ♀	5:45 am	**2:45 am**
☽ ⊔ ⚷	6:29 am	**3:29 am**
☽ ⚹ ♀	10:16 am	**7:16 am**
☉ ⚹ ⚹	10:21 am	**7:21 am**
☽ ⊻ ♂	10:23 am	**7:23 am**
☽ ⊻ ♃	12:00 pm	**9:00 am**
☽ ⚹ ♇	3:06 pm	**12:06 pm**
☽ △ ⚷	3:23 pm	**12:23 pm**
☽ ⊼ ♃	4:44 pm	**1:44 pm**
☽ △ ♄	7:21 pm	**4:21 pm**

2nd ♒

YOM KIPPUR

Eastern Standard Time in medium type
Pacific Standard Time in bold type

2001   **SEPTEMBER**   **2001**

28 FRIDAY

☽	⚷	☉	6:22 am	**3:22 am**
☽	☌	♅	8:15 am	**5:15 am**
☽	✶	⚴	1:01 pm	**10:01 am**
☽	⦡	♂	6:26 pm	**3:26 pm**
☽	⦡	⚷	6:51 pm	**3:51 pm**
☉	△	♆	11:11 pm	**8:11 pm**
☽	⚷	♃	11:26 pm	**8:26 pm**
☽	△	☿		**9:27 pm** ☽ v/c

☽ enters ♓   2nd ♒
                   10:50 pm

29 SATURDAY

☽	△	☿	12:27 am	☽ v/c
☉	⚷	♅	4:33 am	**1:33 am**
♂	☌	⚴	5:31 am	**2:31 am**
☽	⊼	✷	1:07 pm	**10:07 am**
☽	⚹	♆	2:09 pm	**11:09 am**
☽	⊼	☉	3:30 pm	**12:30 pm**
☽	☍	♀		**9:25 pm**
☽	⦡	♀		**9:41 pm**
☽	✶	⚴		**10:38 pm**
☽	✶	♂		**11:24 pm**

☽ enters ♓   1:50 am   2nd ♒

30 SUNDAY

☽	☍	♀	12:25 am	
☽	⦡	⚴	12:41 am	
☽	✶	⚷	1:38 am	
☽	✶	♂	2:24 am	
♀	⦡	☿	3:50 am	**12:50 am**
☽	⦡	♇	3:57 am	**12:57 am**
☽	⦡	♆	4:29 am	**1:29 am**
☽	△	♃	6:00 am	**3:00 am**
☽	⚷	☿	7:18 am	**4:18 am**
☽	⦡	♄	8:02 am	**5:02 am** ☽ v/c
♀	△	⚴	1:56 pm	**10:56 am**
♆	☍	✷	2:53 pm	**11:53 am**
☽	⦡	✷	8:18 pm	**5:18 pm**
☽	⚷	✷	8:32 pm	**5:32 pm**
☽	⚺	♅	8:42 pm	**5:42 pm**
☽	⦡	⚷		**10:46 pm**

       2nd ♓

SEPTEMBER

S	M	T	W	T	F	S
						1
2	3	4	5	6	7	8
9	10	11	12	13	14	15
16	17	18	19	20	21	22
23	24	25	26	27	28	29
30						

Eastern Standard Time in medium type
Pacific Standard Time in bold type

2001   **OCTOBER**   **2001**

LIBRA ♎
Duality: Masculine
Quality: Cardinal
Element: Air
House: 7th
Planetary Ruler: Venus
Rules: Kidneys, Lower Back
Keyword: Harmony
Keynote: We are.

1 MONDAY

☽ □ ♇	1:46 am	
♂ ⚺ ♇	9:18 am	**6:18 am**
♀ □ ♇	11:12 am	**8:12 am**
♀ △ ♂	1:03 pm	**10:03 am**
☽ ⚻ ☿	1:30 pm	**10:30 am**
♀ □ ⚹	5:38 pm	**2:38 pm**
♂ ⚻ ⚹	10:37 pm	**7:37 pm**
☽ ✶ ♆		**11:09 pm**
☽ ⚺ ♅		**11:30 pm**

2nd ♓
☽ enters ♈   2:08 pm   **11:08 am**
☿ ℞   2:24 pm   **11:24 am**

2 TUESDAY

☽ ✶ ♆	2:09 am	
☽ ⚺ ♅	2:30 am	
☽ △ ⚹	3:34 am	**12:34 am**
☽ ☍ ☉	8:49 am	**5:49 am**
♀ ✶ ♃	10:49 am	**7:49 am**
☽ △ ♀	2:07 pm	**11:07 am**
☽ □ ♃	2:19 pm	**11:19 am**
☽ △ ♇	3:48 pm	**12:48 pm**
☽ ✶ ⚹	4:29 pm	**1:29 pm**
☽ □ ♂	5:22 pm	**2:22 pm**
☽ □ ♃	6:11 pm	**3:11 pm**
☽ ⚻ ♀	6:56 pm	**3:56 pm**
☿ ⚺ ♀	7:23 pm	**4:23 pm**
☽ ✶ ♄	7:39 pm	**4:39 pm**
♀ □ ♄		**10:54 pm**

2nd ♈
Full Moon   8:49 am   **5:49 am**

SUKKOT BEGINS

3 WEDNESDAY

♀ □ ♄	1:54 am		
♃ ⚺ ♀	7:27 am	**4:27 am**	
☽ ✶ ♅	7:56 am	**4:56 am**	
♂ ☍ ♃	12:09 pm	**9:09 am**	
☽ △ ⚸	1:15 pm	**10:15 am**	
☽ ⚼ ♀	8:13 pm	**5:13 pm**	
☽ ⚼ ♇	9:09 pm	**6:09 pm**	
☽ ⚺ ⚹	9:53 pm	**6:53 pm**	
☽ ☍ ☿	11:44 pm	**8:44 pm**	☽ v/c
☽ ⚺ ♄		**9:52 pm**	

3rd ♈
☽ enters ♉   **10:01 pm**

Eastern Standard Time in medium type
Pacific Standard Time in bold type

2001 OCTOBER 2001

4 THURSDAY — 3rd ♈

☽	⊥	♄	12:52 am		
☽	⚃	♀	3:25 am	**12:25 am**	
☽	□	♆	12:41 pm	**9:41 am**	
♂	⊼	♄	1:21 pm	**10:21 am**	
☽	□	⚹	4:19 pm	**1:19 pm**	
☽	⚃	⚷	6:22 pm	**3:22 pm**	
☽	⊼	☉		**9:10 pm**	
☽	△	⚴		**10:25 pm**	
☽	⊼	♀		**10:53 pm**	
☽	⊼	♇		**11:05 pm**	
☽	⋎	♇		**11:49 pm**	

☽ enters ♉ 1:01 am

5 FRIDAY — 3rd ♉

☽	⊼	☉	12:10 am		
☽	△	⚴	1:25 am		
☽	⊼	♀	1:53 am		
☽	⊼	♇	2:05 am		
☽	⋎	♇	2:49 am		
☽	✶	♃	4:43 am	**1:43 am**	
☽	⋎	♄	5:39 am	**2:39 am**	
☽	△	♂	6:32 am	**3:32 am**	
♇	☌	♀	9:55 am	**6:55 am**	
☽	△	♀	11:19 am	**8:19 am**	
☽	□	♅	5:33 pm	**2:33 pm**	☽ v/c
☉	□	⚴	7:40 pm	**4:40 pm**	
☽	⊼	⚷	11:03 pm	**8:03 pm**	
☉	✶	♇		**10:00 pm**	
☿	⚃	♇		**10:49 pm**	

6 SATURDAY — 3rd ♉

☉	✶	♇	1:00 am		
☿	⚃	♇	1:49 am		
☽	⚃	⚴	6:18 am	**3:18 am**	
☿	⊥	♀	6:51 am	**3:51 am**	
☽	⚃	☉	7:00 am	**4:00 am**	
☽	⊼	☿	7:03 am	**4:03 am**	
☉	✶	♀	7:59 am	**4:59 am**	
☽	⊥	♃	9:18 am	**6:18 am**	
☉	△	♇	10:47 am	**7:47 am**	
☽	⚃	♂	12:21 pm	**9:21 am**	
♀	☍	♇	4:43 pm	**1:43 pm**	
☿	⊥	♇	4:44 pm	**1:44 pm**	
☽	△	♆	9:27 pm	**6:27 pm**	
♇	⋎	⚴		**10:07 pm**	

☽ enters ♊ 10:12 am **7:12 am**

7 SUNDAY — 3rd ♊

♇	⋎	⚴	1:07 am		
☽	✶	♅	3:02 am	**12:02 am**	
☽	⚃	☿	9:35 am	**6:35 am**	
⚷	⚃	♅	9:48 am	**6:48 am**	
☽	☍	♇	10:31 am	**7:31 am**	
☽	⊼	⚴	10:39 am	**7:39 am**	
☽	⊼	♆	11:14 am	**8:14 am**	
☽	☌	♀	11:42 am	**8:42 am**	
☽	△	☉	1:12 pm	**10:12 am**	
☽	⋎	♃	1:20 pm	**10:20 am**	
☽	☌	♄	1:48 pm	**10:48 am**	
☉	□	♃	3:08 pm	**12:08 pm**	
☽	⊼	♂	5:34 pm	**2:34 pm**	
☉	△	♄	8:58 pm	**5:58 pm**	
☽	□	♀		**10:08 pm**	
☽	△	♅		**10:15 pm**	
♀	⊼	♅		**11:25 pm**	
☽	⚃	♆		**10:04 pm**	
♀	☌	♆		**9:28 pm**	

Eastern Standard Time in medium type
Pacific Standard Time in bold type

2001 OCTOBER 2001

8 MONDAY

♀	⊡	♆	12:28 am		
☽	⊡	♆	1:04 am		
☽	□	♀	1:08 am		
☽	△	♅	1:15 am		
♀	⊼	♅	2:25 am		
☽	☍	⚷	6:52 am	3:52 am	
☽	⊾	⚹	7:30 am	4:30 am	
☽	△	☿	11:23 am	8:23 am	☽ v/c
♄	⊼	♆		9:57 pm	

☽ enters ♋ 5:19 pm **2:19 pm**

3rd ♊

SUKKOT ENDS
COLUMBUS DAY (OBSERVED)

9 TUESDAY

♄	⊼	♆	12:57 am		
☽	⊼	♆	4:04 am	1:04 am	
☽	⊡	♅	4:14 am	1:14 am	
☽	⊻	⚹	11:16 am	8:16 am	
☽	⊼	♇	4:41 pm	1:41 pm	
☽	⊻	⚷	5:17 pm	2:17 pm	
☽	☍	♃	5:32 pm	2:32 pm	
☽	⊼	♀	7:03 pm	4:03 pm	
☽	♂	♃	7:35 pm	4:35 pm	
☽	⊻	♄	7:37 pm	4:37 pm	
☽	□	☉	11:20 pm	8:20 pm	
☽	☍	♂		10:55 pm	
♃	⊻	♄		11:03 pm	

⚷ ℞ 6:20 am **3:20 am**
4th Quarter 11:20 pm **8:20 pm**

3rd ♋

10 WEDNESDAY

☽	☍	♂	1:55 am		
♃	⊻	♄	2:03 am		
☽	⊼	♅	6:33 am	3:33 am	
☽	⚹	♀	11:43 am	8:43 am	
☽	⊼	⚷	12:12 pm	9:12 am	
☽	□	☿	12:47 pm	9:47 am	☽ v/c
♄	☍	♀	5:10 pm	2:10 pm	
♀	□	⚷	5:23 pm	2:23 pm	
☿	⊻	♀	6:34 pm	3:34 pm	
☽	⊡	♇	6:46 pm	3:46 pm	
☽	⊾	⚹	7:18 pm	4:18 pm	
☿	⚹	⚷	7:45 pm	4:45 pm	
☽	⊾	♄	9:33 pm	6:33 pm	
☽	⊡	♀	9:40 pm	6:40 pm	
♃	⊼	♀	10:45 pm	7:45 pm	

☽ enters ♌ 9:54 pm **6:54 pm**

4th ♋

11 THURSDAY

☽	☍	♆	8:07 am	5:07 am	
☽	⊡	⚷	1:52 pm	10:52 am	
☽	⊾	♀	3:42 pm	12:42 pm	
☽	♂	⚹	4:35 pm	1:35 pm	
☽	△	♇	8:12 pm	5:12 pm	
☽	⚹	⚷	8:38 pm	5:38 pm	
☽	⊼	♃	9:42 pm	6:42 pm	
☽	⚹	♄	10:49 pm	7:49 pm	
☽	⊻	♃	11:07 pm	8:07 pm	
☽	△	♀	11:35 pm	8:35 pm	

4th ♌

Eastern Standard Time in medium type
Pacific Standard Time in bold type

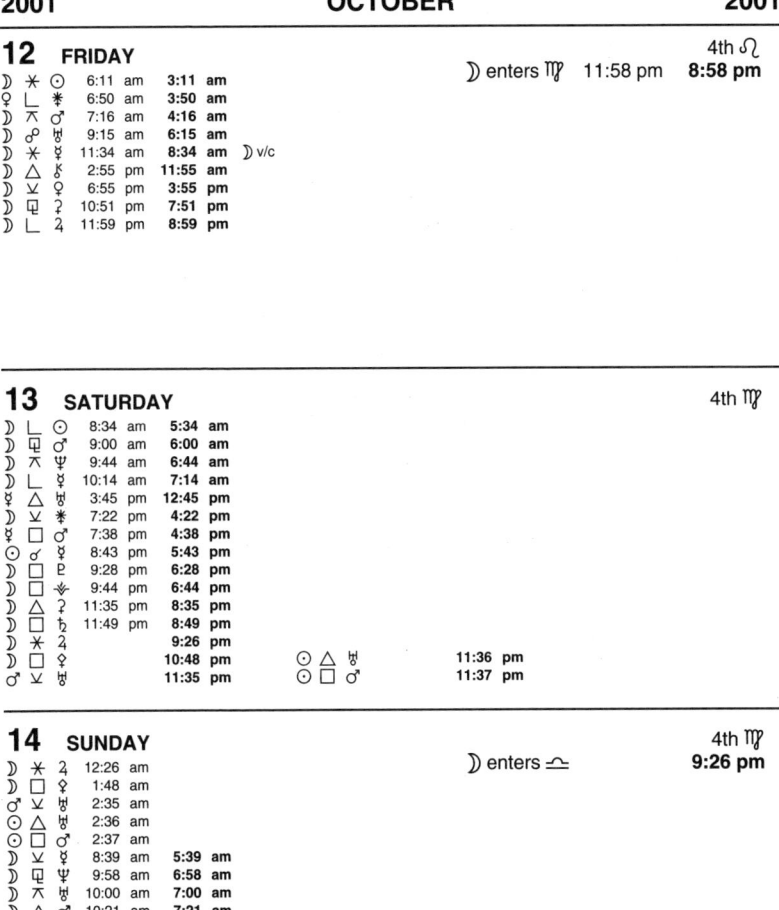

2001 OCTOBER 2001

15 MONDAY
4th ♍

☽ △ ♆	10:04 am	7:04 am		
☽ ⚼ ♅	10:06 am	7:06 am		
☽ ✶ ✳	9:04 pm	6:04 pm		
☽ ✶ ♇	9:51 pm	6:51 pm		
☽ △ ⚸	9:53 pm	6:53 pm		
☽ △ ♄		9:00 pm		
☽ □ ⚷		9:38 pm		
☽ □ ♃		9:55 pm		

☽ enters ♎ 12:26 am
♀ enters ♎ 6:42 am **3:42 am**

16 TUESDAY
4th ♎

☽ △ ♄	12:00 am			
☽ □ ⚷	12:38 am			
☽ □ ♃	12:55 am			
☽ ✶ ♀	3:15 am	12:15 am		
♇ ☍ ⚸	3:59 am	12:59 am		
☽ ☌ ☿	5:32 am	2:32 am		
☽ △ ♅	10:19 am	7:19 am		
☽ □ ♂	12:58 pm	9:58 am		
☽ ☌ ☉	2:23 pm	11:23 am	☽ v/c
☽ ✶ ⚴	4:27 pm	1:27 pm		
☽ ⚼ ⚸	10:11 pm	7:11 pm		
☽ ∟ ♇	10:18 pm	7:18 pm		
✳ ✶ ⚸	10:49 pm	7:49 pm		
♃ ☍ ⚷		9:13 pm		
☽ ⚼ ♄		9:23 pm		
♇ △ ✳		11:47 pm		

New Moon 2:23 pm **11:23 am**
☽ enters ♏ **10:03 pm**

17 WEDNESDAY
1st ♎

♃ ☍ ⚷	12:13 am			
☽ ⚼ ♄	12:23 am			
♇ △ ✳	2:47 am			
☽ ∟ ♀	4:20 am	1:20 am		
☽ ⚺ ♀	4:59 am	1:59 am		
☿ ✶ ♀	5:48 am	2:48 am		
☽ □ ♆	10:57 am	7:57 am		
☽ ∟ ⚴	5:21 pm	2:21 pm		
☽ ⊼ ⚸	11:00 pm	8:00 pm		
☉ ✶ ⚴	11:13 pm	8:13 pm		
☽ ⚺ ♇	11:15 pm	8:15 pm		
☽ □ ✳	11:49 pm	8:49 pm		
☽ ⊼ ♄		10:17 pm		
☽ △ ♃		11:33 pm		
☽ ✶ ⚷		11:54 pm		

☽ enters ♏ 1:03 am
♆ D 8:48 pm **5:48 pm**

18 THURSDAY
1st ♏

☽ ⊼ ♄	1:17 am			
☽ △ ♃	2:33 am			
☽ ✶ ⚷	2:54 am			
☽ ⚺ ☿	4:02 am	1:02 am		
☽ ⚺ ♀	6:02 am	3:02 am		
☽ ∟ ♀	8:30 am	5:30 am		
☽ □ ♅	12:11 pm	9:11 am		
☽ ✶ ♂	5:30 pm	2:30 pm	☽ v/c
☽ ⚺ ⚴	6:57 pm	3:57 pm		
☿ □ ⚷	7:40 pm	4:40 pm		
☽ ⚺ ☉	8:21 pm	5:21 pm		

Eastern Standard Time in medium type
Pacific Standard Time in bold type

2001 — **OCTOBER** — **2001**

19 FRIDAY

1st ♏

☽ ⚌ ♃	4:24 am	**1:24 am**			
☽ ⊥ ☿	4:31 am	**1:31 am**			
☽ ⊥ ♀	5:09 am	**2:09 am**			
☿ □ ♃	6:48 am	**3:48 am**			
☽ ⚹ ♀	1:05 pm	**10:05 am**			
☽ ⚹ ♆	2:20 pm	**11:20 am**			
☽ ⊥ ♂	9:11 pm	**6:11 pm**			
♄ ⚹ ⛢	10:30 pm	**7:30 pm**			
☽ ⊥ ☉		**9:53 pm**			
♀ ⚌ ⛢		**10:53 pm**			
♀ △ ♆		**11:36 pm**			
☽ ☍ ⚷		**11:56 pm**			

☽ enters ♐ 3:47 am **12:47 am**

20 SATURDAY

1st ♐

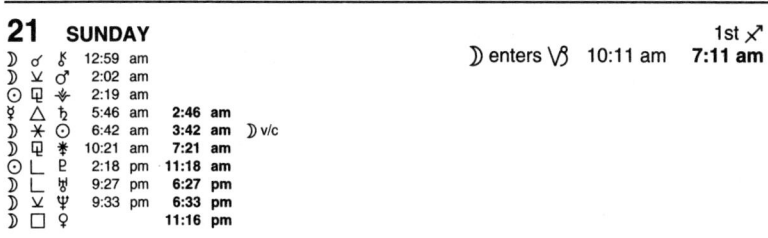

☽ ⊥ ☉ 12:53 am
♀ ⚌ ⛢ 1:53 am
♀ △ ♆ 2:36 am
☽ ☍ ⚷ 2:56 am
♂ ⚺ ⚸ 3:20 am **12:20 am**
☽ ☌ ♇ 3:37 am **12:37 am**
☽ ☍ ♄ 5:31 am **2:31 am**
☽ △ ⛢ 5:46 am **2:46 am**
☽ ⚹ ☿ 6:08 am **3:08 am**
☽ ⊼ ♃ 7:13 am **4:13 am**
☽ ⚺ ♀ 8:23 am **5:23 am**
☿ ⚹ ⛢ 11:39 am **8:39 am**
☽ ☌ ♀ 12:13 pm **9:13 am**
☽ ⚹ ⛢ 5:21 pm **2:21 pm**
☽ ⊥ ♆ 5:25 pm **2:25 pm**
☽ ☌ ⚸ 9:59 pm
☽ ⚺ ♂ 11:02 pm
☉ ⚌ ⚷ 11:19 pm

21 SUNDAY

1st ♐

☽ ☌ ⚸ 12:59 am
☽ ⚺ ♂ 2:02 am
☉ ⚌ ⚷ 2:19 am
☿ △ ♄ 5:46 am **2:46 am**
☽ ⚹ ☉ 6:42 am **3:42 am** ☽ v/c
☽ ⚌ ⛢ 10:21 am **7:21 am**
☉ ⊥ ♇ 2:18 pm **11:18 am**
☽ ⊥ ⛢ 9:27 pm **6:27 pm**
☽ ⚺ ♆ 9:33 pm **6:33 pm**
☽ □ ♀ **11:16 pm**

☽ enters ♑ 10:11 am **7:11 am**

OCTOBER

S	M	T	W	T	F	S
	1	2	3	4	5	6
7	8	9	10	11	12	13
14	15	16	17	18	19	20
21	22	23	24	25	26	27
28	29	30	31			

Eastern Standard Time in medium type
Pacific Standard Time in bold type

2001   **OCTOBER**   **2001**

22 MONDAY

1st ♑

☽	□	♀	2:16 am	
☽	⊼	♆	10:42 am	**7:42 am**
♃	⚻	⚳	10:48 am	**7:48 am**
☽	⚻	♇	11:57 am	**8:57 am**
☉	⚎	♄	12:24 pm	**9:24 am**
☽	□	☿	1:21 pm	**10:21 am**
☽	⊼	♄	1:41 pm	**10:41 am**
☽	☍	♃	3:52 pm	**12:52 pm**
☽	⊼	⚳	4:01 pm	**1:01 pm**
☽	♂	♀	6:07 pm	**3:07 pm**
☽	⚻	♀	10:44 pm	**7:44 pm**
☽	⚻	♅		11:30 pm

☿ D   7:24 pm   **4:24 pm**

23 TUESDAY

1st ♑

☽	⚻	♅	2:30 am		
☽	⚻	⚴	11:02 am	**8:02 am**	
☽	♂	♂	3:11 pm	**12:11 pm**	☽ v/c
☽	⚎	♆	3:53 pm	**12:53 pm**	
☽	⌐	♇	5:30 pm	**2:30 pm**	
☽	⚎	♄	7:05 pm	**4:05 pm**	
☿	△	♄	9:42 pm	**6:42 pm**	
☽	□	☉	9:58 pm	**6:58 pm**	
♂	⚎	♆		11:05 pm	

☉ enters ♏   3:26 am   **12:26 am**
☽ enters ♒   8:26 pm   **5:26 pm**
2nd Quarter   9:58 pm   **6:58 pm**

SUN ENTERS SCORPIO

24 WEDNESDAY

2nd ♒

♂	⚎	♆	2:05 am	
☽	⌐	♀	5:22 am	**2:22 am**
☽	♂	♆	8:26 am	**5:26 am**
☽	⌐	⚴	5:12 pm	**2:12 pm**
☽	△	♀	8:16 pm	**5:16 pm**
☽	△	♆	9:40 pm	**6:40 pm**
☽	⚹	♇	11:39 pm	**8:39 pm**
☽	△	♄		10:03 pm
☽	△	☿		10:53 pm

25 THURSDAY

2nd ♒

☽	△	♄	1:03 am		
☽	△	☿	1:53 am		
☽	⊼	♃	3:43 am	**12:43 am**	
☽	☍	⚳	5:45 am	**2:45 am**	
☽	⚻	⚳	7:14 am	**4:14 am**	
♀	△	♆	8:34 am	**5:34 am**	
♂	⌐	♇	10:10 am	**7:10 am**	
☽	⚹	♀	12:31 pm	**9:31 am**	
☽	♂	♅	2:32 pm	**11:32 am**	☽ v/c
☽	⚹	⚴	11:44 pm	**8:44 pm**	

Eastern Standard Time in medium type
Pacific Standard Time in bold type

2001   **OCTOBER**   **2001**

26 FRIDAY

♀	⚹	♇	5:19 am	**2:19**	**am**
☽	⚻	♀	6:11 am	**3:11**	**am**
☽	⚺	♂	7:15 am	**4:15**	**am**
♂	⚻	♄	7:58 am	**4:58**	**am**
☽	⚻	☿	9:37 am	**6:37**	**am**
☽	⚻	♃	10:10 am	**7:10**	**am**
☽	☌	⚷	2:18 pm	**11:18**	**am**
☽	△	☉	4:03 pm	**1:03**	**pm**
♀	△	♄	4:24 pm	**1:24**	**pm**
☿	□	♃	7:55 pm	**4:55**	**pm**
☽	⚺	♆	9:06 pm	**6:06**	**pm**

           ☽ enters ♓   8:56 am   **5:56 am**   2nd ♒

27 SATURDAY

☽	□	⚷	9:44 am	**6:44**	**am**
☽	□	♇	12:30 pm	**9:30**	**am**
☽	□	♄	1:29 pm	**10:29**	**am**
☽	☌	♂	3:25 pm	**12:25**	**pm**
☽	⚻	♀	4:03 pm	**1:03**	**pm**
☽	△	♃	4:31 pm	**1:31**	**pm** ☽ v/c
☽	⚻	☿	5:51 pm	**2:51**	**pm**
☽	⚻	✶	8:25 pm	**5:25**	**pm**
♀	□	♃	8:36 pm	**5:36**	**pm**
☽	⚹	⚷	9:17 pm	**6:17**	**pm**
☽	⚻	☉		**10:03**	**pm**

           ♂ enters ♒   12:19 pm   **9:19 am**   2nd ♓

28 SUNDAY

☽	⚻	☉	1:03 am		
☽	□	♀	3:01 am	**12:01**	**am**
☽	⚺	♅	3:07 am	**12:07**	**am**
☽	☌	♆	3:20 am	**12:20**	**am**
♅	⚹	♀	6:20 am	**3:20**	**am**
☽	□	⚸	12:38 pm	**9:38**	**am**
♆	☌	♀	1:52 pm	**10:52**	**am**
☽	⚹	♂	11:14 pm	**8:14**	**pm**

           ☽ enters ♈   9:15 pm   **6:15 pm**   2nd ♓

DAYLIGHT SAVING TIME ENDS AT 2 AM

OCTOBER

S	M	T	W	T	F	S
	1	2	3	4	5	6
7	8	9	10	11	12	13
14	15	16	17	18	19	20
21	22	23	24	25	26	27
28	29	30	31			

Eastern Standard Time in medium type
Pacific Standard Time in bold type

2001   **OCTOBER**   **2001**

29 MONDAY

2nd ♈

☽ ⚼ ⚴	3:18 am	**12:18 am**
☉ □ ♆	4:31 am	**1:31 am**
☽ ⊥ ♅	8:57 am	**5:57 am**
☽ ✶ ♆	9:11 am	**6:11 am**
☽ ⊼ ☉	9:36 am	**6:36 am**
☉ ⊥ ♀	12:39 pm	**9:39 am**
☽ ✶ ⚸	8:45 pm	**5:45 pm**
☿ ✶ ⚴	10:47 pm	**7:47 pm**
☽ △ ♇		**9:17 pm**
☽ ✶ ♄		**9:50 pm**
♀ ✶ ⚴		**10:36 pm**

30 TUESDAY

♅ D   5:55 pm   **2:55 pm**   2nd ♈

☽ △ ♇	12:17 am	
☽ ✶ ♄	12:50 am	
♀ ✶ ⚴	1:36 am	
☽ □ ♃	4:06 am	**1:06 am**
☿ □ ♃	5:11 am	**2:11 am**
♀ □ ♃	6:32 am	**3:32 am**
☽ △ ⚴	9:38 am	**6:38 am**
☽ □ ♃	9:59 am	**6:59 am**
☽ ☍ ♀	10:17 am	**7:17 am**
☽ ☍ ☿	10:19 am	**7:19 am**
☿ ☌ ♀	1:54 pm	**10:54 am**
☽ ✶ ♅	2:17 pm	**11:17 am** ☽ v/c
☽ △ ♀	3:58 pm	**12:58 pm**
☽ △ ⚷	11:53 pm	**8:53 pm**
☽ ⊥ ⚸		**10:31 pm**

31 WEDNESDAY

☽ enters ♉   7:48 am   **4:48 am**   2nd ♈
Full Moon   **9:41 pm**

☽ ⊥ ⚸	1:31 am	
☽ ⚼ ♇	5:25 am	**2:25 am**
☽ □ ♄	5:44 am	**2:44 am**
☽ □ ♂	1:06 pm	**10:06 am**
☽ □ ♆	7:20 pm	**4:20 pm**
☽ ⚼ ♀	9:34 pm	**6:34 pm**
☽ ☍ ☉		**9:41 pm**
♀ △ ♅		**10:59 pm**

SAMHAIN • HALLOWEEN

SCORPIO ♏
Duality: Feminine
Quality: Fixed
Element: Water
House: 8th
Planetary Ruler: Pluto
Rules: Genitals, Colon
Keyword: Determined
Keynote: I desire.

Eastern Standard Time in medium type
Pacific Standard Time in bold type

2001 NOVEMBER 2001

1 THURSDAY

☽ ☍ ☉	12:41 am			
♀ △ ♅	1:59 am			
☿ △ ♅	4:04 am	1:04 am		
☽ ⚻ ⚸	4:41 am	1:41 am		
☽ ⚺ ⚹	5:44 am	2:44 am		
☽ ⚻ ♇	10:00 am	7:00 am		
☽ ⚺ ♄	10:06 am	7:06 am		
♀ ⚻ ⚶	11:40 am	8:40 am		
☽ ⚹ ♃	1:33 pm	10:33 am		
☽ △ ♀	8:27 pm	5:27 pm		
☽ □ ⚶	8:30 pm	5:30 pm		
☽ □ ♅	11:20 pm	8:20 pm	☽ v/c
♄ ☍ ♇		10:08 pm	
☽ ⚻ ☿		10:27 pm	
☽ ⚻ ♀		10:37 pm	
☽ ⚻ ♀		11:36 pm	

Full Moon 12:41 am

2nd ♉

ALL SAINTS' DAY

2 FRIDAY

♄ ☍ ♇	1:08 am			
☽ ⚻ ☿	1:27 am			
☽ ⚻ ♀	1:37 am			
☽ ⚻ ♀	2:36 am			
☽ ⚻ ⚸	8:57 am	5:57 am		
♀ ⚹ ♀	3:30 pm	12:30 pm		
☿ ⚹ ♀	4:38 pm	1:38 pm		
☽ ⊥ ♃	5:29 pm	2:29 pm		
☽ △ ♂		9:28 pm		
☽ ⚻ ♃		9:53 pm		
☿ ☌ ♀		11:28 pm		

♃ ℞ 10:35 am **7:35 am**
☽ enters ♊ 4:12 pm **1:12 pm**

3rd ♉

3 SATURDAY

☽ △ ♂	12:28 am			
☽ ⚻ ♃	12:53 am			
☿ ☌ ♀	2:28 am			
☽ △ ♆	3:23 am	12:23 am		
☉ ⊥ ⚸	7:48 am	4:48 am		
☉ ⚻ ⚹	8:05 am	5:05 am		
☽ ⚻ ♀	8:16 am	5:16 am		
☽ ⚻ ☿	8:20 am	5:20 am		
☽ ☌ ⚹	12:40 pm	9:40 am		
☽ ⚻ ☉	1:07 pm	10:07 am		
☽ ☌ ♄	5:21 pm	2:21 pm		
☽ ☍ ♇	5:39 pm	2:39 pm		
☽ ⚺ ♃	8:56 pm	5:56 pm		

3rd ♊

4 SUNDAY

☽ ⚻ ♃	4:49 am	1:49 am		
☽ ⚹ ⚶	5:09 am	2:09 am		
☽ ⚻ ♂	5:20 am	2:20 am		
☽ △ ♅	6:25 am	3:25 am		
☽ ⚻ ♆	6:42 am	3:42 am		
☽ ☍ ♀	11:07 am	8:07 am		
☽ △ ♀	2:18 pm	11:18 am		
☽ △ ☿	2:45 pm	11:45 am	☽ v/c
☽ ☍ ⚸	4:04 pm	1:04 pm		
☽ ⚻ ☉	6:27 pm	3:27 pm		
☿ ⚻ ⚹	8:35 pm	5:35 pm		
♀ ⚻ ⚹		10:04 pm		

☽ enters ♋ 10:44 pm **7:44 pm**

3rd ♊

Eastern Standard Time in medium type
Pacific Standard Time in bold type

2001   **NOVEMBER**   **2001**

5 MONDAY
3rd ♋

♀	⚏	♇	1:04 am		
☿	⚹	⚷	3:43 am	**12:43 am**	
♂	☌	♆	7:44 am	**4:44 am**	
☽	⚌	※	8:45 am	**5:45 am**	
☽	⚏	♅	9:18 am	**6:18 am**	
☽	⚻	♆	9:35 am	**6:35 am**	
☽	⚻	♂	9:41 am	**6:41 am**	
♀	⚹	⚷	10:30 am	**7:30 am**	
☽	⚺	♇	5:49 pm	**2:49 pm**	
☉	⚻	♄	5:50 pm	**2:50 pm**	
☽	⚺	♄	10:51 pm	**7:51 pm**	
☽	△	☉	11:16 pm	**8:16 pm**	
☽	⚻	♇	11:30 pm	**8:30 pm**	
☽	☌	♃		**11:32 pm**	
☉	⚺	♇		**11:40 pm**	

6 TUESDAY
3rd ♋

☽	☌	♃	2:32 am		
☉	⚺	♇	2:40 am		
♅	☍	※	7:09 am	**4:09 am**	
☽	☍	?	11:22 am	**8:22 am**	
☽	⚻	♅	11:46 am	**8:46 am**	
☽	⚺	※	11:53 am	**8:53 am**	
☿	⚌	♄	3:31 pm	**12:31 pm**	
☽	⚻	♀	5:46 pm	**2:46 pm**	
☽	⚌	♇	7:46 pm	**4:46 pm**	
☽	⚻	⚷	9:27 pm	**6:27 pm**	
☿	⚌	♇	10:49 pm	**7:49 pm**	
☽	□	♀		**9:41 pm**	
☽	⚌	♄		**9:58 pm**	
☽	⚌	♇		**10:49 pm**	
☽	□	☿		**11:10 pm**	☽ v/c

GENERAL ELECTION DAY

7 WEDNESDAY
3rd ♋

☽	□	♀	12:41 am		
☽	⚌	♄	12:58 am		
☽	⚌	♇	1:49 am		
☽	□	☿	2:10 am		☽ v/c
♀	⚌	♄	3:37 am	**12:37 am**	
♅	⚺	?	6:22 am	**3:22 am**	
♀	⚌	♇	1:26 pm	**10:26 am**	
☽	☍	♆	2:08 pm	**11:08 am**	
☽	☍	♂	4:58 pm	**1:58 pm**	
☉	△	♃	7:01 pm	**4:01 pm**	
☽	⚌	♀	8:26 pm	**5:26 pm**	
☽	⚹	⚷	9:19 pm	**6:19 pm**	
☽	⚌	⚷	11:32 pm	**8:32 pm**	
☽	⚹	♄		**11:41 pm**	

☽ enters ♌   3:34 am   **12:34 am**
☿ enters ♏   2:53 pm   **11:53 am**

8 THURSDAY
3rd ♌

☽	⚹	♄	2:41 am		
☽	△	♇	3:43 am	**12:43 am**	
☽	⚺	♃	6:27 am	**3:27 am**	
☽	□	☉	7:21 am	**4:21 am**	
☽	☍	♅	3:30 pm	**12:30 pm**	☽ v/c
☽	⚻	?	4:11 pm	**1:11 pm**	
☽	☌	※	4:48 pm	**1:48 pm**	
☽	△	♀	10:41 pm	**7:41 pm**	
☽	△	⚷		**10:13 pm**	

♀ enters ♏   8:29 am   **5:29 am**

Eastern Standard Time in medium type
Pacific Standard Time in bold type

2001 NOVEMBER 2001

9 FRIDAY

☽ △ ⚷	1:13 am			
☽ ⚼ ♃	7:51 am		**4:51 am**	
☽ ✶ ♀	8:58 am		**5:58 am**	
☽ ✶ ☿	11:39 am		**8:39 am**	
☽ ⚻ ♆	5:08 pm		**2:08 pm**	
☽ ⚿ ⚴	6:02 pm		**3:02 pm**	
☽ ⚻ ♂	10:28 pm		**7:28 pm**	
☽ □ ⚶	11:21 pm		**8:21 pm**	

☽ enters ♍ 6:49 am **3:49 am**

4th ♌

10 SATURDAY

☽ □ ♄	5:05 am		**2:05 am**	
☽ □ ♇	6:27 am		**3:27 am**	
☽ ✶ ♃	8:55 am		**5:55 am**	
♂ △ ⚶	12:26 pm		**9:26 am**	
☽ ⚼ ♀	12:28 pm		**9:28 am**	
☽ ✶ ☉	1:40 pm		**10:40 am**	☽ v/c
☽ ⚼ ☿	3:47 pm		**12:47 pm**	
☽ ⚻ ♅	5:52 pm		**2:52 pm**	
☽ ⚿ ♆	6:11 pm		**3:11 pm**	
☽ △ ⚴	7:36 pm		**4:36 pm**	
☽ ⚹ ⚶	8:16 pm		**5:16 pm**	
☽ ⚿ ♂			**9:45 pm**	
☽ □ ♀			**11:12 pm**	

4th ♍

11 SUNDAY

☽ ⚿ ♂	12:45 am			
☽ □ ♀	2:12 am			
☽ □ ⚷	3:42 am		**12:42 am**	
☿ □ ♆	1:59 pm		**10:59 am**	
☽ ⚹ ♀	3:44 pm		**12:44 pm**	
☽ ⚼ ☉	4:26 pm		**1:26 pm**	
☽ ⚿ ♅	6:47 pm		**3:47 pm**	
☽ △ ♆	7:06 pm		**4:06 pm**	
☽ ⚹ ☿	7:44 pm		**4:44 pm**	
☽ ⚼ ⚶	9:41 pm		**6:41 pm**	
☽ △ ⚴			**9:28 pm**	
☽ △ ♂			**11:54 pm**	

☽ enters ♎ 8:53 am **5:53 am**

4th ♍

VETERANS DAY

NOVEMBER

S	M	T	W	T	F	S
				1	2	3
4	5	6	7	8	9	10
11	12	13	14	15	16	17
18	19	20	21	22	23	24
25	26	27	28	29	30	

Eastern Standard Time in medium type
Pacific Standard Time in bold type

2001   **NOVEMBER**   **2001**

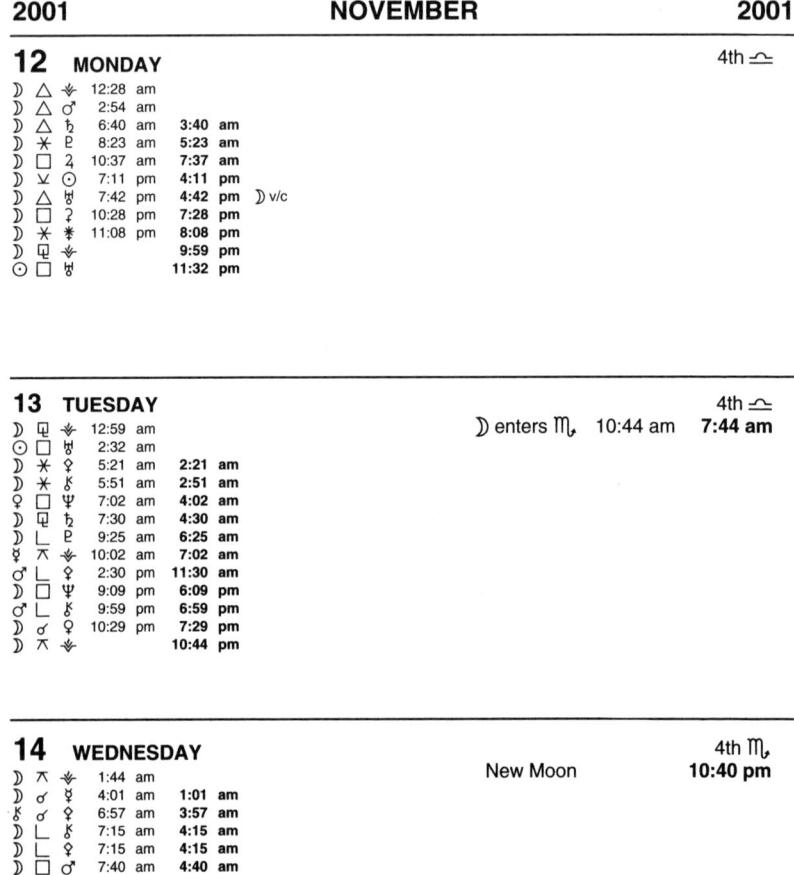

2001 NOVEMBER 2001

16 FRIDAY
1st ♐

☽	✶	♆	12:46 am		
☉	□	⚸	1:15 am		
☽	☍	♅	4:37 am	1:37	am
☽	∟	⚵	5:04 am	2:04	am
☽	⚺	♀	7:22 am	4:22	am
☿	□	♂	11:33 am	8:33	am
☽	☍	♄	12:27 pm	9:27	am
☽	✶	♂	2:39 pm	11:39	am
☽	⚺	☿	2:53 pm	11:53	am
☽	☌	♇	3:09 pm	12:09	pm
☽	⚻	♃	4:58 pm	1:58	pm
☿	⚺	♇	5:08 pm	2:08	pm
♂	✶	♇		9:26	pm

17 SATURDAY
1st ♐

♂	✶	♇	12:26 am		
☽	✶	♅	3:14 am	12:14 am	☽ v/c
☽	∟	♆	3:37 am	12:37 am	
☿	△	♃	7:57 am	4:57 am	
☽	⚺	⚵	8:41 am	5:41 am	
☽	△	⚸	9:14 am	6:14 am	
☽	⚺	☉	11:09 am	8:09 am	
☽	∟	♀	1:16 pm	10:16 am	
☽	☌	⚴	3:03 pm	12:03 pm	
☽	☌	♀	4:49 pm	1:49 pm	
☽	∟	♂	7:30 pm	4:30 pm	
☽	∟	☿	9:59 pm	6:59 pm	

☽ enters ♑ 7:40 pm **4:40 pm**

RAMADAN BEGINS

18 SUNDAY
1st ♑

☽	∟	♅	6:56 am	3:56 am
☽	⚺	♆	7:20 am	4:20 am
♂	⚻	♃	7:32 am	4:32 am
♀	∟	⚴	9:12 am	6:12 am
☽	⚻	⚵	10:19 am	7:19 am
♀	⚻	♄	11:13 am	8:13 am
☽	⚼	⚸	1:43 pm	10:43 am
☽	∟	☉	5:30 pm	2:30 pm
☽	⚻	♄	7:23 pm	4:23 pm
☽	✶	♀	8:21 pm	5:21 pm
☽	⚺	♇	10:45 pm	7:45 pm
☽	☍	♃		9:18 pm
☽	⚺	♂		10:24 pm

NOVEMBER

S	M	T	W	T	F	S
				1	2	3
4	5	6	7	8	9	10
11	12	13	14	15	16	17
18	19	20	21	22	23	24
25	26	27	28	29	30	

Eastern Standard Time in medium type
Pacific Standard Time in bold type

2001 NOVEMBER 2001

19 MONDAY
1st ♑

☽	☌	♃	12:18 am	
☽	⊻	♂	1:24 am	
☽	⚹	☿	6:24 am	3:24 am
☽	⊻	♅	11:32 am	8:32 am
☽	⚻	♆	2:25 pm	11:25 am
♀	⦣	♀	4:27 pm	1:27 pm
☉	⊻	⚷	6:37 pm	3:37 pm
☽	☌	⚷	6:46 pm	3:46 pm
☽	⚻	⚸	7:06 pm	4:06 pm
♀	⊻	♇	9:07 pm	6:07 pm
☽	⚻	♄		9:08 pm
☽	⊻	⚷		9:29 pm
☽	⚹	☉		9:57 pm ☽ v/c

20 TUESDAY
1st ♑
☽ enters ♒ 4:55 am **1:55 am**

☽	⚻	♄	12:08 am	
☽	⊻	⚷	12:29 am	
☽	⚹	☉	12:57 am	☽ v/c
☽	⊻	♀	3:42 am	12:42 am
☽	⦣	♇	3:52 am	12:52 am
♀	△	♃	10:31 am	7:31 am
☽	☌	♆	5:22 pm	2:22 pm
☽	△	⚸	7:14 pm	4:14 pm
☿	□	♅	10:51 pm	7:51 pm

21 WEDNESDAY
1st ♒
♀ enters ♑ 6:39 pm **3:39 pm**
☉ enters ♐   **10:00 pm**

☽	△	♄	5:36 am	2:36 am
☽	⦣	⚷	6:23 am	3:23 am
☽	⚹	♇	9:41 am	6:41 am
☽	⦣	♀	10:24 am	7:24 am
☽	⚻	♃	10:51 am	7:51 am
☽	□	♀	1:50 pm	10:50 am
☽	☌	♂	4:01 pm	1:01 pm
☽	☌	♅	10:57 pm	7:57 pm
☉	⚻	♃		11:11 pm
☽	□	☿		11:37 pm ☽ v/c

SUN ENTERS SAGITTARIUS PST

22 THURSDAY
1st ♒
☉ enters ♐ 1:00 am
☽ enters ♓ 4:52 pm **1:52 pm**
2nd Quarter 6:21 pm **3:21 pm**

☉	⚻	♃	2:11 am	
☽	□	☿	2:37 am	☽ v/c
☉	⊻	♀	4:50 am	1:50 am
☽	⊻	⚷	8:03 am	5:03 am
☽	☍	⚸	8:03 am	5:03 am
⚷	⚻	⚸	8:14 am	5:14 am
☽	⚹	⚷	12:48 pm	9:48 am
☽	⚻	♃	4:53 pm	1:53 pm
☽	⚹	♀	5:36 pm	2:36 pm
☽	□	☉	6:21 pm	3:21 pm

THANKSGIVING DAY • SUN ENTERS SAGITTARIUS EST

Eastern Standard Time in medium type
Pacific Standard Time in bold type

2001   **NOVEMBER**   **2001**

23 FRIDAY

☽	⚹	♆	5:44 am	**2:44 am**
☽	□	⚷	6:15 am	**3:15 am**
♀	□	♂	11:43 am	**8:43 am**
☽	⊥	♃	3:14 pm	**12:14 pm**
☽	□	♄	5:41 pm	**2:41 pm**
☽	□	♇	10:24 pm	**7:24 pm**
☽	△	♃	11:03 pm	**8:03 pm**
☿	□	⚹		**10:37 pm**

2nd ♓

24 SATURDAY

☿	□	⚹	1:37 am	
♆	△	⚷	4:08 am	**1:08 am**
☿	⚹	♃	4:24 am	**1:24 am**
☽	⚹	♂	8:30 am	**5:30 am**
☽	△	♀	9:32 am	**6:32 am**
☽	⚹	♅	11:39 am	**8:39 am**
☽	⊥	♆	12:05 pm	**9:05 am**
☽	⊼	⚹	9:51 pm	**6:51 pm**
☽	⚹	♃	10:19 pm	**7:19 pm**
☽	△	☿		9:29 pm ☽ v/c
☽	□	⚷		**10:51 pm**

2nd ♓

25 SUNDAY

☽	△	☿	12:29 am		☽ v/c
☽		⚷	1:51 am		
♀	□	♅	5:50 am	**2:50 am**	
☽	□	♀	8:03 am	**5:03 am**	
☿	⚹	⚷	11:24 am	**8:24 am**	
☽	△	☉	12:21 pm	**9:21 am**	
☽	⊥	♂	4:26 pm	**1:26 pm**	
☽	⚹	⚷	5:15 pm	**2:15 pm**	
☽	⊥	♅	5:41 pm	**2:41 pm**	
☽	⚹	♆	6:07 pm	**3:07 pm**	
☽	⚼	♀	7:02 pm	**4:02 pm**	

☽ enters ♈   5:21 am   **2:21 am**

2nd ♓

NOVEMBER

S	M	T	W	T	F	S
				1	2	3
4	5	6	7	8	9	10
11	12	13	14	15	16	17
18	19	20	21	22	23	24
25	26	27	28	29	30	

Eastern Standard Time in medium type
Pacific Standard Time in bold type

NOVEMBER 2001

26 MONDAY
2nd ♈

☽	⚻	※	4:15 am	**1:15 am**
☽	⚹	♄	5:17 am	**2:17 am**
☿	⚻	♃	9:30 am	**6:30 am**
☽	△	♇	10:27 am	**7:27 am**
☽	□	♃	10:32 am	**7:32 am**
☽	⚻	☿	10:42 am	**7:42 am**
♄	⚻	♀	1:59 pm	**10:59 am**
♂	☌	♅	2:07 pm	**11:07 am**
♃	⚼	♇	7:16 pm	**4:16 pm**
☽	⚻	☉	8:33 pm	**5:33 pm**
☽	⊥	⚻	10:05 pm	**7:05 pm**
☽	⚹	♅	11:11 pm	**8:11 pm**
☽	⚹	♂	11:43 pm	**8:43 pm** ☽ v/c

☿ enters ♐ 1:23 pm **10:23 am**

27 TUESDAY
2nd ♈

☽	⚼	♀	3:46 am	**12:46 am**
☽	△	※	9:59 am	**6:59 am**
☽	⊥	♄	10:17 am	**7:17 am**
☽	□	♃	10:58 am	**7:58 am**
☉	☍	⚻	11:46 am	**8:46 am**
☽	△	⚸	1:13 pm	**10:13 am**
☽	⚻	♇	3:36 pm	**12:36 pm**
☽	⚼	☿	7:56 pm	**4:56 pm**
☽	△	♀	8:31 pm	**5:31 pm**
☿	⚺	♀		**10:51 pm**
☽	⚺	⚻		**11:17 pm**

☽ enters ♉ 4:06 pm **1:06 pm**

28 WEDNESDAY
2nd ♉

☿	⚺	♀	1:51 am	
☽	⚺	⚻	2:17 am	
☽	⚼	☉	3:52 am	**12:52 am**
☽	□	♆	4:24 am	**1:24 am**
☉	⚹	♆	10:35 am	**7:35 am**
☽	⚺	♄	2:35 pm	**11:35 am**
☽	⚻	⚸	5:52 pm	**2:52 pm**
☽	⚹	♃	7:35 pm	**4:35 pm**
☽	⚼	♇	8:02 pm	**5:02 pm**
☽	⚻	♀		**10:36 pm**

29 THURSDAY
2nd ♉

☽	⚻	♀	1:36 am	
☽	□	♅	8:05 am	**5:05 am**
☽	□	♂	11:50 am	**8:50 am**
☿	☍	⚻	4:25 pm	**1:25 pm**
☽	☍	♀	6:21 pm	**3:21 pm** ☽ v/c
☽	□	※	7:10 pm	**4:10 pm**
☽	△	♃	8:40 pm	**5:40 pm**
☽	⚼	⚸	9:46 pm	**6:46 pm**
☽	⊥	♃	11:03 pm	**8:03 pm**

☽ enters ♊ **9:04 pm**

Eastern Standard Time in medium type
Pacific Standard Time in bold type

2001 NOVEMBER/DECEMBER 2001

30 FRIDAY

♀	□	⚹	4:27 am	1:27 am	
☽	⊼	♀	5:55 am	2:55 am	
☽	☌	⚸	8:41 am	5:41 am	
☽	☍	☿	11:14 am	8:14 am	
☽	△	♆	11:52 am	8:52 am	
☽	☍	☉	3:49 pm	12:49 pm	
☿	⚹	♆	4:40 pm	1:40 pm	
☽	☌	♄	9:08 pm	6:08 pm	
☽	□	⚷		9:26 pm	
☽	⊻	♃		10:53 pm	
☽	☍	♇		11:50 pm	
♀	⚹	⚷		11:51 pm	

2nd ♉

☽ enters ♊   12:04 am
Full Moon   3:49 pm   **12:49 pm**

SAGITTARIUS ♐
Duality: Masculine
Quality: Mutable
Element: Fire
House: 9th
Planetary Ruler: Jupiter
Rules: Liver, Hips, Thighs
Keyword: Freedom
Keynote: I see.

---

1 SATURDAY

☽	□	♃	12:26 am			
☽	⊻	♃	1:53 am			
☽	☍	♇	2:50 am			
♀	⚹	⚷	2:51 am			
♀	⊻	⚸	9:09 am	6:09 am		
☽	△	♅	2:17 pm	11:17 am		
☽	□	♆	2:39 pm	11:39 am		
♀	□	♃	4:43 pm	1:43 pm		
☽	△	♂	8:48 pm	5:48 pm	☽ v/c	
☽	⚹	⚹		10:35 pm		

3rd ♊

---

2 SUNDAY

☽	⚹	⚹	1:35 am		
☽	⊼	♃	3:37 am	12:37 am	
☽	☍	⚸	3:43 am	12:43 am	
☽	⊼	♀	5:26 am	2:26 am	
⚸	⊻	♃	9:24 am	6:24 am	
☽	☍	♀	12:40 pm	9:40 am	
☽	⊻	⚷	12:49 pm	9:49 am	
♀	⊼	⚷	4:00 pm	1:00 pm	
☽	□	♅	4:36 pm	1:36 pm	
☽	⊼	♆	4:57 pm	1:57 pm	
☽	⊼	☿	11:03 pm	8:03 pm	
☽	□	♂		9:24 pm	
☽	⊼	☉		9:51 pm	
☽	⊻	♄		10:30 pm	

3rd ♊

☽ enters ♋   5:30 am   **2:30 am**
♀ enters ♐   6:11 am   **3:11 am**

Eastern Standard Time in medium type
Pacific Standard Time in bold type

DECEMBER 2001

3 MONDAY
3rd ♋

☽	⛛	♂	12:24	am		
☽	☌	☉	12:51	am		
☽	⊻	♄	1:30	am		
☽	∟	⚴	4:01	am	1:01	am
☽	☌	♃	6:04	am	3:04	am ☽ v/c
☽	⛛	♇	7:28	am	4:28	am
☉	☍	♄	9:13	am	6:13	am
☽	⛛	♀	10:03	am	7:03	am
☽	∟	⚷	2:17	pm	11:17	am
☽	⛛	♅	6:32	pm	3:32	pm
☿	☍	♄	7:47	pm	4:47	pm

4 TUESDAY
3rd ♋
☽ enters ♌ 9:15 am **6:15 am**

☽	∟	♄	3:08	am	**12:08**	**am**
☽	⛛	♂	3:36	am	**12:36**	**am**
☽	⛛	☿	4:07	am	**1:07**	**am**
☽	⛛	☉	4:39	am	**1:39**	**am**
☽	⊻	⚴	6:06	am	**3:06**	**am**
☽	⛛	⚵	7:54	am	**4:54**	**am**
☽	☍	⚶	8:43	am	**5:43**	**am**
☽	⛛	♇	9:16	am	**6:16**	**am**
☽	△	♀	2:16	pm	**11:16**	**am**
☽	✶	⚷	3:29	pm	**12:29**	**pm**
☉	☌	☿	4:36	pm	**1:36**	**pm**
☽	⛛	♀	5:42	pm	**2:42**	**pm**
☽	☍	♆	8:33	pm	**5:33**	**pm**
♀	☍	⚷			**10:49**	**pm**

5 WEDNESDAY
3rd ♌
♃ enters ♒ 6:38 am **3:38 am**

♀	☍	⚷	1:49	am		
☽	✶	♄	4:33	am	**1:33**	**am**
☽	△	☉	8:10	am	**5:10**	**am**
☽	△	☿	8:52	am	**5:52**	**am**
☽	⊻	♃	8:59	am	**5:59**	**am**
♇	∟	⚶	9:30	am	**6:30**	**am**
☽	⛛	⚵	9:38	am	**6:38**	**am**
☿	⛛	♃	9:51	am	**6:51**	**am**
☽	△	♇	10:51	am	**7:51**	**am**
☉	⛛	♃	6:26	pm	**3:26**	**pm**
☽	⛛	♀	7:53	pm	**4:53**	**pm**
☽	☍	♅	9:44	pm	**6:44**	**pm**

6 THURSDAY
3rd ♌
☽ enters ♍ 12:11 pm **9:11 am**

☿	☌	♇	3:12	am	**12:12**	**am**
☿	∟	⚶	7:42	am	**4:42**	**am**
☽	☍	♂	9:20	am	**6:20**	**am** ☽ v/c
☽	☌	⚴	9:39	am	**6:39**	**am**
☽	∟	♃	10:12	am	**7:12**	**am**
☽	△	⚵	11:13	am	**8:13**	**am**
☽	⛛	⚶	12:55	pm	**9:55**	**am**
♂	☍	⚴	4:58	pm	**1:58**	**pm**
☽	□	⚷	5:28	pm	**2:28**	**pm**
♀	⊻	♀	8:11	pm	**5:11**	**pm**
☽	△	♀	9:58	pm	**6:58**	**pm**
☽	□	♀	10:06	pm	**7:06**	**pm**
☉	☌	♇	10:53	pm	**7:53**	**pm**
☽	⛛	♆	11:29	pm	**8:29**	**pm**
♂	⛛	♃			**9:17**	**pm**

Eastern Standard Time in medium type
Pacific Standard Time in bold type

2001 **DECEMBER** **2001**

7 FRIDAY
3rd ♍

♂	⚻	♃	12:17 am		
☽	□	♄	7:03 am	**4:03 am**	
☽	⚹	♃	11:23 am	**8:23 am**	
☽	□	♇	1:45 pm	**10:45 am**	
♀	⚹	♆	1:59 pm	**10:59 am**	
☽	□	☉	2:52 pm	**11:52 am**	
☽	⚻	♀	2:56 pm	**11:56 am**	
☉	☍	♀	4:19 pm	**1:19 pm**	
♃	☍	⚹	4:47 pm	**1:47 pm**	
☽	□	☿	5:57 pm	**2:57 pm**	☽ v/c
☽	⚻	♅		**9:35 pm**	
☽	⚻	♆		**9:54 pm**	

4th Quarter 2:52 pm **11:52 am**

8 SATURDAY
4th ♍

☽	⚻	♅	12:35 am		
☽	⚻	♆	12:54 am		
♂	⚹	♄	4:14 am	**1:14 am**	
☽	⚺	⚹	12:56 pm	**9:56 am**	
☽	□	♄	2:22 pm	**11:22 am**	
☽	⚻	♂	2:50 pm	**11:50 am**	
☽	△	♃	4:59 pm	**1:59 pm**	
☽	△	⚹	7:23 pm	**4:23 pm**	
♅	☍	♀	9:20 pm	**6:20 pm**	
☽	⚻	♅		**11:05 pm**	
☽	□	♀		**11:12 pm**	
☽	△	♆		**11:23 pm**	

☽ enters ♎ 2:57 pm **11:57 am**
♂ enters ♓ 4:52 pm **1:52 pm**

9 SUNDAY
4th ♎

☽	⚻	♅	2:05 am		
☽	□	♀	2:12 am		
☽	△	♆	2:23 am		
☽	⚹	♀	5:52 am	**2:52 am**	
♆	⚺	♀	9:19 am	**6:19 am**	
☽	△	♄	9:37 am	**6:37 am**	
☽	□	♃	1:53 pm	**10:53 am**	
☽	☍	⚹	2:41 pm	**11:41 am**	
☽	⚹	♇	4:48 pm	**1:48 pm**	
☽	⚻	♂	5:44 pm	**2:44 pm**	
☽	⚻	⚹	8:30 pm	**5:30 pm**	
☽	⚹	☉	9:45 pm	**6:45 pm**	

DECEMBER

S	M	T	W	T	F	S
						1
2	3	4	5	6	7	8
9	10	11	12	13	14	15
16	17	18	19	20	21	22
23	24	25	26	27	28	29
30	31					

Eastern Standard Time in medium type
Pacific Standard Time in bold type

2001 DECEMBER 2001

10 MONDAY

☽	⚹	☿	3:19 am	12:19 am	
☽	△	♅	3:43 am	12:43 am	☽ v/c
☿	⚹	♅	6:56 am	3:56 am	
☿	⊥	♆	9:36 am	6:36 am	
☽	⊥	♀	10:00 am	7:00 am	
☽	⚼	♄	11:06 am	8:06 am	
☽	⚹	⚵	4:36 pm	1:36 pm	
☽	⚹	⚷	5:58 pm	2:58 pm	
☽	⊥	♇	6:35 pm	3:35 pm	
☽	△	♂	8:52 pm	5:52 pm	
♀	☍	♄	9:32 pm	6:32 pm	
☽	□	⚴	9:33 pm	6:33 pm	
☽	⚻	⚵	9:48 pm	6:48 pm	
☽	⊥	☉		10:32 pm	

☽ enters ♏ 6:09 pm **3:09 pm**

4th ♎

HANUKKAH BEGINS

11 TUESDAY

☽	⊥	☉	1:32 am		
⚴	△	⚵	3:39 am	12:39 am	
☽	□	♆	5:53 am	2:53 am	
☽	⚹	♀	7:04 am	4:04 am	
☽	⊥	☿	8:26 am	5:26 am	
♂	□	⚵	10:40 am	7:40 am	
☽	⚻	♄	12:51 pm	9:51 am	
☽	⚺	♀	2:29 pm	11:29 am	
☽	△	♃	5:05 pm	2:05 pm	
☽	⊥	⚷	8:09 pm	5:09 pm	
☽	⚺	♇	8:38 pm	5:38 pm	
♂	⚺	⚴	9:42 pm	6:42 pm	

⚷ enters ♑ 6:04 pm **3:04 pm**

4th ♏

12 WEDNESDAY

☽	⚺	☉	5:42 am	2:42 am	
☽	□	♅	7:48 am	4:48 am	☽ v/c
☽	⊥	♀	9:59 am	6:59 am	
☽	⚺	☿	2:02 pm	11:02 am	
♀	⚻	♃	4:49 pm	1:49 pm	
☽	⚼	♃	7:10 pm	4:10 pm	
☽	□	⚵	9:21 pm	6:21 pm	
☽	⚺	⚷	10:43 pm	7:43 pm	
☽	☍	⚵		10:24 pm	

☽ enters ♐ 10:30 pm **7:30 pm**

4th ♏

13 THURSDAY

☽	☍	⚵	1:24 am		
☽	⚹	⚴	3:26 am	12:26 am	
☽	□	♂	4:18 am	1:18 am	
☽	⚹	♆	10:42 am	7:42 am	
☉	⚹	♅	10:49 am	7:49 am	
☽	⚺	♀	1:23 pm	10:23 am	
☉	⊥	♆	2:32 pm	11:32 am	
☽	☍	♄	5:29 pm	2:29 pm	
☽	⚻	♃	9:44 pm	6:44 pm	
☽	☌	♀		10:02 pm	
☽	☌	♇		11:02 pm	

4th ♐

Eastern Standard Time in medium type
Pacific Standard Time in bold type

DECEMBER

2001 — **2001**

14 FRIDAY

4th ♐

☽ ☌ ♀	1:02 am			
☽ ☌ ♇	2:02 am			
☽ ⊥ ♃	7:08 am	**4:08 am**		
♀ ☌ ♇	11:51 am	**8:51 am**		
☽ ⚹ ♅	1:37 pm	**10:37 am**		
☽ ⊥ ♆	1:53 pm	**10:53 am**		
☽ ☌ ☉	3:47 pm	**12:47 pm**		

New Moon 3:47 pm **12:47 pm**

SOLAR ECLIPSE ☌ (22° ♐ 56') 3:53 PM EST/12:53 AM PST

15 SATURDAY

1st ♐

☽ ☌ ☿	3:24 am	**12:24 am**	☽ v/c
☽ △ ※	4:01 am	**1:01 am**	
☽ ☌ ⚸	5:29 am	**2:29 am**	
☽ ⊼ ♆	6:55 am	**3:55 am**	
☿ △ ※	8:44 am	**5:44 am**	
☽ ⚺ ♃	11:31 am	**8:31 am**	
☽ ⚹ ♂	2:08 pm	**11:08 am**	
☽ ⊥ ♅	5:26 pm	**2:26 pm**	
☽ ⚺ ♆	5:41 pm	**2:41 pm**	
☿ ☌ ⚸	9:43 pm	**6:43 pm**	
☽ ☌ ♀	10:05 pm	**7:05 pm**	
☽ ⊼ ♄		**9:19 pm**	

☽ enters ♑ 4:48 am **1:48 am**
☿ enters ♑ 2:55 pm **11:55 am**

RAMADAN ENDS

16 SUNDAY

1st ♑

☽ ⊼ ♄	12:19 am			
☽ ☍ ♃	4:35 am	**1:35 am**	☽ v/c
☿ ⊼ ♆	5:20 am	**2:20 am**	
☽ ⚼ ※	8:17 am	**5:17 am**	
☽ ⚺ ♇	9:47 am	**6:47 am**	
☽ ⚼ ♆	10:38 am	**7:38 am**	
☽ ⚺ ♀	2:44 pm	**11:44 am**	
☽ ⊥ ♂	8:14 pm	**5:14 pm**	
☽ ⚺ ♅	9:56 pm	**6:56 pm**	

DECEMBER

S	M	T	W	T	F	S
						1
2	3	4	5	6	7	8
9	10	11	12	13	14	15
16	17	18	19	20	21	22
23	24	25	26	27	28	29
30	31					

Eastern Standard Time in medium type
Pacific Standard Time in bold type

2001 DECEMBER 2001

17 MONDAY

☽	⊡	♄	4:44 am	**1:44 am**
☽	⊻	☉	5:04 am	**2:04 am**
☽	⊼	✱	1:15 pm	**10:15 am**
☽	∟	♇	2:42 pm	**11:42 am**
☽	⊻	⚷	2:57 pm	**11:57 am**
☽	△	⚸	3:00 pm	**12:00 pm**
♀	∟	⚴	4:35 pm	**1:35 pm**
⚷	⊼	⚸	5:27 pm	**2:27 pm**
☽	⊻	☿	8:37 pm	**5:37 pm**
☽	♂	⚴	10:30 pm	**7:30 pm**
☽	∟	♀	10:59 pm	**7:59 pm**

1st ♑

☽ enters ♒ 1:43 pm **10:43 am**

HANUKKAH ENDS

18 TUESDAY

☽	⊻	♂	3:09 am	**12:09 am**
☽	♂	♆	3:23 am	**12:23 am**
♂	⊻	♆	7:07 am	**4:07 am**
☽	⊻	♀	9:44 am	**6:44 am**
☽	△	♄	9:49 am	**6:49 am**
♄	⊼	♀	12:03 pm	**9:03 am**
☽	∟	☉	1:01 pm	**10:01 am**
☽	⊼	♃	2:03 pm	**11:03 am**
☿	⊻	⚴	3:02 pm	**12:02 pm**
☽	✱	♇	8:17 pm	**5:17 pm**
☽	∟	⚷	8:42 pm	**5:42 pm**

1st ♒

19 WEDNESDAY

☽	∟	☿	6:42 am	**3:42 am**	
☽	✱	♀	8:05 am	**5:05 am**	
☽	♂	♅	8:58 am	**5:58 am**	
☽	∟	♀	4:34 pm	**1:34 pm**	
♀	✱	♅	4:41 pm	**1:41 pm**	
♀	∟	♆	6:47 pm	**3:47 pm**	
☽	⊡	♃	7:39 pm	**4:39 pm**	
☽	✱	☉	9:41 pm	**6:41 pm**	☽ v/c
☿	∟	♅		**9:14 pm**	
☽	☍	✱		**9:58 pm**	
☽	□	⚸		**10:33 pm**	
☿	⊻	♆		**10:51 pm**	
☽	✱	⚷		**11:59 pm**	

1st ♒

☽ enters ♓ **10:49 pm**

20 THURSDAY

☿	∟	♅	12:14 am	
☽	☍	✱	12:58 am	
☽	□	⚸	1:33 am	
☿	⊻	♆	1:51 am	
☽	✱	⚷	2:59 am	
☽	⊻	⚴	12:07 pm	**9:07 am**
☽	⊻	♆	3:25 pm	**12:25 pm**
☽	✱	☿	5:28 pm	**2:28 pm**
☽	♂	♂	6:58 pm	**3:58 pm**
☽	□	♄	9:30 pm	**6:30 pm**
☽	✱	♀	11:49 pm	**8:49 pm**
☽	△	♃		**10:35 pm**

1st ♒

☽ enters ♓ 1:09 am

Eastern Standard Time in medium type
Pacific Standard Time in bold type

2001 — **DECEMBER** — **2001**

21 FRIDAY

☽ △ ♃	1:35 am			
⚹ □ ⚷	8:27 am		5:27 am	
☽ □ ♇	8:46 am		5:46 am	
☉ ⚻ ⚷	12:47 pm		9:47 am	
☿ ⚹ ♂	12:47 pm		9:47 am	
☉ △ ⚹	1:43 pm		10:43 am	
☽ ⊻ ⚴	7:25 pm		4:25 pm	
☽ ⊻ ♅	9:40 pm		6:40 pm	
☽ ⊻ ♆	9:50 pm		6:50 pm	
☿ ⚻ ♄	10:23 pm		7:23 pm	

⚷ enters ♉   3:43 am   **12:43 am**
☉ enters ♑   2:21 pm   **11:21 am**

1st ♓

SUN ENTERS CAPRICORN
YULE (WINTER SOLSTICE) 2:21 PM EST/11:21 PST

22 SATURDAY

☽ □ ♀	3:44 am		**12:44 am**	☽ v/c
♂ □ ♄	8:35 am		**5:35 am**	
☽ ⚹ ⚷	1:16 pm		**10:16 am**	
☽ ⚻ ⚹	1:46 pm		**10:46 am**	
☽ □ ☉	3:56 pm		**12:56 pm**	
☽ □ ⚵	4:08 pm		**1:08 pm**	
♃ ☍ ♀	4:41 pm		**1:41 pm**	
☉ ☌ ⚵	6:25 pm		**3:25 pm**	
☿ ☍ ♃			**10:59 pm**	
☽ ⚹ ⚴			**11:37 pm**	

⚹ enters ♍   9:57 am   **6:57 am**
☽ enters ♈   1:45 pm   **10:45 am**
2nd Quarter   3:56 pm   **12:56 pm**

1st ♓

23 SUNDAY

☿ ☍ ♃	1:59 am			
☽ ⚹ ⚴	2:37 am			
☽ ⊻ ♅	3:58 am		**12:58 am**	
☽ ⚹ ♆	4:08 am		**1:08 am**	
☿ ☌ ♀	5:59 am		**2:59 am**	
☽ ⚹ ♄	9:37 am		**6:37 am**	
☽ ⊻ ♂	11:24 am		**8:24 am**	
☽ □ ♃	1:21 pm		**10:21 am**	
☽ □ ♀	2:16 pm		**11:16 am**	
☽ □ ☿	3:13 pm		**12:13 pm**	
☽ ⊻ ⚷	6:53 pm		**3:53 pm**	
☽ ⚻ ⚹	7:50 pm		**4:50 pm**	
☽ △ ♇	9:15 pm		**6:15 pm**	

2nd ♈

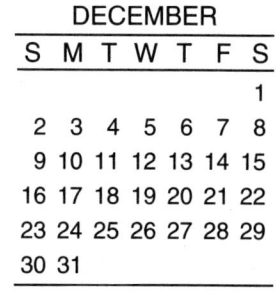

DECEMBER						
S	M	T	W	T	F	S
						1
2	3	4	5	6	7	8
9	10	11	12	13	14	15
16	17	18	19	20	21	22
23	24	25	26	27	28	29
30	31					

Eastern Standard Time in medium type
Pacific Standard Time in bold type

2001 DECEMBER 2001

24 MONDAY

☽	⚹	♅	9:51 am	**6:51 am**
♂	△	♃	2:54 pm	**11:54 am**
☽	⊥	♄	3:06 pm	**12:06 pm**
☿	⊡	⚸	4:52 pm	**1:52 pm**
☽	⊥	♂	6:54 pm	**3:54 pm**
☽	△	♀	10:21 pm	**7:21 pm** ☽ v/c
☽	⋎	⚸	11:59 pm	**8:59 pm**
☽	△	⚹		**10:18 pm**
☿	⊡	⚹		**11:26 pm**
☽	⊡	♇		**11:44 pm**

☽ enters ♉   2nd ♈   **10:12 pm**

CHRISTMAS EVE

25 TUESDAY

☽	△	⚹	1:18 am	
☿	⊡	⚹	2:26 am	
☽	⊡	♇	2:44 am	
☽	△	⚷	4:01 am	**1:01 am**
♆	☌	⚴	8:19 am	**5:19 am**
☽	△	☉	8:36 am	**5:36 am**
♀	⊼	⚸	12:48 pm	**9:48 am**
☿	⋎	♇	1:58 pm	**10:58 am**
☽	□	♆	3:08 pm	**12:08 pm**
☽	□	⚴	3:20 pm	**12:20 pm**
☽	⋎	♄	7:53 pm	**4:53 pm**
☽	⚹	♃	11:10 pm	**8:10 pm**
☽	⚹	♂		**10:30 pm**
☽	△	♀		**11:29 pm**

☽ enters ♉   1:12 am
⚹ ℞   6:09 pm   **3:09 pm**
♀ enters ♑   **11:25 pm**

2nd ♉

CHRISTMAS DAY

26 WEDNESDAY

☽	⚹	♂	1:30 am	
☽	△	♀	2:29 am	
♀	△	⚹	3:18 am	**12:18 am**
☽	⊡	♀	6:14 am	**3:14 am**
☽	⊼	♇	7:26 am	**4:26 am**
☽	⊡	⚷	8:50 am	**5:50 am**
☽	△	☿	9:51 am	**6:51 am**
☽	⊡	☉	3:29 pm	**12:29 pm**
☽	□	♅	7:22 pm	**4:22 pm** ☽ v/c
☽	⊥	♃		**11:52 pm**

♀ enters ♑   2:25 am

2nd ♉

KWANZAA BEGINS

27 THURSDAY

☽	⊥	♃	2:52 am	
☽	⊡	♀	7:12 am	**4:12 am**
☽	☌	⚸	7:53 am	**4:53 am**
☽	□	⚹	9:43 am	**6:43 am**
♀	☌	⚷	10:46 am	**7:46 am**
♂	⚹	♀	12:07 pm	**9:07 am**
☽	⊼	⚷	12:45 pm	**9:45 am**
☽	⊼	♀	12:56 pm	**9:56 am**
☽	⊡	☿	5:16 pm	**2:16 pm**
☽	⊼	☉	9:14 pm	**6:14 pm**
☽	△	♆	10:52 pm	**7:52 pm**
♀	⊡	⚸		**9:22 pm**
☽	△	⚴		**9:30 pm**
☽	☌	♄		**11:54 pm**

☽ enters ♊   9:39 am   **6:39 am**

2nd ♉

Eastern Standard Time in medium type
Pacific Standard Time in bold type

2001   **DECEMBER**   **2001**

28 FRIDAY

♀	⚏	⚷	12:22 am		
☽	△	♃	12:30 am		
☽	☌	♄	2:54 am		
☽	⚺	♃	5:43 am	**2:43 am**	
☽	⚻	♀	10:59 am	**7:59 am**	
☽	□	♂	11:36 am	**8:36 am**	
☽	☍	♇	2:10 pm	**11:10 am**	
☉	⚼	♅	6:52 pm	**3:52 pm**	
☉	⚺	♆	7:21 pm	**4:21 pm**	
☽	⚻	☿	11:24 pm	**8:24 pm**	
☽	△			**10:24 pm**	☽ v/c
☽	⚏	♆		**10:26 pm**	

                                           ※ enters ♌   2nd ♊
                                                               11:11 pm

29 SATURDAY

☽	△	♅	1:24 am		☽ v/c
☽	⚏	♆	1:26 am		
☽	⚏	♃	3:41 am	**12:41 am**	
☽	⚻	⚷	12:31 pm	**9:31 am**	
☽	⚹	※	2:38 pm	**11:38 am**	
☿	⚺	♅	5:25 pm	**2:25 pm**	
☽	☍	♀	6:00 pm	**3:00 pm**	
☽	☍	♀	10:58 pm	**7:58 pm**	

                                           ※ enters ♌   2:11 am   2nd ♊
                                           ☽ enters ♋   2:40 pm   **11:40 am**

30 SUNDAY

☽	⚏	♅	3:16 am	**12:16 am**	
☽	⚻	♆	3:17 am	**12:17 am**	
☽	☍	☉	5:40 am	**2:40 am**	
☽	⚻	♃	6:07 am	**3:07 am**	
☽	⚺	♄	6:44 am	**3:44 am**	
☽	☌	♃	9:09 am	**6:09 am**	
☽	□	⚷	1:50 pm	**10:50 am**	
♂	□	♇	1:50 pm	**10:50 am**	
♀	⚏	※	2:59 pm	**11:59 am**	
☉	⚺	♃	3:05 pm	**12:05 pm**	
☽	⚼	※	4:03 pm	**1:03 pm**	
☽	☍	♀	4:05 pm	**1:05 pm**	
☽	⚻	♇	5:49 pm	**2:49 pm**	

☽	△	♂	6:02 pm	**3:02 pm**	
☿	⚏	♄		**9:17 pm**	
♄	△	♃		**11:00 pm**	

                                          Full Moon   5:40 am   **2:40 am**   2nd ♋

LUNAR ECLIPSE ☍ (8º ♋ 48') 5:30 AM EST/2:30 AM PST

DECEMBER

S	M	T	W	T	F	S
						1
2	3	4	5	6	7	8
9	10	11	12	13	14	15
16	17	18	19	20	21	22
23	24	25	26	27	28	29
30	31					

Eastern Standard Time in medium type
Pacific Standard Time in bold type

2001   **DECEMBER/JANUARY**   **2002**

31 MONDAY

3rd ♋

☿ ⚎ ♄ 12:17 am
♄ △ ♃ 2:00 am
☽ ⚻ ♅ 4:34 am   1:34 am
☽ ⚺ ♄ 7:47 am   4:47 am
☽ ☍ ☿ 8:43 am   5:43 am   ☽ v/c
☽ ✶ ♇ 2:42 pm   11:42 am
☽ ⚺ ♆ 4:59 pm   1:59 pm
☽ ⚎ ♇ 6:52 pm   3:52 pm
☽ ⚎ ♂ 8:20 pm   5:20 pm
☽ ⚻ ⚷ 8:45 pm   5:45 pm
♀ ⚺ ♆   9:33 pm
☉ ☍ ♃   9:53 pm
♀ ⚺ ♅   9:53 pm

☽ enters ♌   5:09 pm   **2:09 pm**

NEW YEAR'S EVE

CAPRICORN ♑
Duality: Feminine
Quality: Cardinal
Element: Earth
House: 10th
Planetary Ruler: Saturn
Rules: Knees, Bones, Joints
Keyword: Ambition
Keynote: I use.

1 TUESDAY

3rd ♌

♀ ⚺ ♆ 12:33 am
☉ ☍ ♃ 12:53 am
☽ ☍ ♆ 5:29 am   **2:29 am**
☽ ⚻ ♀ 5:56 am   **2:56 am**
☽ ✶ ♄ 8:29 am   **5:29 am**
☽ ☍ ♃ 9:26 am   **6:26 am**
☽ ⚺ ♃ 10:37 am   **7:37 am**
☽ ⚻ ☉ 11:27 am   **8:27 am**
☽ ⚻ ♀ 7:11 pm   **4:11 pm**
☽ △ ♇ 7:40 pm   **4:40 pm**
☽ ⚻ ♂ 10:22 pm   **7:22 pm**

NEW YEAR'S DAY • KWANZAA ENDS

2 WEDNESDAY

3rd ♌

☽ ☍ ♅ 6:16 am   **3:16 am**
♀ ⚻ ♄ 10:17 am   **7:17 am**
☿ △ ⚷ 2:00 pm   **11:00 am**
♇ ⚺ ♀ 2:57 pm   **11:57 am**
☽ □ ⚷ 3:49 pm   **12:49 pm**
☽ ⚻ ☿ 4:02 pm   **1:02 pm**
☽ ♂ ⚹ 6:13 pm   **3:13 pm**   ☽ v/c
♃ ⚻ ♃ 7:29 pm   **4:29 pm**
☽ △ ⚸ 10:31 pm   **7:31 pm**

☽ enters ♍   6:34 pm   **3:34 pm**

Eastern Standard Time in medium type
Pacific Standard Time in bold type

2002 JANUARY 2002

3 THURSDAY
3rd ♍

☽	⊼	♆	6:59 am	**3:59 am**
♀	☍	♃	7:22 am	**4:22 am**
☽	□	♄	9:41 am	**6:41 am**
☽	⚹	♃	11:34 am	**8:34 am**
☽	△	♀	12:01 pm	**9:01 am**
☽	⊼	⚷	12:09 pm	**9:09 am**
☿	⊼	⚴	12:15 pm	**9:15 am**
♀	⚺	⚷	2:18 pm	**11:18 am**
☽	△	☉	4:36 pm	**1:36 pm**
☽	□	♇	9:15 pm	**6:15 pm**
☽	△	♀	10:00 pm	**7:00 pm**
☽	☍	♂		**11:30 pm** ☽ v/c

☿ enters ♒   4:38 pm   **1:38 pm**

4 FRIDAY
3rd ♍

☽	☍	♂	2:30 am		☽ v/c
☽	⊼	♅	8:02 am	**5:02 am**
☽	△	⚷	5:18 pm	**2:18 pm**
☽	⚺	⚴	7:45 pm	**4:45 pm**
☽	△	☿	11:35 pm	**8:35 pm**
☽	□	⚴		**9:48 pm**

☽ enters ♎   8:23 pm   **5:23 pm**

5 SATURDAY
3rd ♎

☽	□	⚴	12:48 am	
☽	△	♆	9:14 am	**6:14 am**
☽	△	♄	11:39 am	**8:39 am**
☿	⚺	⚴	12:23 pm	**9:23 am**
☽	□	♃	1:20 pm	**10:20 am**
☽	△	⚷	3:47 pm	**12:47 pm**
☽	□	♀	7:11 pm	**4:11 pm**
☽	□	☉	10:55 pm	**7:55 pm**
☽	⚹	♇	11:54 pm	**8:54 pm**
☽	□	♀		**10:58 pm**

4th Quarter   10:55 pm   **7:55 pm**

6 SUNDAY
4th ♎

☽	□	♀	1:58 am	
☽	⊼	♂	7:59 am	**4:59 am**
☽	△	♅	11:05 am	**8:05 am**	☽ v/c
☉	⚺	♇	12:54 pm	**9:54 am**
☽	⊼	⚷	8:14 pm	**5:14 pm**
☽	⚹	⚴	10:41 pm	**7:41 pm**

☽ enters ♏   11:41 pm   **8:41 pm**

EPIPHANY

Eastern Standard Time in medium type
Pacific Standard Time in bold type

January 2001

DATE	SID.TIME	SUN	MOON	NODE	MERCURY	VENUS	MARS	JUPITER	SATURN	URANUS	NEPTUNE	PLUTO	CERES	PALLAS	JUNO	VESTA	CHIRON
1 M	6:42:50	10 ♑ 38 00	18 ♓ 42	31 ♋ 31	14 ♑ 16	26 ♒ 58	4 ♏ 56	2 ♊ R 11	24 ♉ R 35	18 ♒ 39	5 ♒ 20	13 ♐ 46	16 ♐ 28	22 ♍ 37	6 ♓ 08	26 ♒ 21	22 ♐ 32
2 T	6:46:47	11 39 7	0 ♈ 54	15 R 31	15 54	28 04	5 31	2 07	24 33	18 42	5 22	13 48	16 52	23 01	6 34	26 49	22 39
3 W	6:50:44	12 40 19	13 23	15 31	17 32	29 10	6 06	2 02	24 30	18 45	5 24	13 50	17 17	23 24	7 01	27 16	22 46
4 Th	6:54:40	13 41 29	26 13	15 31	19 10	0 ♓ 16	6 41	2 58	24 28	18 48	5 26	13 52	17 41	23 47	7 28	27 44	22 52
5 F	6:58:37	14 42 37	9 ♉ 27	15 D 31	20 48	1 21	7 16	1 54	24 26	18 51	5 28	13 54	18 06	24 10	7 55	28 11	22 59
6 Sa	7:02:33	15 43 46	23 09	15 31	22 27	2 26	7 51	1 50	24 24	18 54	5 30	13 56	18 30	24 33	8 22	28 39	23 05
7 Su	7:06:30	16 44 54	7 ♊ 17	15 31	24 06	3 31	8 26	1 46	24 22	18 57	5 33	13 59	18 54	24 56	8 50	29 07	23 12
8 M	7:10:26	17 46 02	21 52	15 31	25 45	4 36	9 01	1 42	24 20	19 00	5 35	14 01	19 18	25 19	9 17	29 34	23 19
9 T	7:14:23	18 47 10	6 ♋ 47	15 R 31	27 25	5 40	9 35	1 39	24 18	19 03	5 37	14 03	19 42	25 42	9 45	0 ♓ 02	23 25
10 W	7:18:19	19 48 17	21 56	15 31	29 04	6 44	10 10	1 36	24 16	19 06	5 39	14 05	20 06	26 04	10 12	0 30	23 31
11 Th	7:22:16	20 49 24	7 ♌ 08	15 31	0 ♒ 44	7 47	10 44	1 32	24 14	19 09	5 41	14 06	20 30	26 27	10 40	0 58	23 38
12 F	7:26:13	21 50 31	22 16	15 31	2 24	8 51	11 19	1 30	24 13	19 12	5 44	14 08	20 54	26 49	11 08	1 26	23 44
13 Sa	7:30:09	22 51 38	7 ♍ 08	15 30	4 04	9 54	11 53	1 27	24 12	19 16	5 46	14 10	21 18	27 12	11 36	1 54	23 51
14 Su	7:34:06	23 52 44	21 40	15 29	5 43	10 56	12 28	1 25	24 10	19 19	5 48	14 12	21 42	27 34	12 04	2 21	23 57
15 M	7:38:02	24 53 50	5 ♎ 47	15 28	7 23	11 58	13 02	1 22	24 09	19 22	5 50	14 14	22 06	27 56	12 33	2 49	24 03
16 T	7:41:59	25 54 56	19 27	15 D 28	9 02	13 00	13 36	1 20	24 08	19 25	5 53	14 16	22 29	28 18	13 01	3 17	24 10
17 W	7:45:55	26 56 02	2 ♏ 41	15 28	10 40	14 02	14 11	1 18	24 07	19 29	5 55	14 18	22 53	28 40	13 30	3 45	24 16
18 Th	7:49:52	27 57 08	15 33	15 28	12 18	15 03	14 45	1 17	24 06	19 32	5 57	14 20	23 17	29 01	13 59	4 13	24 22
19 F	7:53:48	28 58 14	28 09	15 29	13 55	16 04	15 19	1 15	24 06	19 35	5 59	14 22	23 40	29 23	14 27	4 42	24 28
20 Sa	7:57:45	29 59 19	10 ♐ 27	15 31	15 30	17 04	15 53	1 14	24 05	19 39	6 02	14 23	24 04	29 44	14 56	5 10	24 34
21 Su	8:01:42	1 ♒ 00 23	22 33	15 32	17 04	18 03	16 27	1 13	24 04	19 42	6 04	14 25	24 27	0 ♎ 06	15 25	5 38	24 40
22 M	8:05:38	2 01 28	4 ♑ 30	15 R 33	18 35	19 02	17 00	1 12	24 04	19 45	6 06	14 27	24 50	0 27	15 55	6 06	24 46
23 T	8:09:35	3 02 31	16 22	15 33	20 04	20 01	17 34	1 12	24 04	19 49	6 08	14 28	25 13	0 48	16 24	6 34	24 52
24 W	8:13:31	4 03 34	28 10	15 33	21 30	20 59	18 08	1 11	24 04	19 52	6 11	14 30	25 37	1 09	16 54	7 03	24 58
25 Th	8:17:28	5 04 37	9 ♒ 58	15 31	22 53	21 57	18 41	1 11	24 D 04	19 55	6 13	14 32	26 00	1 29	17 23	7 31	25 04
26 F	8:21:24	6 05 38	21 47	15 28	24 11	22 54	19 15	1 11	24 04	19 59	6 15	14 33	26 23	1 50	17 53	7 59	25 10
27 Sa	8:25:21	7 06 38	3 ♓ 39	15 25	25 25	23 51	19 48	1 12	24 04	20 02	6 17	14 35	26 46	2 10	18 23	8 28	25 15
28 Su	8:29:18	8 07 38	15 36	15 21	26 32	24 47	20 22	1 12	24 04	20 06	6 20	14 37	27 08	2 31	18 52	8 56	25 21
29 M	8:33:14	9 08 36	27 41	15 17	27 33	25 43	20 55	1 13	24 04	20 09	6 22	14 38	27 31	2 51	19 22	9 24	25 27
30 T	8:37:11	10 09 33	9 ♈ 56	15 13	28 28	26 38	21 28	1 13	24 05	20 13	6 24	14 40	27 54	3 11	19 52	9 53	25 32
31 W	8:41:07	11 10 29	22 24	15 11	29 14	27 32	22 01	1 15	24 06	20 16	6 27	14 41	28 16	3 30	20 22	10 21	25 38

Ephemeris is calculated for midnight Greenwich Mean Time

February 2001

DATE	SID.TIME	SUN	MOON	NODE	MERCURY	VENUS	MARS	JUPITER	SATURN	URANUS	NEPTUNE	PLUTO	CERES	PALLAS	JUNO	VESTA	CHIRON
1 Th	8:45:04	12≈11 24	5♉10	15♋D09	29≈51	28♓25	22♍34	1♊16	24♉06	20≈19	6≈29	14✗43	28✗39	3✗50	20♓52	10♓50	25✗43
2 F	8:49:00	13 12 17	18 16	15 09	0♓18	29 18	23 07	1 17	24 07	20 23	6 31	14 44	29 01	4 10	21 23	11 18	25 49
3 Sa	8:52:57	14 13 09	1♊45	15 10	0 35	0♈10	23 40	1 19	24 08	20 26	6 33	14 46	29 23	4 29	21 53	11 47	25 54
4 Su	8:56:53	15 14 00	15 40	15 12	0 R 42	1 02	24 12	1 21	24 09	20 30	6 36	14 47	29 46	4 48	22 24	12 15	25 59
5 M	9:00:50	16 14 49	0♋00	15 13	0 40	1 52	24 45	1 23	24 10	20 33	6 38	14 48	0♑08	5 07	22 54	12 44	26 04
6 T	9:04:47	17 15 37	14 44	15 R 14	0 27	2 42	25 18	1 25	24 12	20 37	6 40	14 50	0 30	5 26	23 25	13 12	26 10
7 W	9:08:43	18 16 23	29 47	15 13	0 05	3 31	25 50	1 28	24 13	20 40	6 42	14 51	0 52	5 44	23 56	13 41	26 15
8 Th	9:12:40	19 17 08	15♌01	15 11	29≈34	4 19	26 22	1 30	24 15	20 44	6 45	14 52	1 14	6 03	24 27	14 09	26 20
9 F	9:16:36	20 17 52	0♍16	15 07	28 56	5 06	26 54	1 33	24 16	20 47	6 47	14 53	1 35	6 21	24 58	14 38	26 25
10 Sa	9:20:33	21 18 35	15 22	15 01	27 38	5 52	27 26	1 36	24 18	20 51	6 49	14 55	1 57	6 39	25 29	15 06	26 30
11 Su	9:24:29	22 19 16	0♎09	14 56	26 37	6 37	27 58	1 39	24 20	20 54	6 51	14 56	2 18	6 56	26 00	15 35	26 34
12 M	9:28:26	23 19 56	14 30	14 50	25 31	7 21	28 30	1 43	24 22	20 58	6 54	14 57	2 40	7 14	26 31	16 03	26 39
13 T	9:32:22	24 20 35	28 23	14 46	24 22	8 04	29 02	1 46	24 24	21 01	6 56	14 58	3 01	7 31	27 03	16 32	26 44
14 W	9:36:19	25 21 13	11♏46	14 43	23 12	8 46	29 34	1 50	24 26	21 05	6 58	14 59	3 22	7 49	27 34	17 01	26 49
15 Th	9:40:15	26 21 49	24 46	14 D 42	22 03	9 27	0✗05	1 54	24 28	21 08	7 00	15 00	3 44	8 06	28 06	17 29	26 53
16 F	9:44:12	27 22 25	7✗16	14 42	20 56	10 06	0 36	1 58	24 31	21 12	7 02	15 01	4 04	8 22	28 37	17 58	26 58
17 Sa	9:48:09	28 22 59	19 30	14 44	19 53	10 45	1 08	2 02	24 33	21 15	7 04	15 02	4 25	8 39	29 09	18 26	27 02
18 Su	9:52:05	29 23 33	1♑30	14 45	18 56	11 22	1 39	2 07	24 36	21 19	7 07	15 03	4 46	8 55	29 41	18 55	27 06
19 M	9:56:02	0♓24 24	13 22	14 R 46	18 04	11 57	2 10	2 12	24 38	21 22	7 09	15 04	5 06	9 11	0♈12	19 24	27 11
20 T	9:59:58	1 24 35	25 09	14 46	17 19	12 32	2 41	2 17	24 41	21 25	7 11	15 05	5 27	9 27	0 44	19 52	27 15
21 W	10:03:55	2 25 04	6≈55	14 43	16 42	13 05	3 11	2 22	24 44	21 29	7 13	15 06	5 48	9 43	1 16	20 21	27 19
22 Th	10:07:51	3 25 32	18 44	14 38	16 12	13 36	3 42	2 27	24 47	21 32	7 15	15 07	6 08	9 58	1 48	20 50	27 23
23 F	10:11:48	4 25 58	0♓37	14 30	15 49	14 06	4 12	2 33	24 50	21 36	7 17	15 08	6 28	10 13	2 21	21 18	27 27
24 Sa	10:15:44	5 26 22	12 37	14 21	15 34	14 34	4 43	2 38	24 53	21 39	7 19	15 08	6 48	10 28	2 53	21 47	27 31
25 Su	10:19:41	6 26 44	24 44	14 11	15 D 26	15 00	5 13	2 44	24 57	21 43	7 21	15 09	7 08	10 43	3 25	22 16	27 35
26 M	10:23:38	7 27 05	7♈01	14 00	15 25	15 25	5 43	2 50	25 00	21 46	7 23	15 10	7 28	10 57	3 57	22 44	27 38
27 T	10:27:34	8 27 24	19 27	13 51	15 31	15 48	6 13	2 56	25 03	21 49	7 25	15 10	7 48	11 11	4 30	23 13	27 42
28 W	10:31:31	9 27 41	2♉04	13 43	15 42	16 09	6 42	3 02	25 07	21 53	7 27	15 11	8 07	11 25	5 02	23 42	27 46

Ephemeris is calculated for midnight Greenwich Mean Time

March 2001

DATE	SID.TIME	SUN	MOON	NODE	MERCURY	VENUS	MARS	JUPITER	SATURN	URANUS	NEPTUNE	PLUTO	CERES	PALLAS	JUNO	VESTA	CHIRON
1 Th	10:35:27	10 ♓ 27 56	14 ♌ 55	13 ♋ R 38	16 ♒ 00	16 ♈ 28	7 ♐ 12	3 ♊ 09	25 ♉ 11	21 ♒ 56	7 ♒ 29	15 ♐ 12	8 ♑ 26	11 ♐ 38	5 ♈ 35	24 ♓ 10	27 ♐ 49
2 F	10:39:24	11 28 09	28 01	13 34	16 23	16 45	7 41	3 15	25 15	21 59	7 31	15 12	8 08	11 52	6 08	24 39	27 52
3 Sa	10:43:20	12 28 20	11 ♊ 24	13 D 34	16 51	17 00	8 10	3 22	25 19	22 03	7 33	15 13	8 45	12 05	6 40	25 07	27 56
4 Su	10:47:17	13 28 29	25 07	13 34	17 24	17 13	8 39	3 29	25 23	22 06	7 35	15 13	9 24	12 17	7 13	25 36	27 59
5 M	10:51:13	14 28 36	9 ♋ 11	13 R 35	18 01	17 24	9 08	3 36	25 27	22 09	7 37	15 14	9 42	12 30	7 46	26 05	28 02
6 T	10:55:10	15 28 41	23 36	13 34	18 42	17 33	9 36	3 43	25 31	22 13	7 39	15 14	10 01	12 42	8 19	26 33	28 05
7 W	10:59:07	16 28 43	8 ♌ 13	13 32	19 27	17 39	10 05	3 50	25 35	22 16	7 41	15 15	10 20	12 54	8 52	27 02	28 08
8 Th	11:03:03	17 28 44	23 02	13 27	20 16	17 42	10 33	3 58	25 39	22 19	7 43	15 15	10 38	13 05	9 25	27 31	28 11
9 F	11:07:00	18 28 42	8 ♍ 19	13 20	21 08	17 R 44	11 01	4 06	25 44	22 22	7 45	15 15	10 56	13 16	9 58	27 59	28 14
10 Sa	11:10:56	19 28 39	23 23	13 10	22 03	17 43	11 29	4 13	25 48	22 25	7 47	15 16	11 14	13 27	10 31	28 28	28 17
11 Su	11:14:53	20 28 33	8 ♎ 32	13 00	23 01	17 39	11 57	4 21	25 53	22 29	7 48	15 16	11 32	13 38	11 04	28 56	28 19
12 M	11:18:49	21 28 26	22 41	12 49	24 02	17 33	12 24	4 29	25 58	22 32	7 50	15 16	11 49	13 48	11 38	29 25	28 22
13 T	11:22:46	22 28 17	6 ♏ 49	12 40	25 05	17 24	12 51	4 38	26 02	22 35	7 52	15 16	12 07	13 58	12 11	29 53	28 24
14 W	11:26:42	23 28 06	20 33	12 33	26 11	17 13	13 18	4 46	26 07	22 38	7 54	15 16	12 25	14 07	12 44	29 22 ♈	28 27
15 Th	11:30:39	24 27 54	3 ♐ 55	12 29	27 19	17 00	13 45	4 54	26 12	22 41	7 55	15 16	12 42	14 16	13 18	0 ♈ 22	28 29
16 F	11:34:36	25 27 39	15 58	12 D 27	28 29	16 44	14 12	5 03	26 17	22 44	7 57	15 17	12 59	14 25	13 51	0 51	28 31
17 Sa	11:38:32	26 27 24	27 58	12 27	29 41	16 25	14 38	5 12	26 22	22 47	7 59	15 17	13 16	14 34	14 25	1 19	28 33
18 Su	11:42:29	27 27 06	9 ♑ 59	12 R 27	0 ♓ 56	16 04	15 04	5 21	26 27	22 50	8 00	15 17	13 32	14 42	14 58	1 47	28 35
19 M	11:46:25	28 26 47	21 51	12 27	2 12	15 41	15 30	5 30	26 33	22 53	8 02	15 17	13 49	14 50	15 32	2 16	28 37
20 T	11:50:22	29 26 26	3 ♒ 38	12 25	3 29	15 15	15 55	5 39	26 38	22 56	8 04	15 17	14 05	14 57	16 06	2 44	28 39
21 W	11:54:18	0 ♈ 26 03	15 25	12 21	4 49	14 49	16 21	5 48	26 43	22 59	8 05	15 16	14 21	15 04	16 40	3 13	28 41
22 Th	11:58:15	1 25 38	27 17	12 13	6 10	14 20	16 46	5 57	26 49	23 02	8 07	15 16	14 37	15 11	17 13	3 41	28 42
23 F	12:02:11	2 25 12	9 ♓ 16	12 03	7 33	13 49	17 11	6 07	26 54	23 05	8 08	15 16	14 53	15 17	17 47	4 10	28 44
24 Sa	12:06:08	3 24 43	21 25	11 51	8 57	13 18	17 35	6 16	27 00	23 08	8 10	15 16	15 09	15 23	18 21	4 38	28 45
25 Su	12:10:05	4 24 13	3 ♈ 46	11 38	10 23	12 42	17 59	6 26	27 05	23 11	8 11	15 16	15 24	15 28	18 55	5 07	28 47
26 M	12:14:01	5 23 40	16 17	11 24	11 51	12 07	18 23	6 36	27 11	23 14	8 13	15 15	15 39	15 33	19 29	5 35	28 48
27 T	12:17:58	6 23 06	29 01	11 11	13 20	11 31	18 47	6 46	27 17	23 16	8 14	15 15	15 54	15 38	20 03	6 03	28 49
28 W	12:21:54	7 22 29	11 ♉ 56	11 00	14 50	10 54	19 10	6 56	27 23	23 19	8 15	15 15	16 09	15 42	20 38	6 32	28 50
29 Th	12:25:51	8 21 50	25 02	10 52	16 22	10 16	19 33	7 06	27 29	23 22	8 17	15 14	16 23	15 46	21 12	7 00	28 51
30 F	12:29:47	9 21 09	8 ♊ 18	10 47	17 56	9 38	19 56	7 16	27 35	23 24	8 18	15 14	16 38	15 49	21 46	7 28	28 52
31 Sa	12:33:44	10 20 26	21 44	10 44	19 30	9 01	20 18	7 26	27 41	23 27	8 19	15 14	16 52	15 52	22 20	7 57	28 53

Ephemeris is calculated for midnight Greenwich Mean Time

April 2001

DATE	SID.TIME	SUN	MOON	NODE	MERCURY	VENUS	MARS	JUPITER	SATURN	URANUS	NEPTUNE	PLUTO	CERES	PALLAS	JUNO	VESTA	CHIRON
1 Su	12:37:40	11♈19 40	5♋31	10♋R44	21♓06	8♈R23	20♐40	7♊37	27♉47	23♒30	8♒21	15♐R13	17♑06	15♐55	22♈54	8♈53	28♐53
2 M	12:41:37	12 18 52	19 27	10 44	22 23	7 46	21 02	7 47	27 53	23 32	8 22	15 13	17 19	15 57	23 29	8 21	28 54
3 T	12:45:33	13 18 02	3♌19	10 43	24 23	7 10	21 23	7 58	27 59	23 35	8 23	15 12	17 33	15 58	24 03	9 50	28 54
4 W	12:49:30	14 17 09	18 10	10 40	26 03	6 34	21 44	8 09	28 06	23 37	8 24	15 12	17 46	15 59	24 38	10 18	28 55
5 Th	12:53:27	15 16 14	2♍38	10 34	27 45	6 00	22 05	8 20	28 12	23 40	8 26	15 11	17 59	16 00	25 12	10 46	28 55
6 F	12:57:23	16 15 16	17 13	10 26	29 29	5 27	22 25	8 31	28 19	23 42	8 27	15 11	18 12	16♐R00	25 47	11 14	28 55
7 Sa	13:01:20	17 14 17	1♎51	10 16	1♈13	4 56	22 45	8 42	28 25	23 45	8 28	15 10	18 24	16 00	26 21	11 42	28♐R55
8 Su	13:05:16	18 13 15	16 21	10 04	3 00	4 27	23 05	8 53	28 31	23 47	8 29	15 09	18 36	16 00	26 56	12 10	28 55
9 M	13:09:13	19 12 11	0♏34	9 52	4 47	3 59	23 24	9 04	28 38	23 49	8 30	15 08	18 48	15 58	27 30	12 38	28 55
10 T	13:13:09	20 11 06	14 27	9 42	6 36	3 33	23 42	9 15	28 45	23 52	8 31	15 08	19 00	15 57	28 03	13 06	28 55
11 W	13:17:06	21 09 58	27 55	9 34	8 27	3 10	24 01	9 27	28 51	23 54	8 32	15 07	19 12	15 55	28 40	13 34	28 55
12 Th	13:21:02	22 08 49	10♐59	9 29	10 19	2 49	24 19	9 38	28 58	23 56	8 33	15 07	19 23	15 52	29 14	14 02	28 55
13 F	13:24:59	23 07 38	23 41	9 26	12 13	2 30	24 36	9 50	29 05	23 58	8 34	15 06	19 34	15 49	29 49	14 30	28 54
14 Sa	13:28:56	24 06 25	5♑57	9 25D	14 08	2 14	24 53	10 01	29 12	24 00	8 35	15 05	19 45	15 46	0♉24	14 58	28 54
15 Su	13:32:52	25 05 11	18 01	9♋R25	16 05	2 00	25 10	10 13	29 19	24 02	8 36	15 04	19 55	15 42	0 59	15 26	28 53
16 M	13:36:49	26 03 55	29 55	9 25	18 03	1 49	25 26	10 25	29 25	24 04	8 36	15 03	20 05	15 37	1 34	15 54	28 52
17 T	13:40:45	27 02 37	11♒44	9 24	20 03	1 40	25 41	10 37	29 32	24 06	8 37	15 02	20 15	15 32	2 09	16 22	28 52
18 W	13:44:42	28 01 17	23 33	9 21	22 04	1 33	25 56	10 48	29 39	24 08	8 38	15 01	20 25	15 27	2 44	16 49	28 51
19 Th	13:48:38	28 59 56	5♓26	9 15	24 06	1 29	26 11	11 00	29 46	24 10	8 39	15 00	20 34	15 21	3 19	17 17	28 50
20 F	13:52:35	29 58 33	17 30	9 07	26 10	1D27	26 25	11 12	29 53	24 12	8 39	14 59	20 43	15 15	3 54	17 45	28 49
21 Sa	13:56:31	0♉57 08	29 48	8 57	28 14	1 28	26 39	11 25	0♊01	24 14	8 40	14 58	20 52	15 08	4 29	18 12	28 47
22 Su	14:00:28	1 55 41	12♈23	8 46	0♉20	1 31	26 52	11 37	0 08	24 16	8 41	14 57	21 01	15 01	5 04	18 40	28 46
23 M	14:04:25	2 54 13	25 10	8 34	2 27	1 37	27 04	11 49	0 15	24 18	8 41	14 56	21 09	14 53	5 39	19 08	28 45
24 T	14:08:21	3 52 42	8♉13	8 24	4 35	1 44	27 16	12 01	0 22	24 20	8 42	14 55	21 17	14 45	6 14	19 35	28 43
25 W	14:12:18	4 51 10	21 30	8 14	6 43	1 54	27 28	12 14	0 29	24 21	8 42	14 54	21 24	14 36	6 49	20 03	28 42
26 Th	14:16:14	5 49 36	4♊58	8 07	8 52	2 06	27 38	12 26	0 37	24 23	8 43	14 53	21 32	14 27	7 24	20 30	28 40
27 F	14:20:11	6 48 00	18 37	8 03	11 00	2 20	27 48	12 39	0 44	24 25	8 43	14 52	21 39	14 17	7 59	20 58	28 39
28 Sa	14:24:07	7 46 23	2♋25	8 02D	13 09	2 36	27 58	12 51	0 51	24 26	8 44	14 51	21 45	14 07	8 35	21 25	28 37
29 Su	14:28:04	8 44 43	16 19	8 02	15 17	2 54	28 07	13 04	0 59	24 28	8 44	14 49	21 52	13 56	9 10	21 53	28 35
30 M	14:32:00	9 43 01	0♌21	8♋R02	17 24	3 13	28 15	13 17	1 06	24 29	8 45	14 48	21 58	13 45	9 45	22 20	28 33

Ephemeris is calculated for midnight Greenwich Mean Time

May 2001

DATE	SID.TIME	SUN	MOON	NODE	MERCURY	VENUS	MARS	JUPITER	SATURN	URANUS	NEPTUNE	PLUTO	CERES	PALLAS	JUNO	VESTA	CHIRON
1 T	14:35:57	10♉41 16	14♌28	8♋℞03	19♉31	3♈35	28✓23	13♊29	1♊14	24≈30	8≈45	14✓℞47	22♑03	13✓℞34	10♉21	22♈47	28✓℞31
2 W	14:39:54	11 39 30	28 11	8 01	21 31	3 58	28 36	13 42	1 21	24 32	8 45	14 46	22 09	13 22	10 56	23 15	28 29
3 Th	14:43:50	12 37 42	12♍54	7 58	23 39	4 23	28 36	13 55	1 29	24 33	8 46	14 44	22 14	13 09	11 31	23 42	28 27
4 F	14:47:47	13 35 51	27 08	7 52	25 41	4 50	28 42	14 08	1 36	24 34	8 46	14 43	22 19	12 57	12 06	24 09	28 25
5 Sa	14:51:43	14 33 59	11♎19	7 45	27 40	5 18	28 47	14 21	1 44	24 35	8 46	14 42	22 23	12 44	12 42	24 36	28 22
6 Su	14:55:40	15 32 05	25 22	7 37	29 37	5 47	28 51	14 34	1 51	24 37	8 46	14 40	22 27	12 30	13 17	25 03	28 20
7 M	14:59:36	16 30 09	9♏11	7 28	1♊31	6 19	28 55	14 47	1 59	24 38	8 46	14 39	22 31	12 -6	13 53	25 30	28 17
8 T	15:03:33	17 28 11	22 45	7 21	3 22	6 51	28 58	15 00	2 06	24 39	8 46	14 38	22 34	12 02	14 28	25 58	28 15
9 W	15:07:29	18 26 12	5✓59	7 15	5 10	7 25	29 00	15 13	2 14	24 40	8 47	14 36	22 37	11 48	15 03	26 24	28 12
10 Th	15:11:26	19 24 11	18 55	7 11	6 55	8 00	29 02	15 26	2 22	24 41	8 47	14 35	22 40	11 33	15 39	26 51	28 10
11 F	15:15:23	20 22 09	1♑35	7 D 09	8 37	8 37	29℞03	15 40	2 29	24 42	8 ℞ 47	14 33	22 42	11 17	16 14	27 18	28 07
12 Sa	15:19:19	21 20 06	13 59	7 10	10 16	9 14	29 03	15 53	2 37	24 43	8 47	14 32	22 44	11 02	16 50	27 45	28 04
13 Su	15:23:16	22 18 01	25 51	7 11	11 51	9 53	29 02	16 06	2 45	24 43	8 47	14 30	22 46	10 46	17 25	28 12	28 01
14 M	15:27:12	23 15 55	7≈46	7 12	13 22	10 33	29 01	16 19	2 52	24 44	8 46	14 29	22 47	10 30	18 01	28 39	27 58
15 T	15:31:09	24 13 48	19 29	7 ℞ 13	14 50	11 14	28 59	16 33	3 00	24 45	8 46	14 28	22 48	10 14	18 36	29 05	27 55
16 W	15:35:05	25 11 39	1♓14	7 13	16 14	11 56	28 56	16 46	3 08	24 46	8 46	14 26	22 49	9 57	19 12	29 32	27 52
17 Th	15:39:02	26 09 29	13 06	7 11	17 35	12 39	28 52	16 59	3 15	24 46	8 46	14 25	22 ℞ 49	9 49	19 47	29 59	27 49
18 F	15:42:58	27 07 18	25 08	7 08	18 51	13 23	28 48	17 13	3 23	24 47	8 46	14 23	22 49	9 40	20 23	0♉25	27 46
19 Sa	15:46:55	28 05 06	7♈25	7 03	20 04	14 08	28 43	17 26	3 31	24 47	8 46	14 21	22 48	9 23	20 59	0 52	27 43
20 Su	15:50:52	29 02 53	20 35	6 57	21 13	14 54	28 37	17 40	3 39	24 48	8 45	14 20	22 48	8 48	21 34	1 18	27 39
21 M	15:54:48	0♊00 38	3♉33	6 51	22 18	15 40	28 30	17 53	3 46	24 48	8 45	14 18	22 47	8 31	22 10	1 45	27 36
22 T	15:58:45	0 58 22	16 51	6 45	23 28	16 28	28 22	18 07	3 54	24 49	8 45	14 17	22 46	8 13	22 45	2 11	27 32
23 W	16:02:41	1 56 06	0♊20	6 40	24 24	17 16	28 14	18 21	4 02	24 49	8 44	14 15	22 44	7 55	23 23	2 37	27 29
24 Th	16:06:38	2 53 47	14 37	6 37	25 20	18 05	28 05	18 34	4 10	24 49	8 44	14 14	22 42	7 38	23 57	3 04	27 26
25 F	16:10:34	3 51 28	28 24	6 35	25 57	18 54	27 56	18 48	4 18	24 50	8 43	14 12	22 40	7 20	24 32	3 30	27 22
26 Sa	16:14:31	4 49 07	12♋08	6 35	26 42	19 44	27 45	19 02	4 25	24 50	8 43	14 11	22 37	7 02	25 08	3 56	27 18
27 Su	16:18:27	5 46 45	26 54	6 36	27 22	20 35	27 34	19 15	4 33	24 50	8 43	14 09	22 34	6 44	25 43	4 22	27 15
28 M	16:22:24	6 44 21	11♌12	6 38	27 57	21 27	27 22	19 29	4 41	24 50	8 42	14 07	22 31	6 26	26 19	4 48	27 11
29 T	16:26:21	7 41 56	25 29	6 ℞ 39	28 28	22 19	27 10	19 43	4 49	24 ℞ 50	8 41	14 06	22 28	6 08	26 55	5 14	27 07
30 W	16:30:17	8 39 30	9♍40	6 39	28 55	23 12	26 57	19 57	4 56	24 50	8 41	14 05	22 25	5 50	27 30	5 40	27 04
31 Th	16:34:14	9 37 02	23 46	6 39	29 17	24 05	26 43	20 10	5 04	24 50	8 40	14 03	22 22	5 32	28 06	6 06	27 00

Ephemeris is calculated for midnight Greenwich Mean Time

June 2001

DATE	SID.TIME	SUN	MOON	NODE	MERCURY	VENUS	MARS	JUPITER	SATURN	URANUS	NEPTUNE	PLUTO	CERES	PALLAS	JUNO	VESTA	CHIRON
1 F	16:38:10	10 Ⅱ 34 32	7 ♎ 43	6 ⊛ ℞ 37	29 Ⅱ 34	24 ♈ 59	26 ♐ ℞ 29	20 Ⅱ 24	5 Ⅱ 12	24 ♒ ℞ 50	8 ♒ ℞ 40	14 ♐ ℞ 01	22 ♑ ℞ 08	5 ♐ ℞ 14	28 ♉ 41	6 ♉ 32	26 ♐ ℞ 56
2 Sa	16:42:07	11 32 01	21 31	6 34	29 46	25 53	26 14	20 38	5 20	24 50	8 39	13 59	22 02	4 57	29 17	6 57	26 52
3 Su	16:46:03	12 29 29	5 ♏ 07	6 30	29 54	26 48	25 58	20 51	5 27	24 50	8 38	13 58	21 56	4 39	29 53	7 23	26 48
4 M	16:50:00	13 26 56	18 30	6 27	29 ℞ 58	27 43	25 42	21 05	5 35	24 50	8 38	13 56	21 50	4 22	0 Ⅱ 28	7 49	26 44
5 T	16:53:56	14 24 22	1 ♐ 39	6 22	29 56	28 39	25 26	21 19	5 43	24 49	8 37	13 54	21 44	4 04	1 04	8 15	26 40
6 W	16:57:53	15 21 47	14 33	6 22	29 51	29 35	25 09	21 33	5 51	24 49	8 36	13 53	21 36	3 47	1 39	8 40	26 37
7 Th	17:01:50	16 19 11	27 12	6 D 21	29 41	0 ♉ 32	24 51	21 47	5 58	24 49	8 35	13 51	21 29	3 30	2 15	9 05	26 33
8 F	17:05:46	17 16 34	9 ♑ 39	6 21	29 27	1 29	24 34	22 01	6 06	24 48	8 34	13 50	21 21	3 14	2 51	9 30	26 29
9 Sa	17:09:43	18 13 57	21 57	6 21	29 09	2 27	24 15	22 14	6 14	24 48	8 33	13 48	21 13	2 57	3 26	9 56	26 25
10 Su	17:13:39	19 11 19	3 ♒ 50	6 22	28 47	3 25	23 57	22 28	6 21	24 47	8 33	13 46	21 05	2 41	4 02	10 21	26 21
11 M	17:17:36	20 08 40	15 44	6 24	28 22	4 23	23 38	22 42	6 29	24 47	8 32	13 45	20 56	2 25	4 37	10 46	26 17
12 T	17:21:32	21 06 00	27 35	6 25	27 55	5 22	23 19	22 56	6 37	24 46	8 31	13 43	20 47	2 10	5 13	11 11	26 12
13 W	17:25:29	22 03 21	9 ♓ 27	6 26	27 25	6 21	23 00	23 10	6 44	24 45	8 30	13 42	20 38	1 55	5 48	11 36	26 08
14 Th	17:29:25	23 00 40	21 24	6 ℞ 26	26 53	7 21	22 41	23 24	6 52	24 45	8 29	13 40	20 28	1 40	6 24	12 01	26 04
15 F	17:33:22	23 57 59	3 ♈ 32	6 26	26 20	8 21	22 21	23 37	6 59	24 44	8 28	13 38	20 18	1 25	6 59	12 26	26 00
16 Sa	17:37:19	24 55 18	15 54	6 25	25 46	9 21	22 02	23 51	7 07	24 43	8 27	13 37	20 08	1 11	7 35	12 50	25 56
17 Su	17:41:15	25 52 37	28 35	6 24	25 12	10 22	21 42	24 05	7 14	24 42	8 26	13 35	19 58	0 57	8 10	13 15	25 52
18 M	17:45:12	26 49 55	11 ♉ 37	6 23	24 39	11 23	21 23	24 19	7 22	24 41	8 24	13 34	19 47	0 43	8 46	13 40	25 48
19 T	17:49:08	27 47 13	25 03	6 22	24 08	12 24	21 03	24 33	7 29	24 40	8 23	13 32	19 37	0 30	9 21	14 04	25 44
20 W	17:53:05	28 44 30	8 Ⅱ 51	6 21	23 39	13 25	20 44	24 47	7 37	24 39	8 22	13 31	19 25	0 17	9 57	14 29	25 40
21 Th	17:57:01	29 41 48	23 00	6 D 21	23 12	14 26	20 25	25 00	7 44	24 38	8 21	13 29	19 14	0 04	10 32	14 53	25 36
22 F	18:00:58	0 ⊛ 39 05	7 ⊛ 24	6 20	22 49	15 28	20 06	25 14	7 52	24 37	8 20	13 27	19 03	29 ♏ 52	11 08	15 18	25 32
23 Sa	18:04:54	1 36 21	22 05	6 21	22 30	16 30	19 47	25 28	7 59	24 36	8 19	13 26	18 51	29 41	11 43	15 42	25 28
24 Su	18:08:51	2 33 37	6 ♌ 48	6 21	22 15	17 33	19 29	25 42	8 06	24 35	8 17	13 24	18 39	29 29	12 18	16 06	25 25
25 M	18:12:48	3 30 52	21 30	6 21	22 05	18 36	19 11	25 56	8 14	24 34	8 16	13 23	18 27	29 19	12 54	16 30	25 20
26 T	18:16:44	4 28 07	6 ♍ 05	6 21	22 00	19 39	18 53	26 09	8 21	24 33	8 15	13 21	18 15	29 08	13 29	16 54	25 16
27 W	18:20:41	5 25 21	20 29	6 21	22 19 D	20 42	18 36	26 23	8 28	24 31	8 14	13 20	18 03	28 58	14 04	17 18	25 12
28 Th	18:24:37	6 22 35	4 ♎ 34	6 21	22 16	21 45	18 18	26 37	8 35	24 30	8 12	13 18	17 50	28 49	14 40	17 42	25 08
29 F	18:28:34	7 19 48	18 25	6 21	22 17	22 49	18 03	26 51	8 43	24 29	8 11	13 17	17 37	28 40	15 15	18 05	25 04
30 Sa	18:32:30	8 17 00	1 ♏ 58	6 22	22 23	23 53	17 48	27 04	8 50	24 27	8 10	13 16	17 24	28 31	15 50	18 29	25 00

Ephemeris is calculated for midnight Greenwich Mean Time

July 2001

DATE	SID. TIME	SUN	MOON	NODE	MERCURY	VENUS	MARS	JUPITER	SATURN	URANUS	NEPTUNE	PLUTO	CERES	PALLAS	JUNO	VESTA	CHIRON
1 Su	18:36:27	9♋14 12	15♏15	6♋22	21♊34	24♉57	17♐R,33	27♊18	8♊57	24≈R,26	8≈R,08	13♐R,14	17♑R,11	28♏R,23	16♊25	18♉52	24♐R,56
2 M	18:40:24	10 11 24	28 16	6 22	21 50	26 01	17 18	27 32	9 04	24 24	8 07	13 13	16 58	28 16	17 00	19 16	24 52
3 T	18:44:20	11 08 36	11♐03	6 23	22 11	27 05	17 04	27 45	9 11	24 23	8 06	13 11	16 45	28 08	17 36	19 39	24 49
4 W	18:48:17	12 05 47	23 37	6 23	22 36	28 10	16 51	27 59	9 18	24 21	8 04	13 10	16 32	28 02	18 11	20 02	24 45
5 Th	18:52:13	13 02 59	5♑59	6 23 R,	23 07	29 15	16 39	28 12	9 25	24 20	8 03	13 09	16 29	27 55	18 46	20 25	24 41
6 F	18:56:10	14 00 10	18 10	6 23	23 42	0♊20	16 27	28 26	9 32	24 18	8 01	13 07	16 06	27 50	19 21	20 48	24 37
7 Sa	19:00:06	14 57 21	0≈13	6 22	24 23	1 25	16 16	28 39	9 39	24 17	8 00	13 06	15 52	27 44	19 56	21 11	24 34
8 Su	19:04:03	15 54 33	12 10	6 21	25 08	2 30	16 06	28 53	9 45	24 15	7 58	13 05	15 39	27 39	20 31	21 34	24 30
9 M	19:07:59	16 51 44	24 02	6 20	25 58	3 36	15 57	29 06	9 52	24 13	7 57	13 04	15 26	27 35	21 06	21 57	24 27
10 T	19:11:56	17 48 56	5♓53	6 18	26 52	4 42	15 48	29 20	9 59	24 11	7 55	13 02	15 13	27 31	21 41	22 19	24 23
11 W	19:15:53	18 46 08	17 45	6 17	27 51	5 48	15 40	29 33	10 05	24 10	7 54	13 01	15 00	27 27	22 16	22 42	24 20
12 Th	19:19:49	19 43 21	29 42	6 16	28 55	6 54	15 33	29 47	10 12	24 08	7 52	13 00	14 46	27 24	22 50	23 04	24 16
13 F	19:23:46	20 40 34	11♈49	6 15 D	0♋04	8 00	15 27	0♋00 ⊗	10 19	24 06	7 51	12 59	14 33	27 22	23 25	23 27	24 13
14 Sa	19:27:42	21 37 47	24 08	6 14	1 16	9 06	15 21	0 13	10 25	24 04	7 49	12 57	14 20	27 19	24 00	23 49	24 09
15 Su	19:31:39	22 35 02	6♉46	6 15	2 34	10 13	15 17	0 27	10 32	24 02	7 48	12 56	14 08	27 18	24 35	24 11	24 06
16 M	19:35:35	23 32 16	19 45	6 16	3 55	11 20	15 13	0 40	10 38	24 00	7 46	12 55	13 55	27 16	25 09	24 33	24 03
17 T	19:39:32	24 29 32	3♊09	6 17	5 21	12 26	15 10	0 53	10 44	23 58	7 45	12 54	13 42	27 15	25 44	24 55	24 00
18 W	19:43:28	25 26 48	16 59	6 18	6 51	13 33	15 08	1 06	10 51	23 56	7 43	12 53	13 30	27 15 D	26 19	25 16	23 57
19 Th	19:47:25	26 24 05	1⊗15	6 19	8 25	14 40	15 07	1 19	10 57	23 54	7 41	12 52	13 17	27 15	26 53	25 38	23 53
20 F	19:51:22	27 21 22	15 53	6 19 R,	10 02	15 48	15 06 D	1 32	11 03	23 52	7 40	12 51	13 05	27 15	27 28	25 59	23 50
21 Sa	19:55:18	28 18 40	0♌48	6 18	11 44	16 55	15 07	1 45	11 09	23 50	7 38	12 50	12 53	27 16	28 02	26 21	23 48
22 Su	19:59:15	29 15 58	15 53	6 16	13 29	18 03	15 08	1 58	11 15	23 48	7 37	12 49	12 41	27 17	28 37	26 42	23 45
23 M	20:03:11	0♌13 17	0♍57	6 13	15 17	19 10	15 10	2 11	11 22	23 46	7 35	12 48	12 29	27 19	29 11	27 03	23 42
24 T	20:07:08	1 10 36	15 53	6 09	17 09	20 18	15 13	2 24	11 27	23 44	7 33	12 47	12 18	27 21	29 46 ⊗	27 24	23 39
25 W	20:11:04	2 07 56	0♎34	6 05	19 03	21 26	15 17	2 37	11 33	23 42	7 32	12 46	12 06	27 24	0♍20	27 45	23 36
26 Th	20:15:01	3 05 16	14 56	6 04	21 00	22 34	15 22	2 50	11 39	23 39	7 30	12 45	11 56	27 27	0 54	28 05	23 34
27 F	20:18:57	4 02 36	28 59	6 03	22 59	23 42	15 27	3 03	11 45	23 37	7 29	12 44	11 45	27 30	1 28	28 26	23 31
28 Sa	20:22:54	4 59 56	12♏42	6 03	25 00	24 51	15 34	3 15	11 51	23 35	7 27	12 43	11 34	27 34	2 02	28 46	23 29
29 Su	20:26:51	5 57 17	25 19	6 04	27 03	25 59	15 41	3 28	11 56	23 33	7 25	12 43	11 24	27 38	2 37	29 06	23 26
30 M	20:30:47	6 54 39	8♐06	6 06	29 07	27 07	15 49	3 41	12 02	23 31	7 24	12 42	11 14	27 42	3 11	29 26	23 24
31 T	20:34:44	7 52 01	20 37	6 07	1♌11	28 16	15 57	3 53	12 07	23 29	7 22	12 41	11 05	27 47	3 45	29 46	23 22

Ephemeris is calculated for midnight Greenwich Mean Time

August 2001

DATE	SID.TIME	SUN	MOON	NODE	MERCURY	VENUS	MARS	JUPITER	SATURN	URANUS	NEPTUNE	PLUTO	CERES	PALLAS	JUNO	VESTA	CHIRON
1 W	20:38:40	8 ♌ 49 24	2 ♑ 55	6 ♋ ℞ 08	3 ♌ 17	29 ♊ 25	16 ♐ 07	4 ♋ 06	12 ♊ 13	23 ♒ ℞ 26	7 ♒ ℞ 20	12 ♐ ℞ 40	10 ♑ ℞ 55	27 ♏ 52	4 ⊛ 18	0 ♊ 06	23 ♐ ℞ 20
2 Th	20:42:37	9 46 48	15 03	6 06	5 22	0 ⊛ 28	16 16	4 18	12 18	23 24	7 19	12 40	10 46	27 58	4 52	0 26	23 17
3 F	20:46:33	10 44 12	27 04	6 06	7 28	1 43	16 28	4 31	12 23	23 21	7 17	12 39	10 37	28 04	5 26	0 45	23 15
4 Sa	20:50:30	11 41 37	9 ♒ 00	6 02	9 33	2 52	16 40	4 43	12 29	23 19	7 16	12 38	10 29	28 10	6 00	1 05	23 13
5 Su	20:54:26	12 39 03	20 52	5 57	11 38	4 01	16 52	4 55	12 34	23 17	7 14	12 38	10 20	28 16	6 34	1 24	23 12
6 M	20:58:23	13 36 30	2 ♓ 43	5 51	13 42	5 10	17 05	5 07	12 39	23 14	7 12	12 37	10 12	28 23	7 07	1 43	23 10
7 T	21:02:20	14 33 58	14 34	5 44	15 46	6 19	17 19	5 19	12 44	23 12	7 11	12 37	10 10	28 31	7 41	2 01	23 08
8 W	21:06:16	15 31 27	26 26	5 37	17 48	7 29	17 33	5 31	12 49	23 10	7 09	12 36	10 05	28 38	8 14	2 20	23 06
9 Th	21:10:13	16 28 57	8 ♈ 21	5 31	19 49	8 38	17 48	5 43	12 54	23 07	7 07	12 36	9 58	28 46	8 48	2 39	23 05
10 F	21:14:09	17 26 29	20 20	5 26	21 48	9 48	18 03	5 55	12 58	23 05	7 06	12 36	9 51	28 54	9 21	2 57	23 03
11 Sa	21:18:06	18 24 02	2 ♉ 24	5 23	23 48	10 58	18 18	6 07	13 03	23 04	7 04	12 35	9 44	29 03	9 54	3 15	23 02
12 Su	21:22:02	19 21 36	15	5 ℞ 29	25 45	12 08	18 37	6 19	13 08	23 00	7 03	12 35	9 38	29 12	10 28	3 33	23 01
13 M	21:25:59	20 19 12	28	5 22	27 41	13 18	18 55	6 31	13 12	22 58	7 01	12 34	9 35	29 21	11 01	3 51	22 59
14 T	21:29:55	21 16 49	11 ♊ 28	5 23	29 36	14 28	19 13	6 42	13 17	22 55	7 00	12 34	9 30	29 30	11 34	4 08	22 58
15 W	21:33:52	22 14 28	25 09	5 24	1 ♍ 29	15 38	19 32	6 54	13 21	22 53	6 58	12 33	9 26	29 40	12 07	4 26	22 57
16 Th	21:37:49	23 12 09	9 ⊛ 09	5 24	3 21	16 48	19 51	7 05	13 25	22 51	6 56	12 33	9 21	29 50	12 40	4 43	22 56
17 F	21:41:45	24 09 51	24 10	5 23	5 11	17 59	20 11	7 17	13 30	22 48	6 55	12 33	9 16	0 ♐ 01	13 13	5 00	22 55
18 Sa	21:45:42	25 07 34	9 ♌ 08	5 19	7 00	19 09	20 32	7 28	13 34	22 46	6 53	12 33	9 12	0 11	13 45	5 17	22 55
19 Su	21:49:38	26 05 19	24 21	5 14	8 47	20 20	20 53	7 39	13 38	22 43	6 52	12 32	9 09	0 22	14 18	5 33	22 54
20 M	21:53:35	27 03 05	9 ♍ 38	5 06	10 33	21 31	21 15	7 50	13 42	22 41	6 50	12 32	9 08	0 33	14 51	5 50	22 53
21 T	21:57:31	28 00 52	24 48	4 59	12 18	22 41	21 37	8 01	13 46	22 39	6 49	12 32	9 08	0 45	15 23	6 06	22 53
22 W	22:01:28	28 58 40	9 ♎ 42	4 51	14 01	23 52	22 00	8 12	13 49	22 36	6 47	12 32	9 08	0 56	15 56	6 22	22 52
23 Th	22:05:24	29 56 30	24 12	4 45	15 43	25 03	22 23	8 23	13 53	22 34	6 46	12 32	9 08	1 08	16 28	6 37	22 52
24 F	22:09:21	0 ♍ 54 21	8 ♏ 14	4 40	17 23	26 14	22 47	8 34	13 56	22 32	6 44	12 32 D	9 08	1 21	17 00	6 53	22 52
25 Sa	22:13:18	1 52 13	21 46	4 38 D	19 02	27 25	23 11	8 45	14 00	22 29	6 43	12 32	9 08	1 33	17 33	7 08	22 52
26 Su	22:17:14	2 50 06	4 ♐ 52	4 38	20 40	28 36	23 36	8 55	14 03	22 27	6 41	12 32	9 08	1 46	18 05	7 23	22 52
27 M	22:21:11	3 48 01	17 35	4 38	22 16	29 48	24 01	9 06	14 07	22 25	6 40	12 32	8 08	1 59	18 37	7 38	22 52 D
28 T	22:25:07	4 45 57	29 59	4 ℞ 39	23 51	0 ♌ 59	24 27	9 16	14 10	22 22	6 38	12 33	8 0 D	2 12	19 09	7 53	22 52
29 W	22:29:04	5 43 54	12 ♑ 08	4 39	25 25	2 11	24 53	9 26	14 13	22 22	6 37	12 33	8 08	2 25	19 41	8 07	22 52
30 Th	22:33:00	6 41 53	24 09	4 37	26 57	3 23	25 20	9 37	14 16	22 18	6 36	12 33	8 08	2 39	20 12	8 21	22 52
31 F	22:36:57	7 39 52	6 ♒ 03	4 32	28 28	4 35	25 47	9 47	14 19	22 15	6 35	12 33	8 08	2 53	20 44	8 35	22 52

Ephemeris is calculated for midnight Greenwich Mean Time

September 2001

DATE	SID.TIME	SUN	MOON	NODE	MERCURY	VENUS	MARS	JUPITER	SATURN	URANUS	NEPTUNE	PLUTO	CERES	PALLAS	JUNO	VESTA	CHIRON
1 Sa	22:40:53	8 ♍ 37 54	17 ≈ 54	4 ⊕ ℞ 25	29 ♍ 58	5 ♌ 45	26 ♐ 14	9 ⊕ 57	14 ♊ 22	22 ≈ ℞ 13	6 ≈ ℞ 33	12 ♐ 33	8 ♑ 48	3 ♐ 07	21 ⊕ 16	8 ♊ 48	22 ♐ 53
2 Su	22:44:50	9 35 57	29 ♓ 44	4 16	1 ♎ 26	6 57	26 42	10 07	14 24	22 11	6 32	12 34	8 50	3 21	21 47	9 02	22 53
3 M	22:48:47	10 34 01	11 ♓ 36	4 05	2 53	8 08	27 10	10 16	14 27	22 09	6 31	12 34	8 52	3 36	22 18	9 15	22 54
4 T	22:52:43	11 32 07	23 32	3 52	4 19	9 20	27 39	10 26	14 29	22 06	6 29	12 34	8 54	3 50	22 50	9 27	22 55
5 W	22:56:40	12 30 15	5 ♈ 32	3 40	5 43	10 32	28 08	10 36	14 32	22 04	6 28	12 35	8 57	4 05	23 21	9 40	22 56
6 Th	23:00:36	13 28 25	17 37	3 28	7 06	11 44	28 37	10 45	14 34	22 02	6 27	12 35	8 59	4 20	23 52	9 52	22 57
7 F	23:04:33	14 26 36	29 51	3 19	8 27	12 56	29 07	10 54	14 36	22 00	6 26	12 36	9 03	4 36	24 23	10 04	22 58
8 Sa	23:08:29	15 24 50	12 ♉ 14	3 12	9 47	14 09	29 37	11 04	14 38	21 58	6 25	12 36	9 06	4 51	24 54	10 16	22 59
9 Su	23:12:26	16 23 05	24 51	3 08 D	11 06	15 21	0 ♑ 08	11 13	14 40	21 56	6 23	12 37	9 10	5 07	25 25	10 27	23 00
10 M	23:16:22	17 21 23	7 ♊ 43	3 06 D	12 23	16 33	0 39	11 22	14 42	21 53	6 22	12 37	9 14	5 23	25 55	10 38	23 01
11 T	23:20:19	18 19 42	20 55	3 06 ℞	13 38	17 46	1 10	11 31	14 44	21 51	6 21	12 38	9 19	5 39	26 26	10 49	23 02
12 W	23:24:15	19 18 04	4 ⊕ 28	3 06	14 52	18 58	1 41	11 39	14 46	21 49	6 20	12 38	9 24	5 55	26 56	11 00	23 03
13 Th	23:28:12	20 16 28	18 23	3 05	16 03	20 11	2 13	11 48	14 47	21 47	6 19	12 39	9 29	6 11	27 26	11 10	23 04
14 F	23:32:09	21 14 54	2 ♌ 39	3 02	17 13	21 23	2 45	11 57	14 49	21 45	6 18	12 40	9 35	6 28	27 56	11 20	23 05
15 Sa	23:36:05	22 13 22	17 12	2 57	18 21	22 36	3 18	12 05	14 50	21 43	6 17	12 41	9 41	6 45	28 26	11 29	23 09
16 Su	23:40:02	23 11 53	2 ♍ 46	2 49	19 27	23 49	3 51	12 13	14 52	21 41	6 16	12 41	9 47	7 02	28 56	11 38	23 10
17 M	23:43:58	24 10 25	17 58	2 39	20 31	25 02	4 24	12 22	14 53	21 40	6 15	12 42	9 53	7 19	29 26	11 47	23 12
18 T	23:47:55	25 08 59	2 ⎷ 09	2 28	21 33	26 14	4 57	12 29	14 54	21 38	6 14	12 43	10 00	7 36	29 56	11 56	23 14
19 W	23:51:51	26 07 35	18 08	2 17	22 32	27 27	5 31	12 37	14 55	21 36	6 13	12 44	10 07	7 53	0 ♌ 25	12 04	23 16
20 Th	23:55:48	27 06 12	2 ♏ 44	2 08	23 28	28 40	6 05	12 45	14 56	21 34	6 12	12 45	10 14	8 11	0 55	12 12	23 18
21 F	23:59:44	28 04 52	16 53	2 01	24 22	29 53	6 39	12 52	14 R 56	21 32	6 11	12 45	10 22	8 28	1 24	12 19	23 21
22 Sa	0:03:41	29 03 33	0 ♐ 32	1 56	25 12	1 ♍ 07	7 13	12 59	14 57	21 30	6 11	12 46	10 30	8 46	1 53	12 26	23 23
23 Su	0:07:38	0 ♎ 02 16	13 43	1 54	25 59	2 20	7 48	13 07	14 57	21 29	6 10	12 47	10 38	9 04	2 22	12 33	23 25
24 M	0:11:34	1 01 01	26 27	1 54	26 43	3 33	8 23	13 14	14 58	21 27	6 09	12 48	10 47	9 22	2 51	12 39	23 28
25 T	0:15:31	1 59 47	8 ⛎ 51	1 54	27 23	4 46	8 58	13 21	14 58	21 25	6 08	12 49	10 56	9 41	3 20	12 45	23 30
26 W	0:19:27	2 58 35	20 59	1 53	27 58	6 00	9 34	13 28	14 58	21 24	6 07	12 51	11 05	9 59	3 48	12 51	23 33
27 Th	0:23:24	3 57 25	2 ≈ 56	1 50	28 29	7 13	10 10	13 35	14 58	21 22	6 07	12 52	11 14	10 18	4 17	12 56	23 36
28 F	0:27:20	4 56 16	14 48	1 45	28 55	8 27	10 46	13 41	14 ℞ 58	21 21	6 06	12 52	11 24	10 36	4 45	13 01	23 39
29 Sa	0:31:17	5 55 10	26 38	1 38	29 15	9 40	11 22	13 48	14 58	21 19	6 06	12 54	11 33	10 55	5 13	13 06	23 41
30 Su	0:35:13	6 54 05	8 ♓ 29	1 27	29 30	10 54	11 58	13 54	14 58	21 18	6 05	12 55	11 44	11 14	5 41	13 10	23 44

Ephemeris is calculated for midnight Greenwich Mean Time

October 2001

DATE	SID.TIME	SUN	MOON	NODE	MERCURY	VENUS	MARS	JUPITER	SATURN	URANUS	NEPTUNE	PLUTO	CERES	PALLAS	JUNO	VESTA	CHIRON
1 M	0:39:10	7♎53 02	20♓25	1♋R.04	29♎R.39	12♍35	12♑07	14♋00	14♊R.57	21♒R.16	6♒R.04	12✗56	11♐54	11✗33	6♌09	13♊14	23✗47
2 T	0:43:07	8 52 01	2♈27	1 00	29 41	13 21	13 12	14 06	14 57	21 15	6 04	12 57	12 05	11 52	6 37	13 17	23 51
3 W	0:47:03	9 51 01	14 36	0 46	29 36	14 35	13 49	14 12	14 56	21 14	6 03	12 59	12 16	12 11	7 04	13 20	23 54
4 Th	0:51:00	10 50 04	26 54	0 34	29 24	15 49	14 26	14 17	14 55	21 12	6 03	13 00	12 27	12 31	7 32	13 23	23 57
5 F	0:54:56	11 49 09	9♉23	0 23	29 04	17 02	15 04	14 23	14 55	21 11	6 02	13 01	12 38	12 50	7 59	13 25	24 00
6 Sa	0:58:53	12 48 17	21 56	0 15	28 36	18 16	15 41	14 28	14 54	21 10	6 02	13 03	12 50	13 10	8 26	13 26	24 04
7 Su	1:02:49	13 47 26	4♊42	0 10	28 00	19 30	16 19	14 33	14 53	21 09	6 02	13 04	13 01	13 29	8 53	13 28	24 07
8 M	1:06:46	14 46 38	17 42	0 08	27 17	20 44	16 57	14 38	14 52	21 08	6 01	13 06	13 13	13 49	9 20	13 28	24 11
9 T	1:10:42	15 45 52	0♋56	0 07	26 26	21 58	17 35	14 43	14 51	21 07	6 01	13 07	13 26	14 09	9 46	13♊R.29	24 14
10 W	1:14:39	16 45 09	14 28	0♋R.07	25 28	23 12	18 14	14 47	14 50	21 06	6 01	13 08	13 38	14 29	10 13	13 29	24 18
11 Th	1:18:36	17 44 28	28 18	0 07	24 24	24 27	18 52	14 52	14 49	21 05	6 00	13 10	13 51	14 49	10 39	13 28	24 22
12 F	1:22:32	18 43 49	12♌29	0 05	23 16	25 41	19 31	14 56	14 48	21 04	6 00	13 11	14 04	15 09	11 05	13 27	24 26
13 Sa	1:26:29	19 43 12	26 58	0 00	22 05	26 55	20 10	15 00	14 46	21 03	6 00	13 13	14 17	15 30	11 31	13 26	24 30
14 Su	1:30:25	20 42 38	11♍43	29♊53	20 52	28 09	20 49	15 04	14 44	21 02	6 00	13 15	14 31	15 50	11 56	13 24	24 34
15 M	1:34:22	21 42 06	26 37	29 44	19 37	29 24	21 28	15 07	14 41	21 01	6 00	13 16	14 44	16 11	12 22	13 22	24 38
16 T	1:38:18	22 41 36	11♎32	29 34	18 21	0♎38	22 08	15 11	14 39	21 00	6 00	13 18	14 58	16 31	12 47	13 19	24 42
17 W	1:42:15	23 41 08	26 20	29 24	17 06	1 53	22 47	15 14	14 37	20 59	6 00	13 19	15 12	16 52	13 12	13 16	24 46
18 Th	1:46:11	24 40 42	10♏56	29 15	15 53	3 07	23 27	15 17	14 34	20 58	6 00	13 21	15 26	17 13	13 37	13 13	24 50
19 F	1:50:08	25 40 18	24 57	29 08	14 42	4 21	24 07	15 20	14 32	20 58	6 00 D	13 23	15 41	17 33	14 01	13 09	24 55
20 Sa	1:54:04	26 39 57	8✗37	29 03	13 36	5 36	24 47	15 23	14 30	20 58	6 00	13 24	15 55	17 54	14 26	13 04	24 59
21 Su	1:58:01	27 39 36	21 51	29 D 02	14 35	6 51	25 27	15 26	14 27	20 57	6 00	13 26	16 10	18 15	14 50	12 59	25 04
22 M	2:01:58	28 39 18	4♑39	29 01	14 18	8 05	26 07	15 28	14 25	20 57	6 00	13 28	16 25	18 36	15 15	12 54	25 08
23 T	2:05:54	29 39 02	17 06	29 02	14 D 06	9 20	26 47	15 30	14 22	20 56	6 00	13 30	16 40	18 58	15 38	12 48	25 13
24 W	2:09:51	0♏38 47	29 17	29♊R.03	14 14	10 34	27 28	15 32	14 19	20 56	6 00	13 32	16 55	19 19	16 01	12 42	25 17
25 Th	2:13:47	1 38 33	11♒15	29 02	14 34	11 49	28 09	15 34	14 16	20 55	6 00	13 33	17 11	19 40	16 25	12 35	25 22
26 F	2:17:44	2 38 22	23 05	29 00	15 00	13 03	28 49	15 36	14 13	20 55	6 01	13 35	17 27	20 02	16 48	12 28	25 27
27 Sa	2:21:40	3 38 12	4♓58	28 55	15 36	14 18	29 30	15 37	14 10	20 55	6 02	13 37	17 43	20 23	17 10	12 21	25 32
28 Su	2:25:37	4 38 04	16 51	28 48	16 20	15 33	0♒11	15 38	14 07	20 55	6 01	13 39	17 59	20 45	17 33	12 13	25 37
29 M	2:29:33	5 37 57	28 52	28 39	17 12	16 48	0 53	15 39	14 04	20 55	6 02	13 41	18 15	21 06	17 55	12 04	25 42
30 T	2:33:30	6 37 53	11♈01	28 30	18 11	18 03	1 34	15 40	14 01	20 55	6 02	13 43	18 31	21 28	18 18	11 56	25 47
31 W	2:37:27	7 37 50	23 21	28 21	19 16	19 18	2 15	15 41	13 57	20 55	6 02	13 48	18 48	21 49	18 39	11 46	25 52

Ephemeris is calculated for midnight Greenwich Mean Time

November 2001

DATE	SID.TIME	SUN	MOON	NODE	MERCURY	VENUS	MARS	JUPITER	SATURN	URANUS	NEPTUNE	PLUTO	CERES	PALLAS	JUNO	VESTA	CHIRON
1 Th	2:41:23	8 ♏ 37 49	5 ♉ 52	28 ♊ R 10	20 ♎ 27	20 ♎ 33	2 ♒ 56	15 ♋ 41	13 ♊ R 54	20 ♒ 55	6 ♒ 03	13 ✗ 47	19 ♑ 04	22 ✗ 11	19 ♌ 01	11 ♊ R 37	25 ✗ 57
2 F	2:45:20	9 37 49	18 28	28 36	21 42	21 48	3 38	15 R 41	13 49	20 55	6 03	13 49	19 21	22 33	19 23	11 27	26 02
3 Sa	2:49:16	10 37 52	1 ♊ 31	28 57	23 01	23 03	4 20	15 41	13 46	20 55	6 04	13 51	19 38	22 55	19 44	11 16	26 07
4 Su	2:53:13	11 37 57	14 37	27 54	24 23	24 18	5 01	15 41	13 43	20 55	6 04	13 53	19 55	23 17	20 05	11 06	26 12
5 M	2:57:09	12 38 04	27 55	27 D 54	25 48	25 33	5 43	15 41	13 39	20 55	6 05	13 55	20 13	23 39	20 25	10 55	26 18
6 T	3:01:06	13 38 13	11 ♋ 24	27 54	27 15	26 48	6 25	15 40	13 35	20 56	6 06	13 57	20 30	24 01	20 45	10 43	26 23
7 W	3:05:02	14 38 24	25 04	27 56	28 45	28 03	7 07	15 40	13 31	20 56	6 06	13 59	20 48	24 23	21 06	10 31	26 28
8 Th	3:08:59	15 38 36	8 ♌ 53	27 57	0 ♏ 16	29 18	7 49	15 40	13 27	20 56	6 07	14 01	21 05	24 45	21 25	10 19	26 34
9 F	3:12:56	16 38 51	23 01	27 57	1 48	0 ♏ 33	8 31	15 39	13 23	20 57	6 08	14 03	21 23	25 07	21 45	10 06	26 39
10 Sa	3:16:52	17 39 08	7 ♍ 15	27 55	3 21	1 48	9 13	15 37	13 19	20 57	6 08	14 05	21 41	25 30	22 04	9 54	26 45
11 Su	3:20:49	18 39 27	21 38	27 52	4 55	3 03	9 56	15 35	13 15	20 58	6 09	14 07	21 59	25 52	22 23	9 40	26 51
12 M	3:24:45	19 39 48	6 ♎ 06	27 47	6 30	4 18	10 38	15 33	13 11	20 58	6 10	14 09	22 17	26 14	22 42	9 27	26 56
13 T	3:28:42	20 40 11	20 34	27 41	8 05	5 34	11 21	15 31	13 06	20 59	6 11	14 12	22 36	26 37	23 00	9 13	27 02
14 W	3:32:38	21 40 36	4 ♏ 55	27 35	9 40	6 49	12 03	15 29	13 02	21 00	6 12	14 14	22 55	26 59	23 18	8 59	27 08
15 Th	3:36:35	22 41 02	19 11	27 30	11 16	8 04	12 46	15 26	12 57	21 00	6 13	14 16	23 13	27 22	23 35	8 45	27 13
16 F	3:40:31	23 41 31	2 ✗ 26	27 26	12 52	9 19	13 28	15 24	12 53	21 01	6 14	14 18	23 32	27 44	23 53	8 31	27 19
17 Sa	3:44:28	24 42 00	16 16	27 D 24	14 28	10 35	14 11	15 21	12 48	21 02	6 15	14 20	23 51	28 07	24 10	8 16	27 25
18 Su	3:48:25	25 42 32	29 39	27 23	16 03	11 50	14 54	15 18	12 44	21 03	6 16	14 22	24 10	28 30	24 27	8 01	27 31
19 M	3:52:21	26 43 04	12 ♑ 27	27 24	17 39	13 05	15 37	15 15	12 39	21 04	6 17	14 25	24 29	28 52	24 43	7 46	27 37
20 T	3:56:18	27 43 38	24 56	27 26	19 15	14 20	16 20	15 11	12 35	21 05	6 18	14 27	24 48	29 15	24 59	7 31	27 43
21 W	4:00:14	28 44 13	7 ♒ 08	27 28	20 51	15 36	17 03	15 08	12 30	21 06	6 19	14 29	25 08	29 38	25 15	7 15	27 49
22 Th	4:04:11	29 44 50	19 09	27 29	22 26	16 51	17 46	15 04	12 25	21 07	6 20	14 31	25 27	0 ♑ 00	25 30	7 00	27 55
23 F	4:08:07	0 ✗ 45 27	1 ✗ 26	27 R 29	24 02	18 06	18 29	15 00	12 20	21 08	6 21	14 34	25 47	0 23	25 45	6 44	28 01
24 Sa	4:12:04	1 46 06	12 55	27 29	25 37	19 22	19 12	14 56	12 16	21 09	6 22	14 36	26 07	0 46	25 59	6 29	28 07
25 Su	4:16:00	2 46 46	24 50	27 27	27 12	20 37	19 55	14 52	12 11	21 11	6 24	14 38	26 26	1 09	26 14	6 13	28 13
26 M	4:19:57	3 47 26	6 ♈ 52	27 25	28 47	21 52	20 38	14 47	12 06	21 12	6 25	14 40	26 46	1 32	26 27	5 57	28 19
27 T	4:23:54	4 48 08	19 08	27 21	0 ✗ 21	23 08	21 22	14 43	12 01	21 13	6 26	14 43	27 06	1 55	26 41	5 42	28 25
28 W	4:27:50	5 48 52	1 ♉ 39	27 17	1 55	24 23	22 05	14 38	11 56	21 15	6 27	14 45	27 27	2 17	26 54	5 26	28 31
29 Th	4:31:47	6 49 36	14 24	27 14	3 30	25 39	22 48	14 33	11 51	21 16	6 29	14 47	27 47	2 40	27 07	5 10	28 38
30 F	4:35:43	7 50 21	27 27	27 11	5 06	26 54	23 32	14 28	11 46	21 18	6 30	14 50	28 07	3 03	27 19	4 54	28 44

Ephemeris is calculated for midnight Greenwich Mean Time

December 2001

DATE		SID.TIME	SUN	MOON	NODE	MERCURY	VENUS	MARS	JUPITER	SATURN	URANUS	NEPTUNE	PLUTO	CERES	PALLAS	JUNO	VESTA	CHIRON
1	Sa	4:39:40	8 ♐ 51 08	10 ♊ 30	27 ♋ ℞ 09	6 ♐ 41	28 ♏ 09	24 ♐ 15	14 ♋ ℞ 23	11 ♊ ℞ 42	21 ♒ 19	6 ♒ 32	14 ♐ 52	28 ♑ 27	3 ♑ 26	27 ♌ 31	4 ♊ ℞ 39	28 ♐ 50
2	Su	4:43:36	9 51 56	24 ♊ 01	27 D 08	8 15	29 25	24 59	14 17	11 37	21 21	6 33	14 54	28 48	3 49	27 42	4 23	28 56
3	M	4:47:33	10 52 45	7 ♋ 45	27 09	9 49	0 ♐ 40	25 42	14 12	11 32	21 22	6 34	14 56	29 08	4 12	27 53	4 08	29 03
4	T	4:51:30	11 53 36	21 40	27 10	11 24	1 56	26 26	14 06	11 27	21 24	6 36	14 59	29 29	4 35	28 04	3 52	29 09
5	W	4:55:26	12 54 27	5 ♌ 09	27 11	12 58	3 11	27 09	14 00	11 22	21 26	6 37	15 01	29 50	4 58	28 14	3 37	29 15
6	Th	4:59:23	13 55 20	19 51	27 12	14 32	4 27	27 53	13 54	11 17	21 27	6 39	15 03	0 ♒ 11	5 22	28 24	3 22	29 22
7	F	5:03:19	14 56 15	4 ♍ 02	27 ℞ 13	16 06	5 42	28 37	13 48	11 12	21 29	6 41	15 06	0 32	5 45	28 34	3 07	29 28
8	Sa	5:07:16	15 57 0	18 13	27 13	17 40	6 58	29 20	13 41	11 07	21 31	6 42	15 08	0 53	6 08	28 43	2 52	29 35
9	Su	5:11:12	16 58 07	2 ♎ 23	27 12	19 15	8 13	0 ♑ 04	13 35	11 02	21 33	6 44	15 10	1 14	6 31	28 51	2 37	29 41
10	M	5:15:09	17 59 05	16 30	27 12	20 49	9 28	0 48	13 28	10 57	21 35	6 45	15 13	1 35	6 54	28 59	2 23	29 47
11	T	5:19:05	19 00 04	0 ♏ 31	27 11	22 23	10 44	1 31	13 21	10 52	21 37	6 47	15 15	1 56	7 17	29 07	2 09	29 54
12	W	5:23:02	20 01 05	14 24	27 10	23 58	11 59	2 15	13 14	10 48	21 39	6 49	15 17	2 18	7 40	29 14	1 55	0 ♑ 00
13	Th	5:26:59	21 02 06	28 06	27 09	25 32	13 15	2 59	13 07	10 43	21 41	6 50	15 20	2 39	8 03	29 21	1 41	0 07
14	F	5:30:55	22 03 08	11 ♐ 37	27 08	27 07	14 30	3 43	13 00	10 38	21 43	6 52	15 22	3 00	8 27	29 27	1 28	0 13
15	Sa	5:34:52	23 04 12	24 55	27 D 08	28 41	15 46	4 26	12 53	10 33	21 45	6 54	15 24	3 22	8 50	29 33	1 15	0 20
16	Su	5:38:48	24 05 16	7 ♑ 57	27 08	0 ♑ 16	17 02	5 10	12 46	10 29	21 47	6 56	15 26	3 44	9 13	29 38	1 02	0 26
17	M	5:42:45	25 06 20	20 43	27 08	1 51	18 17	5 54	12 38	10 24	21 50	6 57	15 29	4 05	9 36	29 43	0 50	0 33
18	T	5:46:41	26 07 25	2 ♒ 18	27 09	3 26	19 33	6 38	12 31	10 19	21 52	6 59	15 31	4 27	9 59	29 47	0 38	0 39
19	W	5:50:38	27 08 31	14 55	27 ℞ 09	5 01	20 48	7 22	12 23	10 15	21 54	7 01	15 33	4 49	10 23	29 51	0 26	0 46
20	Th	5:54:34	28 09 37	26 56	27 09	6 36	22 04	8 06	12 16	10 10	21 57	7 03	15 36	5 11	10 46	29 54	0 15	0 52
21	F	5:58:31	29 10 43	8 ♓ 51	27 08	8 12	23 19	8 50	12 08	10 05	21 59	7 05	15 38	5 33	11 09	29 57	0 04	0 59
22	Sa	6:02:28	0 ♑ 11 49	20 43	27 D 08	9 47	24 35	9 34	12 00	10 01	22 01	7 07	15 40	5 55	11 32	29 59	29 ♉ 53	1 05
23	Su	6:06:24	1 12 56	2 ♈ 36	27 08	11 22	25 50	10 18	11 52	9 57	22 04	7 09	15 42	6 17	11 55	0 ♍ 01	29 43	1 12
24	M	6:10:21	2 14 03	14 37	27 08	12 58	27 06	11 02	11 44	9 52	22 06	7 11	15 45	6 39	12 19	0 02	29 33	1 18
25	T	6:14:17	3 15 09	26 48	27 09	14 33	28 21	11 45	11 37	9 48	22 09	7 13	15 47	7 01	12 42	0 03	29 24	1 25
26	W	6:18:14	4 16 16	9 ♉ 16	27 09	16 09	29 37	12 29	11 29	9 44	22 11	7 14	15 49	7 24	13 05	0 ℞ 03	29 15	1 31
27	Th	6:22:00	5 17 24	22 02	27 10	17 44	0 ♑ 52	13 13	11 21	9 39	22 14	7 16	15 51	7 46	13 28	0 03	29 06	1 38
28	F	6:26:07	6 18 31	5 ♊ 10	27 11	19 19	2 08	13 57	11 12	9 35	22 16	7 18	15 53	8 08	13 51	0 02	28 58	1 44
29	Sa	6:30:03	7 19 38	18 40	27 ℞ 12	20 54	3 23	14 41	11 04	9 31	22 19	7 20	15 56	8 31	14 14	0 00	28 50	1 50
30	Su	6:34:00	8 20 46	2 ♋ 32	27 12	22 28	4 39	15 25	10 56	9 27	22 22	7 23	15 58	8 53	14 38	29 ♌ 59	28 43	1 57
31	M	6:37:57	9 21 54	16 42	27 11	24 02	5 54	16 09	10 48	9 23	22 25	7 25	16 00	9 16	15 01	29 56	28 36	2 03

Ephemeris is calculated for midnight Greenwich Mean Time

The Planetary Hours

The selection of an auspicious time for starting any affair is an important matter. When a thing is begun, its existence tends to take on a nature corresponding to the conditions under which it was begun.

Each hour of the day is ruled by a planet, and so the nature of any time during the day corresponds to the nature of the planet ruling it. The nature of the planetary hours is the same as the description of each of the planets, except that you will not need to refer to the descriptions for Uranus, Neptune, and Pluto, as they are considered here as higher octaves of Mercury, Venus, and Mars, respectively. If something is ruled by Uranus, you can use the hour of Mercury.

The only other factor you need to know to use the planetary hours is the time of your local sunrise and sunset for any given day. This is given in the following chart.

Planetary hours for January 2, 2001, 10 degrees latitude

Step One. Find sunrise (table, page 190) and sunset (table, page 191) for January 2, 2001, at 10 degrees latitude by following the 10 degrees latitude column down to the January 2 row. In the case of our example, this is the first entry in the upper left-hand corner of both the sunrise and sunset tables. You will see that sunrise for January 2, 2001, at 10 degrees latitude is at 6 hours and 16 minutes (or 6:16 am) and sunset is at 17 hours and 49 minutes (or 5:49 pm).

Step Two. Subtract sunrise time (6 hours 16 minutes) from sunset time (17 hours 49 minutes) to get the number of astrological daylight hours. It is easier to do this if you convert the hours into minutes. For example, 6 hours and 16 minutes = 376 minutes (6 hours x 60 minutes each = 360 minutes + 16 minutes = 376 minutes). 17 hours and 49 minutes = 1,069 minutes (17 hours x 60 minutes = 1020 minutes + 49 minutes = 1,069 minutes). Now subtract: 1,069 minutes - 376 minutes = 693 minutes. If we then convert this back to hours by dividing by 60, we have 11 hours and 33 minutes of daylight planetary hours. However, it is easier to calculate the next step if you leave the number in minutes.

Step Three. Next you should determine how many minutes are in a daylight planetary hour for that particular day (January 2, 2001, 10 degrees latitude). To do this, divide 693 minutes by 12 (the number of hours of daylight at the equinoxes). The answer is 58, rounded up. Therefore, a daylight planetary hour for January 2, 2001, at 10 degrees latitude has 58 minutes.

Step Four. Now you know that each daylight planetary hour is roughly 58 minutes. You also know, from step one, that sunrise is at 6:16 am. To determine the starting times of each planetary hour, simply add 58 minutes to the sunrise time for the first planetary hour, 58 minutes to that number for the second planetary hour, etc. So the daylight planetary hours for our example are as follows: first hour, 6:16 am–7:14 am; second hour, 7:14 am–8:12 am; third hour, 8:12 am–9:10 am; fourth hour, 9:10 am–10:08 am; fifth hour, 10:08 am–11:06 am; sixth hour, 11:06 am–12:04 am; seventh hour, 12:04 am–1:02 pm; eighth hour, 1:02 pm–2:00 pm; ninth hour, 2:00 pm–2:58 pm; tenth hour, 2:58 pm–3:56 pm; eleventh hour, 3:56 pm–4:54 pm; and twelfth hour, 4:54 pm–5:52 pm. Note that because you rounded up the number of minutes in a sunrise hour, the last hour doesn't end where the sunset table says sunset begins (5:49 pm). This is a good reason to give yourself a little "fudge space" when using planetary hours. (You could also skip the rounding-up step.) For more accurate sunrise or sunset times, consult your local paper.

Step Five. Now, to determine which sign rules which daylight planetary hour, consult your *Daily Planetary Guide* date pages to determine which day of the week January 2 falls on. You'll find it's a Tuesday. Next, turn to page 192 to find the sunrise planetary hour chart. (It's the one on the top.) If you follow down the column for Sunday, you will find the first hour is ruled by Mars, the second by the Sun, the third by Mercury, and so on.

Step Six. Now you've determined the daytime (sunrise) planetary hours. You can use the same formula to determine the nighttime (sunset) planetary hours. You know you have 11 hours and 33 minutes of sunrise planetary hours. Therefore subtract 11 hours and 33 minutes of sunrise hours from the 24 hours in a day to equal the number of sunset hours. 24 hours - 11 hours 13 minutes = 12 hours 47 minutes of sunset time. Now convert this to minutes $(12 \times 60) + 47 = (720) + 47 = 767$ minutes. (This equals 12.783 hours, but remember to leave it in minutes for now.)

Step Seven. Now go to step three and repeat the rest of the process for the sunset hours. When you get to step five, remember to consult the sunset table on page 192 rather than the sunrise table. When you complete these steps you should get the following answers. There are (roughly) 63 minutes in a sunset planetary hour for this example. This means that the times for the sunset planetary hours are (starting from the 17:49 sunset time rather than the 6:16 sunrise time): first hour, 5:49 pm; second hour, 6:52 pm; third hour, 7:55 pm; fourth hour, 8:58 pm; fifth hour, 10:01 pm; sixth hour, 11:04 pm; seventh hour, 12:07 am; eighth hour, 1:10 am; ninth hour, 2:13 am; tenth hour, 3:16 am; eleventh hour, 4:19 am; and twelfth hour, 5:22 am. You see which signs rule the hours by consulting the sunset chart on page 192.

Sunrise

Universal Time for Meridian of Greenwich

Latitude		+10°	+20°	+30°	+40°	+42°	+46°	+50°
		h:m	h:m	h:m	h:m	h:m	h:m	h:m
JAN	2	6:16	6:34	6:57	7:21	7:28	7:42	7:59
	14	6:21	6:34	6:55	7:20	7:26	7:39	7:53
	26	6:23	6:37	6:53	7:14	7:19	7:29	7:42
FEB	7	6:22	6:33	6:46	7:03	7:06	7:15	7:24
	19	6:18	6:27	6:36	6:48	6:50	6:56	7:03
	27	6:15	6:21	6:28	6:37	6:38	6:43	6:48
MAR	7	6:11	6:15	6:19	6:24	6:26	6:28	6:31
	19	6:05	6:05	6:05	6:05	6:05	6:05	6:05
	27	6:00	5:58	5:56	5:52	5:52	5:50	5:49
APR	12	5:51	5:44	5:37	5:27	5:25	5:19	5:14
	20	5:47	5:38	5:28	5:15	5:12	5:05	4:57
	28	5:44	5:33	5:20	5:04	5:00	4:52	4:42
MAY	6	5:41	5:28	5:13	4:54	4:50	4:40	4:28
	18	5:38	5:23	5:05	4:42	4:37	4:25	4:10
	26	5:38	5:21	5:01	4:36	4:30	4:17	4:01
JUN	3	5:38	5:20	4:59	4:32	4:26	4:12	3:54
	15	5:39	5:20	4:58	4:30	4:24	4:09	3:50
	23	5:41	5:22	5:00	4:32	4:25	4:10	3:51
JUL	1	5:43	5:24	5:02	4:35	4:28	4:13	3:55
	9	5:45	5:27	5:06	4:39	4:33	4:19	4:01
	17	5:47	5:30	5:10	4:45	4:39	4:26	4:10
	25	5:48	5:33	5:15	4:52	4:46	4:34	4:20
AUG	2	5:50	5:36	5:19	4:59	4:54	4:43	4:31
	10	5:51	5:38	5:24	5:07	5:02	4:53	4:42
	18	5:51	5:41	5:29	5:14	5:11	5:03	4:54
	26	5:51	5:43	5:34	5:22	5:19	5:13	5:06
SEP	3	5:51	5:45	5:38	5:29	5:27	5:23	5:18
	11	5:50	5:46	5:42	5:37	5:36	5:33	5:30
	19	5:49	5:48	5:47	5:45	5:44	5:43	5:42
	27	5:49	5:50	5:51	5:52	5:53	5:53	5:54
OCT	13	5:48	5:54	6:01	6:08	6:10	6:14	6:19
	21	5:49	5:57	6:06	6:17	6:19	6:25	6:31
	29	5:50	6:00	6:12	6:26	6:29	6:36	6:45
NOV	6	5:52	6:04	6:18	6:35	6:39	6:48	6:58
	14	5:54	6:08	6:24	6:44	6:49	6:59	7:11
	22	5:57	6:13	6:31	6:53	6:58	7:10	7:24
	30	6:01	6:18	6:37	7:02	7:07	7:20	7:35
DEC	8	6:05	6:23	6:44	7:09	7:15	7:29	7:45
	16	6:09	6:28	6:49	7:15	7:22	7:36	7:53
	24	6:13	6:32	6:53	7:20	7:26	7:40	7:57
	30	6:17	6:35	6:56	7:22	7:28	7:42	7:59

Sunset
Universal Time for Meridian of Greenwich

Latitude		+10°	+20°	+30°	+40°	+42°	+46°	+50°
		h:m	h:m	h:m	h:m	h:m	h:m	h:m
JAN	2	17:49	17:30	17:09	16:43	16:37	16:23	16:06
	14	17:57	17:41	17:22	16:58	16:52	16:40	16:25
	26	18:03	17:48	17:32	17:12	17:07	16:57	16:44
FEB	7	18:07	17:55	17:42	17:26	17:23	17:14	17:05
	19	18:09	18:01	17:52	17:40	17:38	17:32	17:25
	27	18:10	18:04	17:58	17:50	17:48	17:44	17:39
MAR	7	18:11	18:07	18:03	17:58	17:57	17:55	17:52
	19	18:11	18:11	18:11	18:11	18:11	18:11	18:11
	27	18:11	18:13	18:16	18:19	18:20	18:22	18:24
APR	12	18:10	18:17	18:25	18:35	18:38	18:43	18:49
	20	18:11	18:20	18:30	18:43	18:47	18:53	19:02
	28	18:11	18:22	18:35	18:52	18:55	19:04	19:14
MAY	6	18:12	18:25	18:41	19:00	19:04	19:14	19:26
	18	18:14	18:30	18:48	19:11	19:17	19:29	19:43
	26	18:16	18:33	18:53	19:18	19:24	19:38	19:54
JUN	3	18:18	18:37	18:57	19:24	19:30	19:45	20:02
	15	18:22	18:43	19:03	19:30	19:37	19:53	20:11
	23	18:23	18:42	19:05	19:33	19:39	19:55	20:13
JUL	1	18:25	18:43	19:05	19:33	19:39	19:54	20:12
	9	18:25	18:43	19:04	19:31	19:37	19:51	20:09
	17	18:25	18:42	19:02	19:27	19:33	19:46	20:02
	25	18:24	18:42	18:58	19:21	19:26	19:38	19:53
AUG	2	18:23	18:36	18:53	19:13	19:18	19:28	19:41
	10	18:20	18:32	18:46	19:03	19:07	19:17	19:28
	18	18:16	18:27	18:38	18:53	18:56	19:04	19:13
	26	18:12	18:20	18:30	18:41	18:44	18:50	18:57
SEP	3	18:08	18:14	18:20	18:28	18:30	18:35	18:40
	11	18:03	18:06	18:10	18:16	18:17	18:19	18:23
	19	17:58	17:59	18:00	18:02	18:03	18:04	18:05
	27	17:53	17:52	17:50	17:49	17:49	17:48	17:47
OCT	13	17:44	17:38	17:32	17:24	17:22	17:18	17:13
	21	17:40	17:32	17:23	17:12	17:09	17:04	16:57
	29	17:37	17:27	17:16	17:01	16:58	16:51	16:42
NOV	6	17:36	17:23	17:09	16:52	16:48	16:39	16:29
	14	17:35	17:21	17:04	16:45	16:40	16:30	16:17
	22	17:35	17:19	17:01	16:39	16:34	16:22	16:08
	30	17:36	17:19	17:00	16:36	16:30	16:17	16:02
DEC	8	17:39	17:21	17:00	16:35	16:28	16:15	15:58
	16	17:42	17:24	17:02	16:36	16:30	16:15	15:59
	24	17:46	17:27	17:06	16:40	16:33	16:19	16:02
	30	17:50	17:32	17:11	16:45	16:39	16:25	16:09

Sunrise and Sunset Hours

Sunrise

Hour	Sun	Mon	Tue	Wed	Thu	Fri	Sat
1	☉	☽	♂	☿	♃	♀	♄
2	♀	♄	☉	☽	♂	☿	♃
3	☿	♃	♀	♄	☉	☽	♂
4	☽	♂	☿	♃	♀	♄	☉
5	♄	☉	☽	♂	☿	♃	♀
6	♃	♀	♄	☉	☽	♂	☿
7	♂	☿	♃	♀	♄	☉	☽
8	☉	☽	♂	☿	♃	♀	♄
9	♀	♄	☉	☽	♂	☿	♃
10	☿	♃	♀	♄	☉	☽	♂
11	☽	♂	☿	♃	♀	♄	☉
12	♄	☉	☽	♂	☿	♃	♀

Sunset

Hour	Sun	Mon	Tue	Wed	Thu	Fri	Sat
1	♃	♀	♄	☉	☽	♂	☿
2	♂	☿	♃	♀	♄	☉	☽
3	☉	☽	♂	☿	♃	♀	♄
4	♀	♄	☉	☽	♂	☿	♃
5	☿	♃	♀	♄	☉	☽	♂
6	☽	♂	☿	♃	♀	♄	☉
7	♄	☉	☽	♂	☿	♃	♀
8	♃	♀	♄	☉	☽	♂	☿
9	♂	☿	♃	♀	♄	☉	☽
10	☉	☽	♂	☿	♃	♀	♄
11	♀	♄	☉	☽	♂	☿	♃
12	☿	♃	♀	♄	☉	☽	♂

☉ Sun; ☿ Mercury; ♄ Saturn; ♂ Mars; ♀ Venus; ☽ Moon; ♃ Jupiter

Quick Table of Rising Signs

Your ascendant is the following if your time of birth was:

Sun sign:	6-8 am	8-10 am	10 am-12 pm	12-2 pm	2-4 pm	4-6 pm
Aries	Taurus	Gemini	Cancer	Leo	Virgo	Libra
Taurus	Gemini	Cancer	Leo	Virgo	Libra	Scorpio
Gemini	Cancer	Leo	Virgo	Libra	Scorpio	Sagittarius
Cancer	Leo	Virgo	Libra	Scorpio	Sagittarius	Capricorn
Leo	Virgo	Libra	Scorpio	Sagittarius	Capricorn	Aquarius
Virgo	Libra	Scorpio	Sagittarius	Capricorn	Aquarius	Pisces
Libra	Scorpio	Sagittarius	Capricorn	Aquarius	Pisces	Aries
Scorpio	Sagittarius	Capricorn	Aquarius	Pisces	Aries	Taurus
Sagittarius	Capricorn	Aquarius	Pisces	Aries	Taurus	Gemini
Capricorn	Aquarius	Pisces	Aries	Taurus	Gemini	Cancer
Aquarius	Pisces	Aries	Taurus	Gemini	Cancer	Leo
Pisces	Aries	Taurus	Gemini	Cancer	Leo	Virgo

Sun sign	6-8 pm	8-10 pm	10 pm-12 am	12-2 am	2-4 am	4-6 am
Aries	Scorpio	Sagittarius	Capricorn	Aquarius	Pisces	Aries
Taurus	Sagittarius	Capricorn	Aquarius	Pisces	Aries	Taurus
Gemini	Capricorn	Aquarius	Pisces	Aries	Taurus	Gemini
Cancer	Aquarius	Pisces	Aries	Taurus	Gemini	Cancer
Leo	Pisces	Aries	Taurus	Gemini	Cancer	Leo
Virgo	Aries	Taurus	Gemini	Cancer	Leo	Virgo
Libra	Taurus	Gemini	Cancer	Leo	Virgo	Libra
Scorpio	Gemini	Cancer	Leo	Virgo	Libra	Scorpio
Sagittarius	Cancer	Leo	Virgo	Libra	Scorpio	Sagittarius
Capricorn	Leo	Virgo	Libra	Scorpio	Sagittarius	Capricorn
Aquarius	Virgo	Libra	Scorpio	Sagittarius	Capricorn	Aquarius
Pisces	Libra	Scorpio	Sagittarius	Capricorn	Aquarius	Pisces

Find your Sun sign in the left column. Determine the correct approximate time of your birth. Line up your Sun sign with birth time to find ascendant. Note: This table will give you the approximate ascendant only. To obtain your exact ascendant you must consult your natal chart.

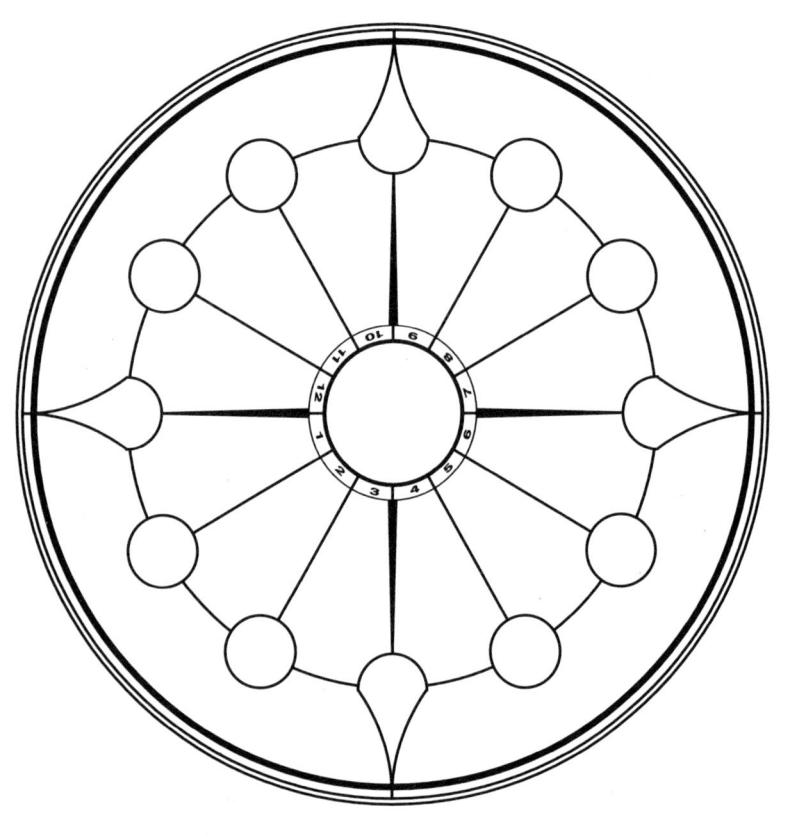

Name	Birthday
Address	
City, State, Zip	
Phone	Office Phone
Fax	E-mail

Name	Birthday
Address	
City, State, Zip	
Phone	Office Phone
Fax	E-mail

Name	Birthday
Address	
City, State, Zip	
Phone	Office Phone
Fax	E-mail

Name	Birthday
Address	
City, State, Zip	
Phone	Office Phone
Fax	E-mail

Name	Birthday
Address	
City, State, Zip	
Phone	Office Phone
Fax	E-mail

Name	Birthday
Address	
City, State, Zip	
Phone	Office Phone
Fax	E-mail

Name	Birthday
Address	
City, State, Zip	
Phone	Office Phone
Fax	E-mail

Name	Birthday
Address	
City, State, Zip	
Phone	Office Phone
Fax	E-mail

Name	Birthday
Address	
City, State, Zip	
Phone	Office Phone
Fax	E-mail
Name	Birthday
Address	
City, State, Zip	
Phone	Office Phone
Fax	E-mail
Name	Birthday
Address	
City, State, Zip	
Phone	Office Phone
Fax	E-mail
Name	Birthday
Address	
City, State, Zip	
Phone	Office Phone
Fax	E-mail

Name	Birthday
Address	
City, State, Zip	
Phone	Office Phone
Fax	E-mail

Name	Birthday
Address	
City, State, Zip	
Phone	Office Phone
Fax	E-mail

Name	Birthday
Address	
City, State, Zip	
Phone	Office Phone
Fax	E-mail

Name	Birthday
Address	
City, State, Zip	
Phone	Office Phone
Fax	E-mail

Llewellyn's 2001 Astrology Datebook

Directory of Products and Services

Llewellyn's Computerized Astrological Services

Llewellyn has been a leading authority in astrological chart readings for more than 30 years. We feature a wide variety of readings with the intent to satisfy the needs of any astrological enthusiast. Our goal is to give you the best possible service so that you can achieve your goals and live your life successfully. An order form follows these listings.

Map the stars with a
Professional Natal Chart

If you are a student or professional astrologer and prefer to do your own interpretations, you need to be sure you are starting with an accurate and detailed birth chart. The *Professional Natal Chart* is generated by Matrix Software's best-selling WinStar 2.0 software. It is loaded with information, including a chart wheel, aspects, declinations, nodes, major asteroids, and more. (Tropical zodiac/Placidus houses, unless specified otherwise.)

APS03-119 ....$5.00

Gain a deeper understanding with an
Astro*Talk Advanced Natal Report

Without a doubt, this is one of the most thorough interpretations of your birth chart you will ever read. Written in plain English by world-famous astrologer Michael Erlewine, these detailed descriptions of the unique effects of the planets on your character and life will amaze and enlighten you. Included in this 30+ page report are: Your Rising Sign; your planets' signs and aspects; your challenges and abilities; your major life periods; your "burn rate;" your soul type; your current influences; your chart's houses; and more. See how your birth chart contains the keys to self-understanding.

APS03-525 ....$30.00

Find out everything you've always wanted to know
about yourself but were afraid to ask with
Heaven Knows What

Get your personality and destiny interpreted by the man most modern astrologers learned their art from. This report contains a classic interpretation of your birth chart and a look at upcoming events, as presented by the time-honored master of the astrological arts, Grant Lewi. Clear and concise, these descriptions of the influences of the planets on your inner self go light-years beyond the one-size-fits-all descriptions found in magazines and popular astrology books. Also included is a look at your year ahead, as laid out in the patterns of the stars and planets.

APS03-532 ....$30.00

Your map to the future is a
TimeLine Transit/Progression Forecast

Love, money, health—everybody wants to know what lies ahead, and this report will keep you one-up on your future. The *TimeLine Forecast* is invaluable for seizing opportunities and timing your moves. Discover how the future can be an open book when you put astrology to work for you with an astrological report that is completely tailored to you—a unique individual with a unique relation to the cosmos. Reports begin the first day of the month you specify.

APS03-526 - 3-month report $12.00

APS03-527 - 6-month report $20.00

APS03-528 - 12-month report $30.00

Stop looking for love in all the wrong places with
Friends and Lovers

Why can't we all just get along? Well, sometimes we can and sometimes we can't, and astrology can shed light on what makes the difference when you start with a custom-made report like *Friends and Lovers*. Go way beyond "does Capricorn get along with Sagittarius?" Find out how you relate to others, and whether you are really compatible with your current or potential lover, spouse, friend, or business partner! This service includes planetary placements for both people, so send birth data for both and specify "friends" or "lovers."

APS03-529 ....$20.00

Find out if you and your lover are truly matched with
Sympaticos

You have a chart, and your love partner has a chart, but did you know that your relationship has a chart, too? It does—the Composite Chart, a blend of the birth charts of two people, and the method behind this amazingly insightful new report. With *Sympaticos*, you will find out the real secrets of what exists between you, and the essence of what you can do and be *together*. Be sure to include birth data for both people.

APS03-533..$20.00

Give your child a jump on life with
Child*Star

We all want the best for our children, and a large part of that comes from understanding who they are and where their latent talents and challenges lie. Every parent knows that each child enters the world with a unique, distinct personality, and astrology can reveal the forces behind that fresh new face. Written by an astrologer who is also a Montessori(c) instructor, *Child*Star* is an astrological look at your child's inner world through a skillful interpretation of his or her unique birth chart—as relevant for teens as it is for newborns. Specify your child's sex.

APS03-530 ....$20.00

Get the feminine perspective with
Woman to Woman

Finally, astrology from a feminine point of view! World-renowned astrologer Gloria Star brings her special style and insight to this detailed look into the mind, soul, and spirit of the modern female. This report will show you the truth about yourself in a way that only another woman could understand. Read about: your projection of your real self; meeting the world on you terms; and power issues of sex, money, and control.

APS03-531 ....$30.00

Now you can take this job and love it with
Opportunities

Your career is more than just a job—it's where the real you meets the real world. If you want to know just what the best fit might be, you need this enlightening and detailed report. Your unique talents are needed by someone out there, and by fulfilling that need you will not only be contributing to the world, but to your soul's growth as well. With the right livelihood, you could actually begin to look forward to Mondays!

APS03-534 ....$20.00

NOTE: Be sure to give accurate and complete birth data on the order form. Llewellyn cannot be held responsible for your mistakes in filling out the proper information. This includes exact time (a.m. or p.m.), date, year, city, county, and country of birth. Noon will be used as your birth time if you do not provide an exact time. Check your birth certificate for this information!

For *Friends and Lovers*, make sure to specify "friends" or "lovers" after your name. For *Child*Star*, make sure to specify your child's sex (male or female) after their name.

Astrological Services Order Form

Report name & number _____

_____

Provide the following data on all persons receiving a report:

1st Person's Full Name, including current middle & last name(s)

_____

Birthplace (city, county, state, country) _____

_____

Birthtime_____ ❑ a.m. ❑ p.m. Month _____ Day _____ Year _____

2nd Person's Full Name, including current middle & last name(s)

_____

Birthplace (city, county, state, country) _____

_____

Birthtime_____ ❑ a.m. ❑ p.m. Month _____ Day _____ Year _____

Billing Information

Name _____
Address _____
_____

City_____State_____ Zip _____
Country_____Day phone: _____

Make check or money order payable to Llewellyn Publications, or charge it!
Check one: ❑ VISA ❑ MasterCard ❑ American Express
Acct. No. _____ Exp. Date _____
Cardholder Signature _____

❑ Yes, send me my free copy of Llewellyn's color catalog, ***New Worlds***!

Mail this form and payment to:
**Llewellyn's Computerized Astrological Services
P.O. Box 64383, Dept. K-971-7 • St. Paul, MN 55164-0383**

Allow 4-6 weeks for delivery

Spells for every occasion, every day

This 384-page, tear-off calendar is packed with spells for all occasions. Featuring a short spell on each page, it also includes crucial information for spell casters—when the spell is appropriate; which implements are necessary; and where the spell should be performed. Icons categorize each spell under a variety of headings: health, love, money, purification, and so on. Users who combine spells with astrology will find daily Moon signs and phases, and Moon void-of-course times.

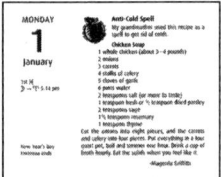

- Sun Spells (Sunday): health, weight loss, fitness
- Moon Spells (Monday): home, family, children's spells, cooking, recipes, animal magic
- Mars Spells (Tuesday): banishment, protection, sports, cleansing, purification, curse-breaking
- Mercury Spells (Wednesday): business, short-term travel, communication
- Jupiter Spells (Thursday): money and prosperity spells
- Venus Spells (Friday): love and relationship spells
- Saturn Spells (Saturday): grab bag of spells (blessings, weather, divination, tarot and rune spells)

LLEWELLYN'S 2001
SPELL-A-DAY CALENDAR
384 pp. • 4¼" x 5¼" • Order #K-974 • $10.95
To order call 1-800-NEW-WRLD

The Ultimate Horoscope Book

Gain amazing insights into yourself and all the people in your life—from that special someone to your coworkers and children—with the upbeat and perceptive horoscopes by astrologer Gloria Star. Why purchase a book about only one zodiac sign, when the *Sun Sign Book* gives you the lowdown on each and every sign in one handy source. PLUS, articles from our trusted experts!

This year's features include:
"How Your Sun Sign Affects Your Career" by Stephanie Clement
"New Age Love: Romance and Your Sun Sign" by Marguerite Elsbeth
"Coming of Age: World Predictions for 2001" by Leeda Alleyn Pacotti
"Economic Forecasts for 2001" by Kaye Shinker

We've got everything under the sun packed into this insightful guide—forecasts for all twelve signs of the zodiac; action tables with the best dates to begin a romance, take a vacation, move, look for a job, and more.

LLEWELLYN'S 2001 SUN SIGN BOOK
480 pp. • 5¼" x 8" • Order #K-965 • $7.95
To order call 1-800-NEW-WRLD

The Almanac for Better Living Naturally

No other book on the market tops the *Moon Sign Book* in supplying useful tips for daily success. Get weather and earthquake forecasts for all U.S. zones year round; economic predictions that help save money; tips on planting sumptuous produce with the help of lunar energy; lively, on-target, monthly lunar horoscopes for every sign; and more than 30 special articles on topics that affect us all.

This year's features include:
"Workplace Politics" by Alice DeVille
"Managing Moods with Herbs and Flowers" by Gretchen Lawlor
"Controlling Climate in the Garden" by Harry MacCormack
"Getting Rid of Emotional Buttons" by Maritha Pottenger

See why *Llewellyn's Moon Sign Book* has been a best-selling guide to successful living for almost a century!

LLEWELLYN'S 2001 MOON SIGN BOOK
and Gardening Almanac
480 pp. • 5¼" x 8" • Order #K-964 • $7.95
To order call 1-800-NEW-WRLD

Save $$ on Llewellyn Annuals

Llewellyn has two ways for you to save money on our annuals. With a four-year subscription, you receive your books as soon as they are published—and your price stays the same every year, even if there's an increase in the cover price! Llewellyn pays postage and handling for subscriptions. Buy 2 subscriptions and take $2 off; buy 3 and take $3 off; buy 4 subscriptions and take an additional $5 off the cost!

Please check boxes below and send this form along with the order form on the next page.

Subscriptions (4 years, 2002–2005):

- ☐ Astrological Calendar $51.80
- ☐ Witches' Calendar $51.80
- ☐ Tarot Calendar $51.80
- ☐ Goddess Calendar $51.80
- ☐ Spell-A-Day Calendar $43.80
- ☐ Daily Planetary Guide $39.80
- ☐ Witches' Datebook $39.80
- ☐ Astrological Pocket Planner $27.80
- ☐ Sun Sign Book $31.80
- ☐ Moon Sign Book $31.80
- ☐ Herbal Almanac $31.80
- ☐ Magical Almanac $31.80

Order a Dozen and Save 40%:
Sell them to your friends or give them as gifts. Llewellyn pays all postage and handling when you order annuals by the dozen.

2001	2002		
☐	☐	Astrological Calendar	$93.24
☐	☐	Witches' Calendar	$93.24
☐	☐	Tarot Calendar	$93.24
☐	☐	Goddess Calendar	$93.24
☐	☐	Spell-A-Day Calendar	$78.84
☐	☐	Daily Planetary Guide	$71.64
☐	☐	Witches' Datebook	$71.64
☐	☐	Astrological Pocket Planner	$50.04
☐	☐	Sun Sign Book	$57.24
☐	☐	Moon Sign Book	$57.24
☐	☐	Herbal Almanac	$57.24
☐	☐	Magical Almanac	$57.24

Individual Copies of Annuals:
Include $4 postage for orders $15 and under and $5 for orders over $15. Llewellyn pays postage for all orders over $100.

2001	2002		
☐	☐	Astrological Calendar	$12.95
☐	☐	Witches' Calendar	$12.95
☐	☐	Tarot Calendar	$12.95
☐	☐	Goddess Calendar	$12.95
☐	☐	Spell-A-Day Calendar	$10.95
☐	☐	Daily Planetary Guide	$9.95
☐	☐	Witches' Datebook	$9.95
☐	☐	Astrological Pocket Planner	$6.95
☐	☐	Sun Sign Book	$7.95
☐	☐	Moon Sign Book	$7.95
☐	☐	Herbal Almanac	$7.95
☐	☐	Magical Almanac	$7.95

Llewellyn Order Form

Call 1-877-NEW-WRLD or use this form to order any of the Llewellyn books or services listed in this publication.

SEND TO: Llewellyn Publications, P.O. Box 64383, Dept. K-971-7, St. Paul, MN 55164-0383

Qty	Order #	Title/Author	Total Price

Postage/handling:
ORDERS $15 AND UNDER: **$4.00**
ORDERS OVER $15: **$5.00**
Subscription orders, dozen orders, or orders over $100: **FREE SHIPPING**
2ND DAY AIR: **$8.00 for one book**
(add $1 for each additional book)
We cannot deliver to P.O. Boxes; please supply a street address. Please allow 4-6 weeks for delivery.

Total price	
MN residents add 7% sales tax	
Postage/handling (see left)	
Total enclosed	

☐ VISA ☐ MasterCard ☐ American Express
☐ Check or money order – U.S. funds, payable to Llewellyn Publications

Account # _____ Expiration Date _____

Cardholder Signature _____

Name _____ Phone ( ) _____

Address _____

City _____ State _____ Zip/PC _____

Questions? Call Customer Service at 1-877-NEW-WRLD